KU-518-403

WITHDRAWN

Research Methods for Human–Computer Interaction

Human–Computer Interaction (HCI) draws on the fields of computer science, psychology, cognitive science, and organisational and social sciences in order to understand how people use and experience interactive technology. Until now, researchers have been forced to return to the individual subjects to learn about research methods and how to adapt them to the particular challenges of HCI. This is the first book to provide a single resource through which a range of commonly used research methods in HCI are introduced. Chapters are authored by internationally leading HCI researchers who use examples from their own work to illustrate how the methods apply in an HCI context. Each chapter also contains key references to help researchers find out more about each method as it has been used in HCI. Topics covered include experimental design, use of eyetracking, qualitative research methods, cognitive modelling, how to develop new methodologies and writing up your research.

PAUL CAIRNS is Senior Lecturer in Human–Computer Interaction in the Department of Computer Science at the University of York.

ANNA L. COX is Lecturer in Human–Computer Interaction at the UCL Interaction Centre, University College London.

LIVERPOOL JMU LIBRARY

3 1111 01506 3157

Research Methods for Human–Computer Interaction

Edited by
Paul Cairns and Anna L. Cox

CAMBRIDGE
UNIVERSITY PRESS

University Printing House, Cambridge CB2 8BS, United Kingdom

Published in the United States of America by Cambridge University Press, New York

Cambridge University Press is part of the University of Cambridge.

It furthers the University's mission by disseminating knowledge in the pursuit of education, learning and research at the highest international levels of excellence.

www.cambridge.org
Information on this title: www.cambridge.org/9780521690317

© Cambridge University Press 2008

This publication is in copyright. Subject to statutory exception
and to the provisions of relevant collective licensing agreements,
no reproduction of any part may take place without the written
permission of Cambridge University Press.

First published 2008
Reprinted 2011

A catalogue record for this publication is available from the British Library

Library of Congress Cataloguing in Publication data
Research methods for human–computer interaction / Edited by Paul Cairns and Anna L. Cox.
    p.   cm.
Includes bibliographical references and index.
ISBN 978-0-521-87012-2 (hardback)
1. Human–computer interaction.   I. Cairns, Paul, 1971–   II. Cox, Anna L., 1972–   III. Title.
QA76.9.H85R45   2008
004.01'9–dc22   2008015935

ISBN 978-0-521-87012-2 Hardback
ISBN 978-0-521-69031-7 Paperback

Cambridge University Press has no responsibility for the persistence or accuracy of
URLs for external or third-party internet websites referred to in this publication,
and does not guarantee that any content on such websites is, or will remain, accurate
or appropriate.

To our girls and boys

Contents

Figures

Tables

Contributors

DR ANNE ADAMS
Lecturer in Practice Centred Education and Development
The Institute of Educational Technology, Open University

PROF. ANN BLANDFORD
Professor of Human–Computer Interaction
UCL Interaction Centre, University College London

DR PAUL CAIRNS
Senior Lecturer in Human–Computer Interaction
Department of Computer Science, University of York

DR ANNA L. COX
Lecturer in Human–Computer Interaction
UCL Interaction Centre, University College London

DR JOSÉ CREISSAC CAMPOS
Lecturer in Informatics
Department of Informatics, School of Engineering, University of Minho

PROF. ALAN DIX
Professor of Computing
Computing Department, Lancaster University

PROF. THOMAS GREEN
Emeritus Professor
School of Computing, University of Leeds

PROF. MICHAEL HARRISON
Professor of Informatics
Informatics Research Institute, University of Newcastle upon Tyne

DR KARSTEN LOER
Department of Strategic Development, Germanischer Lloyd AG, Germany

PROF. PETER LUNT
Professor of Media and Communications
School of Social Sciences and Law, Brunel University

DR DAVID PEEBLES
Senior Lecturer in Cognitive Psychology
Department of Behavioural Sciences, University of Huddersfield

DR TONY RENSHAW
Research Fellow
School of Computing, Leeds Metropolitan University

PROF. HAROLD THIMBLEBY
Professor of Computer Science
Department of Computer Science, University of Wales, Swansea

NATALIE WEBB
Freelance Usability Consultant
London, UK

Preface

Why write this book?

Human–Computer Interaction (HCI) is a clearly multidisciplinary subject. It has historically grown out of both computer science and psychology but in addressing the full complexity of how people use computers it has also grown to encompass social sciences, organisational theories, cognitive ergonomics and even philosophy. These areas all have their own traditions for how to make a useful contribution to knowledge. This means that researchers coming into HCI, be they MSc students, PhD students or even established academics from another area, are rarely aware of the full range of methods that can be used to provide a useful contribution to HCI knowledge. Moreover, it is through awareness of the range of research methods that good researchers realise that a narrow approach to HCI may not be most appropriate in providing a substantial contribution to the area.

The purpose of this book is to describe and demonstrate research methods used in HCI so that new researchers in this area are aware of the possible sorts of research that can be done. In addition, through demonstrating how such research has been done, the book will provide a starting reference for a researcher who is intending to use a particular method. This book will not therefore tell you everything you need to know about a particular method, but it will tell you where you can find out more. Its main aim is to help you to be sure that you have chosen the right method(s) for your particular research project.

Who is this book for?

Our audience is any student (BSc, MSc or PhD) doing a research project in HCI and who needs to know about research methods, that is, methods for producing sound, valid research knowledge. We know that students have very good ideas for research but often do not know how to perform the research in a way that is useful and valid to other researchers. This is not because these students are stupid, but because HCI research is hard. HCI researchers generally come from a single background (psychology, computer science, information science, etc.) and although they are often expert in the research methods used in their own discipline, they are sometimes ignorant of the methods used in another complementary discipline. For example, a computer science student would approach a supervisor to develop a new design for an interface. Whilst the idea can be interesting and useful, they do not necessarily appreciate how they are to evaluate whether their design really does deliver promised improvements. Or conversely, students in psychology sometimes consider it sufficient to merely find out how users behave with a particular interface rather than to think about how the interface could be designed to be better.

We hope that a single resource for anyone planning a research project in HCI will be valuable both to the individuals and to their supervisors, and also to HCI research generally.

What is in each chapter?

As the purpose of the book is to describe and demonstrate research methods, in each chapter we will describe what the method is and how to apply it, how it works and what the expected outcomes are. Each chapter shows how the method has been applied by describing a published piece of research that has employed the method and then highlight the strengths and weaknesses of using the method in the example. We will also point you to other examples that you could look up and tell you where to find out more information about the method itself.

The book is roughly in three parts. The first part is about methods for gathering data, the second for analysing that data and the third for methods that encourage HCI researchers to take a wider perspective on their work.

The first part is made up of three chapters about studying users in order to gather data about what they do, what they think and how they feel. The first chapter is therefore on controlled experiments and describes how to design and run them to evaluate HCI designs, principles and user behaviours. The chapter covers the types of numerical data you can expect to collect and tells you how to go about observing and recording the behaviour of the participants. The second chapter tells you about asking questions, specifically about designing questionnaires, conducting different types of interviews (structured and unstructured) and how to run focus groups. Again the chapter will cover the type of data you can expect to collect from each of these techniques.

Chapter 3 covers a very different way of gathering data through the use of eyetracking. This brings its own particular problems, such as relating what the eye is doing to what you need to know about an interface. This chapter therefore aims to lay the foundations for knowing when to do eyetracking, how to do it and what you can sensibly expect to gain from such a study.

The second part of the book consists of four chapters addressing analysis techniques that can be used to understand user behaviour, perhaps using data gathered through the methods in the previous three chapters. In Chapter 4, we discuss the advances that cognitive modelling has made in the area of HCI and demonstrate how this method can be used to test, confirm and support data collected by other methods. Chapter 5 focuses on formal methods such as statecharts as a different sort of model for interactive systems. Instead of modelling the user like cognitive models, these models consider the system and the context for the system. They can then be reasoned about to ensure that they function as they should. This is particularly important in safety critical systems, like air traffic control or medical monitors, where the cost of failure is never acceptable.

Chapter 6 introduces the use of statistics to analyse quantitative data. This chapter is naturally closely linked to Chapter 1 on controlled experiments and we use the same example in both chapters. However, questionnaires and even interviews can produce quantitative data that statistics summarise and analyse in greater depth. In contrast, Chapter 7 takes a more qualitative look at data arising from questionnaires and interviews in order to develop grounded theories of how users think, their attitudes and what influences their thoughts and attitudes. This chapter therefore uses the same examples as Chapter 2.

The third part is not what you might find in a typical book about research methods but nonetheless covers important aspects of doing good HCI research.

One particular feature of HCI, unlike other disciplines, is that HCI can influence the design and development of the systems that it studies. The usual way of providing designers and developers with the results of research is through methodologies that embody the research findings in some way. However, it is no trivial matter to develop a new methodology. In Chapter 8, we tackle the development of methodologies and the important step of validating the methodology. Without making use of case studies with which to validate new methodologies, we do not have the evidence to be confident that the methodology will really be able to deliver what it claims it can. Even then, developing a methodology is best considered as a long-term project. This does not mean that there cannot be many valuable smaller-scale projects that can contribute to methodology development, but rather that the planning of such projects needs to be done with care and with a view to the bigger picture.

Chapter 9 addresses one of the most important ideas in any research, the theoretical basis for the work. Theory in HCI is very hard to define and so this chapter explores different ways of understanding theory in HCI research. It is perhaps odd to call it a method, but at the same time without theory it is very hard to say exactly what a piece of research is contributing. Theories enable us to generalise our findings to other situations and can then provide us with a focus for our future research and give us something to think and argue about and test.

All research ultimately needs to be communicated to the wider research community if it is to be valuable. This process of writing up work is usually considered at the end of the project. However, in Chapter 10 we make the case that writing is actually a valuable research method that should be begun at the same time as the project. The process of writing helps us to clarify our thoughts not only about what needs to be done, but also about what our results mean.

As already mentioned, HCI is a multidisciplinary area that has been growing to encompass more and more areas of research that were once thought to be distinct. We expect that this is likely to continue in the future as those individual research areas offer us more insights into the interactions between people and computer systems. It is likely therefore that more areas of research will contribute to HCI research and bring with them their own preferred research methods. In the final chapter, Chapter 11, we discuss how the existing methods can still be used to analyse a new area of research, namely user experience, but also how we have found from our own work that there are clearly limitations to the methods. This does not mean the methods are useless, but rather that there is an opportunity to develop new methods that will fill the gap and continue to produce sound, valuable and valid HCI knowledge in these new and challenging areas.

Acknowledgements

We would like to thank all of the authors of this book for agreeing to join us in this enterprise. Though we planned the book, we have been surprised and rewarded by the freshness and enthusiasm that the other authors have brought to their chapters. We have also appreciated the mutual support they have provided to us and each other.

We would like to thank various people other than the authors who have read draft chapters and provided invaluable feedback, particularly Dr Simon Li, Prof. Richard Young, Eduardo Calvillo and Charlene Jennett and the UCLIC students in 2006 and 2007.

Anna would like to thank Paul for his kind generosity in sharing his ideas, opportunities and experience, for not minding too much when she disappeared on maternity leave in the middle of this project and for being a pleasure to work with. She would also like to thank James and Bryn for providing the 'life' part of her work–life balance – it would all be much harder without their smiles, love and support.

Paul would like to thank in particular Harold Thimbleby for countless opportunities, limitless advice and constant friendship that have inspired him over the years of working in HCI and ultimately led to wanting to make this book a reality. He would also like to thank Anna for bringing sanity, good sense and good humour to this project. And of course, Paul would not be able to do very much at all if it were not for the sure support and love of Deb and the joy and distraction provided by Eleanor.

In the end though, this book is our responsibility. We hope you enjoy reading it and, as a result, enjoy even more doing successful research. If not, do let us know because there is always more to learn in HCI.

Paul Cairns and Anna L. Cox

1 Controlled experiments

ANN BLANDFORD, ANNA L. COX AND
PAUL CAIRNS

1.1 Overview

Controlled experiments, an approach that has been adopted from research methods in psychology, feature large in the arsenal of HCI research methods. Controlled experiments are a widely used approach to evaluating interfaces
(e.g. McGuffin and Balakrishnan, 2005) and styles of interaction (e.g. Moyle and
Cockburn, 2005), and to understanding cognition in the context of interactions
with systems (e.g. Li *et al.*, 2006). The question they most commonly answer
can be framed as: does making a change to the value of variable X have a significant effect on the value of variable Y? For example, X might be an interface
or interaction feature and Y might be time to complete task, number of errors or
users' subjective satisfaction from working with the interface. Controlled experiments are more widely used in HCI research than in practice, where the costs of
designing and running a rigorous experiment typically outweigh the benefits.

The purpose of this chapter is to outline matters that need to be considered
when designing experiments to answer questions in HCI.

1.2 The method

We have structured this section about how to design and run a controlled
experiment in the order that the information is usually reported within the method
section of a paper or project report; that is, first we will consider how to go about
choosing the participants who will take part in the experiment before moving on to
consider designing the experiment itself, assembling the materials and apparatus
required, and finally the procedure. We hope that this approach will help you to
find your way around papers that are written up in this way and also help you
when you are considering designing your own experiments.

1.2.1 Participants

For any experiment it is necessary to consider what the appropriate user population
is. For example, if the experiment is designed to test the effect of a changed
display structure for a specialist task, for instance a new air traffic control system,

it is important to recruit participants who are familiar with that task, namely experienced air traffic controllers. Similarly, if the concern is with an interface for older users, it is important to recruit such users to the study. Ideally, for any experiment, a representative sample of the user population is recruited as participants; pragmatically, this is not always feasible (also, it is so much easier to recruit friends, students or members of a psychology department participant database). If a non-representative sample of users is involved in the study then the consequences of this for the findings should be carefully considered. For example, how meaningful is it to have run an experiment on an interface intended for air traffic controllers with undergraduate psychology students? Probably not at all. Sometimes the target population is hard to define. Who, for example, is the audience for a government benefits website? In that case, undergraduate psychology students might not be a bad starting point to begin to study the website.

Having decided on the user population, decisions need to be made on how many participants to recruit, depending on factors such as the power of the statistical tests to be used, the time available for the study, the ease of recruiting participants, funds or other incentives available as participant rewards and so on. Participants can then be recruited through direct approach or by advertising in suitable places.

1.2.2 Ethical considerations

Although not usually reported explicitly, one important consideration is the ethical dimensions of any study. Most professional bodies (e.g. British Psychological Society, 2006) publish codes of practice. Less formally, Blandford *et al.* (2008) have proposed that the three important elements of ethical consideration can be summarised by the mnemonic 'VIP':

- Vulnerable participants
- Informed consent
- Privacy, confidentiality and maintaining trust

Examples of vulnerable participants will include obviously vulnerable groups (such as the young, old or infirm), but may also include less obvious people such as those with whom the investigator has a power relationship (e.g. students may feel obliged to participate in a study for their professor), or who otherwise feel unable to refuse to participate for any reason, or who might feel upset or threatened by some aspect of the study. Some concerns can be addressed simply by making it very clear to participants that it is the system that is being assessed and not them.

It is now recognised as good practice to ensure all participants in any study are informed of the purpose of the study and of what will be done with the data. In particular, the data should normally be made as anonymous as possible (e.g. by using codes in place of names) and individuals' privacy and confidentiality need to be respected. It is now common practice to provide a (short) written information sheet about the experiment and to have a consent form on which participants can indicate that they understand what is expected of them, that they are participating voluntarily and that they are free to withdraw at any time without giving a reason. This is informed consent – a person agrees to take part knowing what they are getting into.

Usually it is possible to offer participants the opportunity to talk about the experiment in a debriefing session after they have finished the tasks they were set. Not only does this help to make the participants feel valued, but sometimes it can be a source of informal feedback that can lead to a better design of experiment or even new ideas for experiments. All data should be stored in accordance with legislation; for example, in the UK the Data Protection Act specifies what information can be held and for what reasons, and it is necessary to register with the government if the data being stored allows individuals to be identified.

1.2.3 Design: dependent and independent variables

A controlled experiment tests a hypothesis – typically about the effects of a designed change on some measurable performance indicator. For example, a hypothesis could be that a particular combination of speech and keypress input will greatly enhance the speed and accuracy of people sending text messages on their mobile. The aim of a classical experiment is, formally, to fail to prove the null hypothesis. That is, for the texting example, you should design an experiment which in all fairness ought not to make any difference to the speed and accuracy of texting. The assumption that there will be no difference between designs is the null hypothesis. By failing to show this, you provide evidence that actually the design is having an effect in the way that you predicted it would.

Put more generally: the study is designed to show that the intervention has no effect, within the bounds of probability. It is by failing to prove that the intervention has had no effect – that the probability of getting this result if the intervention has no effect is very small indeed – that one is led to the conclusion that the intervention did indeed have an effect. More formally, using the terminology defined below, the failure to prove the null hypothesis provides evidence that there is a causal relationship between the independent and dependent variables. This idea is discussed at greater length in Chapter 6.

In an HCI context, the changes to be made might be to interaction design, interface features, participant knowledge, and so on. The variable that is intentionally varied is referred to as the *independent variable* and that which is measured is the *dependent variable*. One way to try to remember which way round these are is to think that the value of the dependent variable *depends* on the value of the independent variable. There may be multiple dependent variables (e.g. time to complete task, error rate) within one experiment, but – at least for simple experiments – there should normally only be one independent variable.

One of the challenges of experimental design is to minimise the chances of there being *confounding variables* – variables that are unintentionally varied between conditions of the experiment and which affect the measured values of the dependent variable. For example, in testing people with different interfaces for text message entry, it could be that you use different messages for people to enter in the different interfaces. The length of message clearly has an effect on how long it takes to enter a message, regardless of the interface. Thus, the message length is a possible confounding variable. Another one might be the complexity of entering certain words. In designing the experiment, you would need to do something to make sure that any differences in text message entry time were solely due to the interface and not to the messages people had to enter. The simplest thing would be to make sure that every message was entered on all the interfaces. This way, even if the messages did take different times, over the course of the whole experiment the effect of the different messages would be evenly spread out across all of the interfaces. This is called counter-balancing.

In designing an experiment, then, the aims are to vary the independent variable in a known manner, to measure the dependent variable(s) and to minimise the effects of confounds on the outcomes of the study.

Within HCI, there are various techniques for minimising the effects of possible confounds. An important starting point is simply to eliminate as many confounds as possible from the experiment, such as those relating to different rooms or different computers. Another approach is to randomise variables wherever possible; for example, if time of day is likely to have an effect on results then either run all experiments at the same time of day (which is likely to be impractical) or randomise the timing of trials so that participants under each condition take part at different times of day.

One particular set of confounds to be aware of is individual differences. This is a general name for how people differ from each other. There are obvious things like the physical differences between men and women but the term also covers a huge range of things such as differences in personality, aesthetic sensibilities, cognitive skills and so on. It is clearly not possible to control for all individual differences in an experiment, but it is advisable to control for the most likely factors that might influence performance or attitudes, such as age, sex and education level. To do this, we must avoid putting all the men in one group and all the women in the other, or having all the older students in one group and all the younger ones in the other. Of course, there might be experiments in which such a difference is an independent variable, for example testing a hypothesis that there will be performance differences with a given interface between women and men or older and younger users. In such cases, a particular difference will be the independent variable – but more on that later!

1.2.4 Design: 'within subjects' or 'between subjects'

Some experiments are most appropriately conducted 'within subjects' and others 'between subjects'. A within-subject experiment involves each participant performing under all sets of conditions, whereas a between-subject experiment involves each participant only performing under one condition. So in a study to compare three websites we might choose to have everybody use all three websites, and that would be a within-subject design; or each participant might use only one website, so that would be a between-subject design. A third design that is common in HCI research is a 'mixed factorial' design in which one independent variable is within subjects and another between subjects. This would not mean that some participants use only one or two of the websites! Instead, there are two independent variables (also called factors in this case) and one factor is within and one factor is between. So if we were comparing differences between the three websites but also between how men and women use the websites, we could have the website as a within factor, so that each person used all three websites. But obviously, the other factor would be a between factor with each person being either a man or a woman but not both.

Note that the terms 'within-subject' and 'between-subject' are a throw-back to the days when the people who took part in experiments were referred to as 'subjects', a term that is now considered inappropriate as it implies a power relationship between experimenter and experimentees and an objectification of the people who take part in experiments. (Indeed, in even earlier times, people who took part in experiments were sometimes called experimental material!) In this enlightened age, the people who take part in an experiment are 'participants', not 'subjects'.

When is it best to choose a within-subject design and when a between-subject one? This is a difficult question to answer. It depends on whether participants are required to compare interfaces (in which case a within-subject design is essential); whether there are likely to be unwelcome learning or interference effects across conditions (in which case a between-subject design is essential); what statistical tests are planned; how long each participant is likely to take in completing each part of the experiment (the longer each task, the less attractive a within-subject design is); and how easy it will be to recruit participants to the study (the more people can be recruited, the more feasible a between-subject design is). One advantage of within-subject designs is that individual differences are less likely to influence results; disadvantages include possible learning effects and more complicated statistics.

In a within-subject design, participants will typically be required to repeat a very similar procedure multiple times with different values of the independent variable. In many cases, it would be inappropriate to repeat literally the same task for each condition, so it is advisable to generate multiple tasks, one for each condition, for each participant to perform. The task becomes, in effect, another independent variable, but one that is of no direct interest in the analysis. The different values are sometimes referred to as 'levels'; for example, in the experiment described in section 1.3 there are two independent variables, the mode of input for message entry (which has three levels) and the mode of input for text entry (which has two levels). Each combination of levels that a participant engages with is referred to as a 'condition', so in the experiment described there are six conditions.

1.2.5 Apparatus/Materials

Every experiment is conducted using some 'instruments'; most commonly (in HCI experiments) the core instrument will be a piece of computer software. For some experiments it is possible to make use of existing software. For others it is necessary to create your own. Many experimental instruments are computer simulations of systems. It is sometimes possible to make use of an experiment generator to simplify the process of creating a suitable instrument. E-prime is one such system commonly used in psychology experiments. Sometimes it is necessary to exploit or acquire programming skills in order to create prototypes that can measure and record task completion times, keystrokes, etc. and that enable you to manipulate the variables of interest.

1.2.6 Procedure

You should create a formal procedure that describes what the participants do during the experiment. This has two purposes. First, it enables you to make sure that every participant in your experiment has the same experience because it is possible that if you use different procedures between different participants, this could be a confounding variable. For instance, if a study was done to see how older users performed compared with younger, and the older users were treated more deferentially (as would be polite), it is possible that the older people would perform better not because of the user interface but because they were more relaxed and felt happier having met this charming experimenter.

The second purpose of a formal procedure is that it allows other people to replicate your experiment. This is the basis of good science. If other people can replicate a study's findings then collectively science can feel confident that the findings are sound and can build on this in future work. The formal procedure removes confounding variables not only within the one experiment but also between separate attempts at the same experiment.

There are a number of issues that we need to consider when designing the experimental procedure:

- Minimising the effect of confounds by controlling the order in which we test the interfaces, the tasks we ask participants to perform and the context in which the study is run
- Making the experiment robust through careful design of instructions, piloting and careful collection and management of data
- Building up to a bigger series of experiments that probes the phenomenon of interest more deeply.

Minimising the effects of confounds

This typically involves considering in which order interfaces are tested, how tasks are assigned to interfaces and the broader context within which trials take place.

If all participants in a study experience interfaces in the same *order*, there are likely to be performance effects due to learning (for example, improving performance with the second interface if learning transfers from one to the other); there may also be changes in attitude due to novelty effects (with the first interface perceived as more novel than the second).

As noted above, in many experiments it is necessary to give participants well-defined *tasks* to complete with the interfaces; it is usually important to devise different tasks to reduce learning effects and also reduce boredom. However, if particular tasks are always associated with the same conditions, this may affect performance in unexpected (or even undetected) ways.

Sometimes in experiments it is more convenient to run one condition (i.e. one value of the independent variable) in a different *context* from the other, for example, using a different computer or a different room, or conducting the experiment at a different time of day. Such apparently innocuous changes can influence results. For example, the first author was once involved in an experiment to study the effects of a training intervention on students' performance. For various reasons, a within-subject design was used (that is, one in which all participants performed under both sets of conditions). In this case it was clearly not possible to control the order of presentation, since it is impossible to undo any effects of training, so all participants had to do the before-training task first, then undergo the training before the second task set. We controlled for task-set variations by allocating half the participants to each task set for the first test then swapping the task sets over for the second set of tests. However, one variable we could not control for was the fact that the participants had a big party in the evening between the first and second tests, so they were all slightly hung over during the second test. Obviously, this should be avoided if possible.

For some variables, a systematic approach to variation is appropriate. One example is to use a 'Latin square' design; a second is to administer the test in every possible sequence to different participants. A Latin square is a square grid in which every element appears precisely once in each row and each column, where a row represents the order in which test elements are administered to a participant and a column represents the sequence of participants in the study. If only two conditions are being considered, and there is no variation in the task participants are being given, then this randomisation is easily achieved by allocating participants to two groups, balanced as far as possible for age, gender, education level, relevant prior experience and any other variables considered relevant to the experiment. If more than two possible conditions are being considered then a Latin square design might look something like that shown in Table 1.1.

If two different tasks are being administered then the design is usually run as 'mixed factorial' and might be organised as shown in Table 1.2. Here, both the order of presentation of the tasks and the order of presentation of the interfaces are being systematically varied to eliminate possible order effects. It should be noted, however, that the statistical test for analysing the resulting data is a three-factor

Table 1.1 *Example Latin square with four different tasks*

Group	First task	Second task	Third task	Fourth task
i	Task A	Task B	Task C	Task D
ii	Task B	Task C	Task D	Task A
iii	Task C	Task D	Task A	Task B
iv	Task D	Task A	Task B	Task C

Table 1.2 *Organising tests for comparing two interfaces with two different tasks*

Group	First task	Second task
i	Interface 1	Interface 2
	Task A	Task B
ii	Interface 1	Interface 2
	Task B	Task A
iii	Interface 2	Interface 1
	Task A	Task B
iv	Interface 2	Interface 1
	Task B	Task A

repeated measures ANOVA (assuming the data is normal), which is not for the faint-hearted.

Making the experiment robust

This includes ensuring clear and consistent task instructions, piloting the experiment to ensure that people behave (roughly) as anticipated and making sure all recording equipment is working properly.

It is important to decide how to *describe tasks* to participants. Some tasks – such as those described by Moyle and Cockburn (2005), which are small tasks involving simple gestures – are easily described to participants. Others require more extensive task descriptions to be given to participants. It is important to consider what level of detail is to be given: if the focus is on whether participants can make sense of interface features then minimal instructions are most appropriate, whereas if the concern is with how actions are performed then greater detail is likely to be required. It is important that tasks are kept to a reasonable time limit, and that they are interesting and engaging enough to keep participants' attention (so that what is actually being measured is that which is intended and not some result of boredom).

It is usually advisable to *pilot* any new experimental design (i.e. to run it with a very small number of participants) to check the design. For example, it is essential to check that the instructions to participants are clear and that participants can complete the experiment in a reasonable time (typically no longer than an hour, and even then there should be opportunities for breaks at realistic intervals). It is also helpful to discover early on if any participants behave in unexpected ways that will result in the experiment not delivering the data intended. These early participants can be asked to give feedback on the experimental design to improve it and their data should be discarded. You might use the data to pilot test the statistical tests you intend to use, recognising that data from a very small number of participants are not going to yield statistically reliable results.

However well designed the experiment, there are always things that might go wrong. These include failures in *recording and retaining data*. Common difficulties are: essential data not being captured (hence the need for piloting the analysis as well as the data recording); recording being lost due to equipment or software failure; and data being subsequently lost. Care should be taken over making sure that you know exactly how equipment works, have sufficient recording media (e.g. tapes, disks or memory cards), have everything fully charged up (or with enough new batteries) and are alert to other kinds of equipment failure. Once gathered, data should be stored securely and systematically so that they can be easily retrieved for analysis and review purposes.

Bigger investigations

To develop a good understanding of a phenomenon, it is usually necessary to investigate it in more than one way, leading to a series of linked experiments each of which involves a single controlled manipulation. It is almost invariably more reliable and easier (if more time consuming) to conduct a series of linked experiments than to increase the complexity of one individual experiment.

1.2.7 Analysis

In controlled experiments the focus is on quantitative data (see Chapters 2 and 7 for approaches to gathering qualitative data). In quantitative analysis, dependent measures might include some or all of: time; errors; particular action types; and user satisfaction ratings. These may be measured by one or more of: automatic logging of user actions; external (video or audio) recording; questionnaires (typically giving numerical ratings); and (less usually) interviews.

Before running any experiment, it is important to decide, at least provisionally, what statistical tests will be performed on the data. Plans may subsequently need to change, for example if data that were expected to have a normal distribution turn out to have a surprisingly different distribution (see Chapter 6 for more details). The choice of statistical test will influence both the detailed design of the experiment and the decision about how many participants to recruit.

1.2.8 Are you addressing the question?

It may seem odd to raise this issue at this point; however, it is an important question. Having gone through all the fine details of designing the experiment, it

LIVERPOOL JOHN MOORES UNIVERSITY
LEARNING SERVICES

is easy to lose sight of the purpose of the experiment. And in adapting the original idea in order to avoid confounds, addressing issues from piloting, setting up the apparatus and so on, it is possible the original design has changed in subtle ways that actually mean that it is not addressing the question intended.

This is best understood with an example. Suppose a researcher was interested, as Dearden and Finlay (2006) were, in studying the effects of using interface patterns in design processes. This sort of question could be answered by having many groups of people doing a design project, some using patterns and some not. To measure the value of patterns, the design produced by each group might be evaluated by a set of users who were not involved in the design. So far so good. But in practice the researcher could not use real designers, partly because they are hard to get hold of and partly because it is unrealistic to expect real designers to waste time producing different systems intended for the same purpose. Instead, then, the researcher might settle for using different groups of students on an HCI course.

For the evaluation, the researcher would want to make sure that there are clear quantitative measures because that is what experiments are all about, so the evaluation might involve timing users in how long they take to achieve various tasks using the different interfaces that the student groups produced.

This all sounds very plausible but now think again about the research question. Suppose the researcher found a significant difference between how users performed with the different designs. Would this tell you anything about the use of patterns in the design process? Actually, all it really tells you is that different groups of students produced different designs that were differently usable! With some careful argument, the researcher may be able to attribute some of the design differences to the patterns, but that would be more of a qualitative argument rather than the conclusion from the experiment. The difference in performance of the users could be attributed to the differences between the groups, the lack of experience of the students in design, the difficulty of learning patterns for inexperienced designers and so on. These are all confounds that undermine the point of the experiment.

One way to avoid losing the plot of the experiment could be to write up the report before devising the experiment. This is the approach advocated in Chapter 10 on writing. That way, as the details of the experiment become clearer, you can check to see if it still fits with the story that you set out to write in the first place.

1.3   Applying the method

The study reported here (Cox *et al.*, in press) is also used as the example in Chapter 6 on statistics. You will therefore be able to use the two chapters together to see how the experimental design and statistical analysis support each other in ensuring a good quality result.

As the mobile phone develops and its set of capabilities grows richer, there is a constant pressure to evolve the user interface and develop more efficient, convenient input methods. Recent attention has focused on changing handset layout (Hirotaka, 2003) or improving word-prediction software (MacKenzie *et al.*, 2001; Butts and Cockburn, 2001; Silfverberg, MacKenzie and Korhonen, 2000). Although these proposed alternatives ease the use of such an interface, they do not solve the problem of shrinking user interfaces driven by consumer demand, nor do they address the issue of truly mobile usage, that is, hands-busy, eyes-busy situations.

The investigation explores the viability of speech recognition as an alternative method of text entry. The intention is not to replace the traditional keypress mode of interaction altogether, but instead to add functionality to the existing user interface, thus addressing the limitations of keypress input. This is motivated by previous research suggesting that user performance and satisfaction could be enhanced by the addition of a separate input channel to provide multimodal functionality (Cohen, 1992). Specifically, it is posited that in the same way as a speech user interface (SUI) and a graphical user interface (GUI) can provide a complementary multimodal interface, there exists a similar relationship between keypress and speech recognition at the text-message interface.

1.3.1 Participants

We decided to recruit 36 undergraduate participants who were all regular mobile phone users. In order to verify this, we asked our participants how long they had been using a mobile phone and how many text messages they sent per month. The users had an average of 3.2 years of mobile phone use and, from the information on their most recent phone bills, they sent on average 72 messages a month.

1.3.2 Design

In order to test whether or not speech recognition would be a useful addition to the mobile phone interface, a number of mock-up interfaces were created which enabled interaction using different combinations of speech and keypress. Speech (S) could be used at two different points in entering text messages: it could be used to actually enter the words of the message and it could be used to allow the user to navigate through the mobile phone menus both to start entering the message and to send it off. For entering the message itself, the two most common ways are predictive text (P) and multi-tap entry (M). Navigating round a phone menu is usually done via the keys on the phone (K). Thus, there were three ways of entering the message, S, P and M, and two ways of doing the navigation, S and K. The more formal way of saying this is that there were two factors (or independent variables) in the design: one for message entry with three levels and one for navigation with two levels; giving rise to six experimental conditions. These six conditions are summarised in Table 1.3, where each condition is describing the mode of navigating (to select message entry), then the mode of message entry, and finally the mode of navigating (to send the message).

Table 1.3 *The design of the experiment showing two factors and six conditions*

		Speech	Message entry Predictive text	Multi-tap
Navigation	Speech	SSS	SPS	SMS
	Keypress	KSK	KPK	KMK

Table 1.4 *Predicted time (in seconds) for each task condition based on the GOMS model*

		Speech	Message entry Predictive text	Multi-tap
Navigation	Speech	10.09	16.89	26.02
	Keypress	9.21	16.01	25.14

Before conducting an experiment a GOMS model (John and Kieras, 1996b) was used to create predictions for the time it would take to complete a task of navigating through the menu, composing a message and then using the menu to send the message, using each of the six different methods (see Chapter 4 for information about GOMS models). These are shown in Table 1.4.

Just looking at the predicted times made us hopeful that we were right in thinking that using speech would improve the interaction. Although for navigation speech was always slightly slower than keypress, for message entry the speech times were quicker than both the predictive text entry and the multi-tap entry.

In order to determine whether our predictions were correct it was important to carry out a user study. We decided to use a within-subject design (so that all participants completed tasks on all interfaces).

We have already described the main dependent variable for this study – the task completion times. However, time alone is not the only thing that can tell us something interesting about whether or not one interaction method is better than another. If we only looked at task completion times we might find that people were very quick using one particular method but not realise that this might be because they were rushing and thus making many mistakes (this is known as a speed/accuracy trade-off). This meant it was important for us to look at number of errors too. The NASA-TLX workload questionnaire enables us to look at how difficult people find it to use each method. There would be little point in proposing the introduction of a particular interaction method, no matter how quick it might be, particularly in the context of mobile phones where interaction often occurs on the move, if people found it more difficult to use than other methods. Having three dependent variables (times, errors, workload) enabled us to be more confident that we would find out whether or not speech interaction would really be of benefit to people using mobile phones.

1.3.3 Apparatus/Materials

For this experiment we needed to:

- develop the prototype mobile phones which made use of the different interaction methods
- develop the tasks that participants would complete
- identify and obtain any questionnaires we wanted to include: in our case, the NASA-TLX and the questionnaire that asked participants about their age, mobile phone usage, SMS usage, and so on.

The experiment was conducted on a PC, running a mobile phone prototype. The prototype supported both keypress and spoken input, and the output was displayed on a 17in colour monitor. The numerical keypad of the keyboard was relabelled to mirror the standard mobile phone keypad interface. Dragon Naturally Speaking Professional 7 was used for the voice-recognition system. The environment supported speaker-dependent, continuous recognition of natural speech. A head-mounted microphone was provided to allow dictation to the system.

This level of detail may seem over the top. However, it is what would be needed if someone else were to repeat this work and to be sure that they could compare their results with ours. For example, if the voice-recognition software was not specified, another person might find very different results due to the difference in quality of the voice recognition that they used. Thus, it would be impossible to build up a secure knowledge of the issues in this area across different groups of researchers.

The ideal experimental procedure would be to test participants' usage and acceptance of a multimodal mobile phone interface. However, the mobile phone handsets currently available are not yet powerful enough to support speech recognition in the text-message interface. Moreover, mobile phones are now so pervasive that participants in the experiment are likely to be experts at text entry on their own handset model. Hence, a study using a Nokia phone, say, would be biased by the prior experience of any owners of Nokia handsets. These two factors therefore led to the decision to carry out the experiment on a mobile phone prototype, running on a desktop PC. In addition, the lack of a familiar interface would produce more consistent results across the population. Finally, such a prototype can be instrumented to accurately measure and record task completion times.

Six experimental text messages, derived from a logging study, were printed in lower case, 14 pt bold type and mounted individually onto A5 card. We used this method of creating the messages so that we could be reasonably sure that we were including words that were commonly used in SMS messages. Four training text messages were also printed in lower case 14 pt bold type and presented as a group, on plain A4 paper. The messages were formulated to mirror the conversational text-sending habits among undergraduate students, utilising their most frequently used words. Each text message consisted of 8 words, averaging 28 characters in length. All punctuation and capital letters were omitted from the messages.

A one-page pre-experiment questionnaire was constructed to elicit background information on the users and their mobile phone usage. This A4 document consisted of nine short questions. An A4 booklet was also provided to the participants consisting of six NASA-TLX task workload evaluation forms. Each page displayed the six workload factors and an unmarked 20-point, equal-interval scale, with endpoints labelled 'low' and 'high'. The final page of the booklet consisted of one question requiring the user to state their preferred method of interaction and give a brief explanation of their choice.

1.3.4 Procedure

All participants were tested individually, seated at a desk in front of the computer monitor and the keyboard. It was explained that the aim of the investigation was to evaluate user satisfaction and performance with different mobile phone navigation and text-entry techniques. These would consist of keypress navigation, multi-tap and predictive text entry, and spoken navigation and text entry. Each participant was informed that the experimental test procedure would consist of using a mobile phone emulator to create and send six different text messages via six different methods of interaction (KMK, KPK, KSK, SMS, SPS, SSS). It was then explained that the experimental procedure would consist of four stages: pre-experiment questionnaire; training the voice-recognition software; practice session using the prototype; experimental testing procedure.

After the participants had consented to continue with the experiment, they were asked to complete the pre-experiment questionnaire and then underwent the training program required by the Dragon Naturally Speaking system. The head-mounted microphone was positioned approximately one inch from the participant's mouth and they were instructed to read aloud the instructional text from the computer screen. Participants were encouraged to speak naturally and clearly. Training continued until the system had successfully completed the enrolment program – this process took approximately 10 minutes, depending on the system and the participant's ability in reading the instructional text. On completion of the speech training, participants were allowed a short break while the system analysed the speech data and constructed a speech model for the participant.

Following speech training, a brief practice session using the prototype was carried out. This was necessary to accustom each participant to the modified numerical keypad and the on-screen interface of the prototype. The keyboard was placed on the desk in front of the monitor and moved by the participant into a comfortable 'texting' position. This practice session consisted of the six experimental conditions used in the main experiment, but the participant was allowed to choose the order in which conditions were practised, with a set of training messages supplied by the experimenter. Participants were allowed to complete each condition once only.

After the practice session, the main experiment was summarised. Each participant was informed that task completion times were being recorded and was encouraged to complete each task as quickly and accurately as possible. They were informed that timing would begin when the experimenter pressed the 'Start' button on the emulator and would stop when the final menu command option was executed. Participants were instructed not to correct any spelling mistakes, although it was explained that any mistakes made would be recorded. Each participant was told that they would be required to complete a task workload form on completion of each task. In addition to an oral explanation of the form, a hard copy explanation for each workload factor was provided. It was then explained that the experiment would conclude with one final question. Once the participants understood and were comfortable with the experimental testing procedure, they were encouraged to ask any questions.

The experiment began when the participants told the experimenter they were ready to start. A Latin square was used to determine the order of task completion (thus minimising any order or practice effects) and at the start of each task the proposed method of interaction was fully explained to the participants and they were presented with a new, unseen text message to enter. They were encouraged to familiarise themselves with the text message by reading through it two or three times. Each test began when the experimenter said 'Go' and pressed the 'Start' button on the prototype. Each test was completed when the last menu command option had been executed. Following completion of each condition, participants were required to rate their experience of the interaction method by circling one of the unmarked values on each task workload scale. On completion of all six conditions, participants were asked to answer the final question on the last page of the booklet. In total, the experiment lasted approximately 45 minutes.

The analysis of the data collected is discussed in Chapter 6. However, the data does show that the differences between the experimental conditions were as predicted by the GOMS model. This suggests that speech-keypress combination could be very useful as a new form of multimodal interface for text messaging. It is, of course, not the last word on the matter. Specifically, this was a formal experiment, and a company interested in such an interface might like to see how it would work for someone sitting on a bus or walking down a street before committing to this as the new design for their latest mobile phone.

1.4   Critique

A well-designed and executed controlled experiment, or series of experiments, can give confidence in the findings. Controlled experiments are well suited to studying details of cognition or interactive behaviour, such as those presented in the preceding example. Other examples include the work of Cockburn, Gutwin and Alexander (2006), who ran a series of controlled experiments on ways of navigating documents, and of Brewster, McGookin and Miller (2006), who studied the use of smell for searching large photographic collections.

The strength of controlled studies can also be their weakness: the causes of success or failure of new interactive systems are commonly to be found in the broader context of activity rather than the details. Controlled experiments are poorly suited to analysing these situations because it is not possible to isolate and control the variables that are pertinent to the interactive behaviour, and it is difficult to design experiments to eliminate all confounds. It is also possible that the experiment measures something other than that which the experimenter believes it is measuring, so that data can be misinterpreted.

Despite the fact that controlled experiments are common within HCI research, we are not aware of any thorough accounts of how to design and conduct such experiments written from an HCI perspective. Nevertheless, there are many text books on the subject of designing and reporting on experiments in the behavioural sciences – for example, Cochran and Cox (1992), Field and Hole (2002) and Harris (2002) all give good overviews of the subject, though with different emphases on the details.

2 Questionnaires, in-depth interviews and focus groups

ANNE ADAMS AND ANNA L. COX

2.1 Overview

With fast changing technologies and related human interaction issues, there is an increased need for timely evaluation of systems with distributed users in varying contexts (Pace, 2004). This has led to the increased use of questionnaires, in-depth interviews and focus groups in commercial usability and academic research contexts. Questionnaires are usually paper based or delivered online and consist of a set of questions which all participants are asked to complete. Once the questionnaire has been created, it can be delivered to a large number of participants with little effort. However, a large number of participants also means a large amount of data needing to be coded and analysed. Interviews, on the other hand, are usually conducted on a one-to-one basis. They require a large amount of the investigator's time during the interviews and also for transcribing and coding the data. Focus groups usually consist of one investigator and a number of participants in any one session. Although the views of any one participant cannot be probed to same degree as in an interview, the discussions that are facilitated within the groups often result in useful data in a shorter space of time than that required by one-to-one interviews.

All too often, however, researchers eager to identify usability problems quickly throw together a questionnaire, interview or focus group that, when analysed, produces very little of interest. What is often lacking is an understanding of how the research method design fits with the research questions (Creswell, 2003) and how to appropriately utilise these different approaches for specific HCI needs. The methods described in this chapter can be useful when used alone but are most useful when used together with other methods. Creswell (2003) provides a comprehensive analysis of the different quantitative and qualitative methods and how they can be mixed and matched for overall better quality research. Depending on what we are investigating, sometimes it is useful to start with a questionnaire and then, for example, follow up some specific points with an experiment, or a series of interviews, in order to fully explore some aspect of the phenomenon under study.

This chapter describes how to choose between and design questionnaires, interviews and focus group studies and, using two examples, illustrates the advantages of combining a number of approaches when conducting HCI research.

2.2   The methods

As with all research, before you start developing your materials, for example by composing questions for a questionnaire, it is important to consider:

- why you are asking the questions
- who the results are for
- what you expect to find from the answers (i.e. hypothesis – see Chapter 9)
- how you are going to analyse the data when you get them (see Chapter 7).

If you stop and reflect on these questions, it will be easier to compose more appropriate, accurate questions that provide useful findings. This reflection should also help you to understand which method will be the most appropriate for your needs. The methods discussed in this chapter enable us to investigate participants' subjective memories of an event or views on a topic whereas experiments and user testing give a more objective measure of what occurs (see Chapter 9). The choice of method therefore depends on the questions that you want answered. If you want to know what people do in a particular situation (e.g. which pieces of software they use and how frequently), then a questionnaire will probably be sufficient. If you want to identify why something has occurred, a questionnaire will provide less valid responses than in-depth interviews or focus groups because in-depth interviews and focus groups allow the respondent the freedom to express things in context that you may not have thought of before. Knowing what questions to ask is the hardest part of constructing a questionnaire. Triangulating between qualitative and quantitative approaches can help with this problem.

This section of the chapter will outline how to design questionnaires, interview schedules and focus groups before considering in more detail the issues of sampling, piloting your study, triangulation of data and trust, privacy and ethics.

2.2.1   Using questionnaires

Questionnaire design

It is important to understand that a questionnaire is a tool and as such it must be usable so that the reader can easily understand, interpret and complete it. This in turn will increase the accuracy of responses. As a research tool, we must consider two important concepts in questionnaire design: 'reliability' and 'validity'. Reliability refers to the consistency of a measure whilst validity refers to its ability to measure what it is supposed to be measuring. There are several ways in which these factors can be statistically analysed (e.g. a 'reliability coefficient' between questions) and several books that deal with these issues in depth (e.g. Aiken, 1996). These concepts and analysis methods are very valuable if you wish your tool to accurately assess attitudes or opinions. In the past researchers have concentrated on reliability as it is easier to measure. However, reliability without validity is useless. You may be reliably testing something completely different from what you want to test. For example, you want to test interface layout but the respondents are actually giving responses for aesthetics. This is an issue that relates strongly to the questionnaire wording and scales (see below).

Questionnaire length and structure

It is commonly accepted that a questionnaire should not be over long. People's short attention spans mean that long questionnaires are completed less accurately as people rush to finish them. This is also true for obvious question repetition with respondents biased towards simply repeating what they said before, whether it is accurate or not. One major problem with very long questionnaires is the likelihood of participants skim reading them, which increases the likelihood of participants misinterpreting complex questions. This is also a problem with background information or instructions given at the beginning of the questionnaire. Many, although not all, of these problems can be counteracted with careful design of the questionnaire (see below). It is important to understand that there is a not a simple golden number of questions that can be given as a limit for questionnaires. The amount of motivation felt by participants to complete the questionnaire can affect how much they are prepared to concentrate on completing it. For example, participants who feel the outcomes of the research will directly benefit them (e.g. the application will be redesigned and used by the participants themselves) may feel more motivated to complete a questionnaire. Participants who feel the research is irrelevant to them (e.g. they rarely use these applications) may feel less motivated to complete it. Since a spread of different types of users is often required, it is important to understand these variations when designing and piloting the questionnaire.

To increase the usability and effectiveness of the questionnaire tool it is important to consider how you structure it. This means reviewing the sequence of questions very carefully. Grouping questions together under a common themed heading will help the respondent contextualise the subsequent questions. This approach will also help you identify how the sequence is likely to affect the respondent. The order in which questions are presented may bias your respondent to give more or less favourable responses. This can also happen with the response scales whereby a respondent gives the same answer throughout a section without reading the questions. To counteract this you can either counterbalance the questions (i.e. a negative and positive statement) or you can counterbalance the response (i.e. going from positive to negative then negative to positive). However, you must be careful how you design this in, as it might cause errors with people not realising that the ordering has changed. Piloting the questionnaire should help you identify these problems and correct them in the final version.

Question wording

When designing questions it is important to consider if each question will have the same meaning for everyone; e.g. networks are a common technology term but the expression 'networking' can be commonly used to mean establishing social relationships. It is, therefore, important to make sure your frame of reference is clear. Providing definitions or examples is a useful way to overcome these problems. Some researchers provide scenarios at the beginning of sections to contextualise the questions. Be careful, however, that these don't bias responses.

Keeping questions as short and simple as possible will increase the likelihood that they will be understood as well as the accuracy of responses. Questions that are complicated by double negatives or loaded words are particularly hard for a respondent to answer (e.g. 'which of these applications did you not consider unreliable?'). It is also important not to ask more than one question at once as you will find the respondent only answering one (e.g. 'How do you rate the system response times to urgent and non-urgent request?'). Similarly it is essential not to ask a question that requires them to interpret your meaning of a term (e.g. 'Do you attend online tutorials on a regular basis?' What is meant by the concept 'regular basis', is it once a day or once a week?). Providing a range within which to choose a response will help to clarify these choices. Ranges can also help respondents feel happier about answering some questions. For example, being asked to write down your age can feel far more invasive than choosing from a selection of age ranges.

Ultimately, it is always important to consider what biases you may be relaying through the wording of a question. Leading questions are frequently the major problem with most questionnaires (e.g. 'Why do you think online assessment is wrong?'). Similarly questions that invite a socially desirable response will produce a biased set of response (e.g. 'In online conferences which description best describes yourself: an "enthusiast", "occasional participant" or "lurker"?' Who would realistically describe themselves as a lurker?). Finally, assuming a respondent will be able to remember accurate details of events several months ago is unrealistic and will produce inaccurate responses.

Different types of questions and scales

It is important to understand the different types of questions that can be included within a questionnaire as they require different levels of interpretation by the reader. This in turn impacts on the level of concentration required by the participant and thus the ease in completing the questionnaire. There are four main types of questions:

- simple factual questions – requiring a yes/no response, e.g. 'Do you have a computer at home?'
- complex factual questions – requiring some interpretation or analysis, e.g. 'How many times have you used this application today?'
- opinion and attitudinal questions – requiring more alternatives and deeper concentration
- open-ended questions – requiring participants' full concentration.

Each of these types of questions suits different scales of responses, e.g. factual questions can be recorded as yes/no answers or with a space to enter an appropriate

The advice on the help pages was:
Very Good   Good   Acceptable   Poor   Very poor

I found the help page advice useful:
Strongly agree   1 2 3 4 5   Strongly disagree

Fig 2.1 *Two types of Likert scale*

quantity. Open-ended questions will require a box large enough to record the amount of detail you want and that participants are likely to give. There is little dispute about these scales and forms of data entry. However, opinion and attitude questions have a wide variety of rating scales and are rife with complex arguments. A full appraisal of these scales would be too lengthy for this chapter (see instead Aiken, 1996). The following paragraph will therefore concentrate on the most popular scales and relevant issues.

The most commonly used attitude/opinion scale is the Likert scale. There are different versions of this scale used in questionnaires (see Figure 2.1). Ideally a full Likert scaling should be undertaken by developing groups of items that are statistically tested to identify the degree to which they measure the same things (Aiken, 1996). However, many designers have neither the time nor the skills to take this approach and so utilise the basic look of the Likert scale (Aldridge and Levine, 2001) in a checklist type format. This means that the importance of each question/item may vary, so adding up across those items would be useless. What is often done is that percentages across users are given, e.g. '85 per cent of users didn't find the help page advice useful'. It is worth noting that this approach will lower both the reliability and validity of the tool. A useful way to counteract this is to triangulate the findings with other approaches.

One continuing debate amongst questionnaire researchers is the question of a middle category. Some researchers feel that it gives the respondent a true representation of the scale. Others argue that respondents opt for the middle category as an opt-out from making a decision either way. Ultimately, a well-designed questionnaire will counteract all of these problems.

2.2.2 Conducting interviews

Conducting interviews is a time-consuming process that requires careful planning. In this section we outline some of these planning issues, notably: interview structure; style; the setting; and recording the data.

One might think that conducting an interview is much like helping someone complete a questionnaire by reading out the questions and writing down their answers. However, as discussed in the overview of this chapter, researchers make use of interviews when they wish to obtain more detailed and thorough information on a topic than might be gleaned from a questionnaire. During an interview the investigator often follows a schedule of pre-prepared questions, but is also able to deviate where necessary in order to maximise the information obtained. These are known as structured or semi-structured interviews. It is important to consider that the more structured an interview is, the less likely it is for a participant to feel at ease and reveal important and relevant issues. However, the less structured it is the harder it is to analyse afterwards. If a structured approach is taken, it is still important to be flexible enough to allow jumping between questions that the participants have started to answer in a previous response. Sticking rigidly to a structure can simply annoy your respondents when you ask a question they've already answered. For semi-structured and unstructured interviews it is important that the interview structure is kept flexible so that key issues not identified before the interview are allowed to emerge through the discussion. If there are key points that need to be discussed, these should flow from the discussion rather than being forced on the interviewee. This takes practice to perform while keeping an informal feel to the structure. A useful aid is to have a list of issues and to tick them off if the interviewee mentions them along the way. It is also good to link things already being discussed to new issues on the list, so the conversation feels natural and not forced. Don't forget that conducting an interview is a skill and the more you complete, the better you will be at doing them.

The format for an in-depth interview or focus group can take on many forms (e.g. scenario-led, reflective accounts, task-led). Yet there are some basic guidelines that can be followed for all of these approaches. Initially, it is important to put participants at their ease with general introductions and permissions (consent) for interviewing and recording the interview/focus group, as for any study involving people (see Chapter 1). Details on confidentiality should also be given about the anonymity of the information and sensitivity concerning its later usage. At this point it is useful to start the talking with a brief background to the study. This helps contextualise the focus of the questions and their responses. However, you must be very careful not to give away too much detail that would bias participants' responses. After this initial introduction it is useful to consider the interview or focus group in four main stages.

1 **Background:** At this point obtain the subjects' background details, such as their experience with equipment and experience in general. Do not attempt to ask any detailed personal background questions here as this will be received much better at the end of an interview, when a trust relationship has been established.
2 **Letting off steam:** It is now useful to ask general questions which allow the participant to 'let off steam'. Often participants have in their mind a set of key points that they want to tell you about (e.g. their pet hates or loves). If you do not allow them to unburden themselves of these issues at the beginning, you will find all your questions resulting in these points repeatedly resurfacing.
3 **Addressing issues:** Any issues that have not naturally been dealt with through (2) should now be introduced. This stage could require further scenario prompting – although this should be used sparingly and with great caution so as not to bias the respondent towards specific issues or responses. If there

are potentially sensitive issues that you want to ask the participant, leave them until the end of this section. This will help to increase a sense of trust between the participant and researcher, making it easier for the participant to talk with more comfort about these issues.

4 **Tying up/debriefing:** There should always be a rounding off of the session with a summing up of all the issues, so that the respondent believes they have presented all the information they want to. There should also be a reaffirmation that the information will be dealt with in the strictest confidence. Finally a short debriefing session may be required to present in more detail what the research will be used for and what the aim of the research is.

An appropriate interviewing style can aid natural interactions without fostering any intimidation from those being interviewed. Although there are many different styles and approaches to choose from, the student–tutor approach is the easiest and quickest to pick up and implement. In this approach the interviewer takes on the role of a student who is asking questions from an expert. This approach should accentuate to the end user how much their opinions will be valued. It is also a useful approach to support novice end-users in revealing problems they have with applications.

The setting for the interview can influence its success as the more natural the setting, for the respondents, the more likely they are to give naturalistic responses. If you are asking them about technologies they would use at home it is easier for them to respond in their home environment. Keeping eye contact during an interview is also imperative for keeping the natural, conversational nature of the interview. This becomes very hard if you are trying to write down most of what is said and makes audio or video recording of the session extremely valuable. It is, however, useful to consider the impact that a recording device will have on the interview structure and responses. A large, imposing recording device will be likely to intimidate the respondent and thus their responses to the questions. However, it is worth noting that after a while the respondent often relaxes and forgets the presence of the recording device. It is important to ask permission to use any recording device and highlight to the participant why you need the device (e.g. 'I can't write down what people say quickly enough'). Again, reiterate here how the information will be kept in the strictest confidence and anonymised before being disseminated in an aggregated form. Although some people refuse permission to be recorded, it is very rare and notes can always be used in these circumstances.

To ensure that the data is complete enough for accurate analysis there are some key points that need to be considered throughout the interview.

- Don't do all the talking, you should talk at most for 5–15 per cent of the time.
- Don't ask leading questions or questions that are too restrictive. If you do, your answers are likely to be reduced to a series of simple yes/no responses.
- Don't let participants drift off the focus, which is more likely in a group than with an individual. But at the same time be flexible about their responses to

questions and don't restrict them to answering your questions in the order you have them.

- Do remember that there are no right or wrong answers, only the respondents' opinions.
- Don't ever give the respondents your opinions on the topic as this may bias them to give responses that will please you.
- Do remember to ask questions that probe but do not prompt a response. If a respondent gives a vague response ask them to qualify it (e.g. 'What do you mean by that?'), but don't give them a response to agree to (e.g. 'Do you mean this ... ?').
- Do ask a respondent to qualify what they mean when they use jargon (e.g. 'What does eTMA mean?').
- Do remember, in a focus group, not to let dominant personalities steal the limelight by giving you all the responses.

2.2.3 Focus groups

Focus groups are very similar to interviews and therefore many of the guidelines for conducting interviews also apply to conducting focus groups. A focus group should not exceed six or seven participants (eight at a maximum) and it should also be no smaller than three people. Too large and people are more likely to break off to talk in sub-groups and leave people out of the discussion. Too small and it is hard to keep the conversation going in enough depth for the participants not to feel intimidated by the situation. It is also easier to have a homogeneous group of people for a focus group as they find it easier to talk to one another. Watch out though, they may be more eager to impress one another and be biased in their responses. To counterbalance this likelihood it is useful to have comparative focus groups to compare responses with (Lunt and Livingstone, 1996).

When choosing whether to complete an interview or focus group often the decision is made for purely logistic reasons (e.g. it is very difficult to get seven software designers from different companies to agree to attend a focus group). However, there are some issues that for ethical or privacy reasons are better dealt with in an in-depth interview. Conversely, a focus group will allow for easier reflection on collaborative experiences (Lunt and Livingstone, 1996; Bruseberg and McDonagh-Philp, 2002).

The role of the investigator during the focus group is to facilitate the discussion of a number of topics and to ensure that the data is recorded. It is often useful to allow the members of the group a few moments to consider each question before you invite them to start the discussion. The investigator needs to ensure that each member of the group gets an opportunity to put forward their views and that no single person dominates the meeting. One might consider ensuring that each person takes a turn at explaining their view on the topic before moving on to the next person in the group. The investigator should also reflect back to the group what the group view or views are on a topic.

2.2.4   Important issues to consider

Sampling

In all research the issue of sampling is a crucial one that is often overlooked. In experiments this is often discussed with reference to participants (see Chapter 1). Within questionnaire research there is a wide variety of sampling methods used (e.g. random, systematic, stratified, multi-stage clustered, quotas) that are reviewed in detail by many other books (e.g. Czaja and Blair, 1996; Creswell, 2003; Aldridge and Levine, 2001). However, there are some key terms and concepts that need to be understood. The 'theoretical population' is the population you may want to generalise your research to (e.g. internet users across the world). The study population is the population you can acquire access to (e.g. computer users within the UK). The 'sampling frame' is the reference point that will allow you to select appropriate people for your study (e.g. a telephone book). But you must realise that whatever sampling frame you use will bias how representative your sample is of the wider population. For example, selecting people from a telephone book will exclude those who are not in the book (e.g. without a phone, ex-directory). With your own research limitations taken into consideration (e.g. time, cost, opportunity) it is useful to remember that you will never get an ideal sample.

Piloting

It is essential to identify potential problems before the expensive, time-consuming, full-scale research is undertaken. Initial, small-scale studies (pilots) help to identify how the questions are likely to be interpreted. It is important to consider seriously any research issues that occur at this point and use them to improve your questionnaire design or interview techniques. These pilots, although small-scale, should attempt to obtain a spread of different types of user so that variations in bias, expectations and abilities can be understood and accounted for. Giving your questionnaire to a selection of colleagues who understand questionnaire design can help to correct some of the problems that are so easy to miss. Be careful, though, not to take criticism too personally – there is no questionnaire that could not be criticised to some extent.

Triangulation

Triangulation is the term given to the use of other qualitative methods, literature and experimentation to evaluate research findings. It enables researchers to overcome the weakness or intrinsic biases that come from qualitative methods where the data is derived from a small number of observations and, rather than viewing quantitative methods as rivals, takes the view that we can gain most by employing a mixture of methods and thereby avoiding the limitations of any single method.

In order to validate the results from a qualitative study we can obtain multiple data sources and multiple observers, employ current theory and make use of multiple methods. Obtaining data from multiple sources might involve interviewing people from different groups (different companies, professions, etc.) and identifying issues that are common across groups. Obtaining data from multiple observers would require having more than one person conducting the interviews and ensuring that issues are identified by all observers/investigators, thus avoiding any experimenter bias. Theoretical triangulation requires looking in the established literature for references that support our findings (and ones that don't!) in order to add weight to our own conclusions. Using methodological triangulation requires the use of multiple methods to investigate the same phenomenon – perhaps by using this book to identify which other methods would be appropriate.

Trust, privacy and ethics

A poorly designed series of questions (e.g. unclear, lengthy, confusing questions with lots of typographic errors) can decrease a respondent's trust in the researcher. Leading questions can also make people believe there is a hidden agenda behind the questions, thus decreasing their trust in the research. Providing additional information where needed can, in contrast, increase a sense of trust. Careful emphasis of the purpose of the research can encourage a sense of purpose in the respondents. However, as with experiments, the respondents' consent (verbal or written) to record and use the data must be obtained. This is often completed at the beginning of an interview or focus groups and in a tick-box format on a questionnaire. Another important ethical requirement is the need to establish a clear understanding with the respondents that they can withdraw from the research at any point.

Trust is closely connected to a respondent's perception of privacy (Adams and Sasse, 2001). If a respondent feels that their answers are likely to risk their personal privacy they will either not complete the research or distort their responses to put themselves in a more favourable light. Participants also need assurances of confidentiality – details of how the information is going to be stored and who will access it. Of key concern is how identifiable the information is. Anonymous information will produce less concern as the information will not be personally identifiable. It can be helpful to emphasise, either verbally or within the questionnaire, that any data will be anonymised. For example, participants may need to know that this means that their data will be merged together with other responses, e.g. 'Twenty per cent of participants gave this response', or 'Eight out of ten agreed with this statement.' Giving participants a number (e.g. participant 246) also helps to increase perceptions of anonymity and thus the likelihood of accurate responses. It is also important to emphasise that information that identifies groups of people (e.g. specific departments or organisations) will also be anonymised in later dissemination of findings. These issues can be summarised as follows:

- Trust and ethics: informed consent, right to withdraw, enhancing trust through question and questionnaire design
- Privacy and ethics: confidentiality, anonymity, sensitive use of information.

2.3   Applying the methods

In this section two examples (Adams and Sasse, 1999; Adams, Blandford and Lunt, 2005) are given for the different methods to help clarify a series of points that were found through each study. The same studies are being used in the chapter on qualitative analysis (see Chapter 7) and so both chapters can be used to cross-reference for the whole research process.

2.3.1 Questionnaire and interview study

Most organisations try to protect their systems from unauthorised access, usually through passwords. Considerable resources are spent designing secure authentication mechanisms, but the number of security breaches and problems is still increasing (Hitchings, 1995). Unauthorised access to systems, and resulting theft of information or misuse of the system, is usually due to hackers 'cracking' user passwords, or obtaining them through social engineering. At the same time many organisations have major problems with users forgetting their passwords. The cost of re-instating passwords is an ever-growing problem within modern organisations. A review of previous research (Adams and Sasse, 1999) identified that there is a need for balance in password construction between secure and memorable passwords. Secure passwords are often considered less memorable and vice versa. The development of usable yet effective system security is a field growing in importance. This study sought to identify relationships between memorability and security to support users in designing memorable yet secure passwords.

Method

A total of 139 questionnaire responses were received, half of which were from one particular telecommunications company. The other half of the responses came from organisations throughout the world. Participants were recruited via email and web interest groups. This approach could be argued to have biased subject sampling to technologically experienced respondents. It should be noted, however, that respondents were varied in both computer experience (less than 1 year to 10 years) and password experience (1 to over 10 passwords, some using over 30 passwords).

A pilot questionnaire was used to obtain initial quantitative and qualitative data to re-design the questionnaire. Although the questionnaire was placed on the web, the pilot feedback ascertained that anonymity was of key importance. Yet ensuring that participants did not complete and submit several copies was also important. This problem led to the development of a small program that would automatically anonymise participants' personal details and return the data entered via email for analysis (uniquely identified according to IP address). There was a personal details section in the questionnaire, but this did not have to be completed, giving the participants the freedom to privacy that they required. This was not

Table 2.1 *Mean correlation coefficients between automaticity, memorability and frequency of password usage*

	Responses	Correlation	Significance
Password usage by Memory problems	137	−0.220	$p < 0.05$
Automaticity by Memory problems	136	−0.634	$p < 0.05$
Required security changes by Memory problems	122	−0.2079	$p < 0.05$

an ideal solution to the problems noted above, but it did provide adequate solutions to most of the problems identified.

The questions ranged from factual to open-ended questions with the appropriate scales as noted above. There was one main open-ended question at the end of the questionnaire that asked participants to add any other issues they felt relevant. The responses identified a very large response rate for this question (some participants wrote over a page) and many of these highlighted the limitations of the questionnaire design, for example identifying questions not previously noted before.

Findings and re-design

Although this questionnaire took a broad approach to the subject area, it focused on password related user behaviours, in particular memorability problems. Several correlations were identified using a Spearman's Correlation Coefficient (see Chapter 6). Several of the significant relationships found (summarised in Table 2.1), although never identified before, were relatively obvious, for example a significant ($p < 0.05$) correlation between 'infrequently used passwords' and 'frequent memory problems' and between 'frequently used passwords' and 'infrequent memory problems'. There were also significant correlations ($p < 0.005$) between 'have to think first' (before password recall) and 'frequent memory problems' (with the same password) and at the opposite end of this relationship between 'automatic' (password recall) and 'infrequent memory problems'. As noted earlier in the chapter, these findings highlight what was happening with the users, their passwords and their behaviours, but not why. The results could suggest that password memorability is partially reliant on frequency of use, which produces automaticity. This would tie in with observations on encoding specificity and the implicit vs. explicit memory models (Graf and Mandler, 1984; Graf and Schacter, 1985). An experiment could have been devised to investigate that this hypothesis was correct (see Chapter 1).

However, there was a surprising significant correlation ($p < 0.05$) between the 'desire to decrease security' and 'frequent memory problems' with the same password. Another interesting finding was that 50 per cent of respondents wrote their passwords down in one form or another. Both of these findings again highlighted a need to know why these issues were occurring. Results from the open-ended sections of the questionnaire also suggested that this narrow approach was not addressing key problems with password usage as an authentication device. It was then decided that the questionnaire required a follow-up study to incorporate a more in-depth exploratory analysis of these issues. In-depth interviews with 30 participants from two comparable organisations (the original telecommunications company and a building research organisation) were then used to gather more detailed data.

The in-depth interviews uncovered a whole raft of relevant usability issues that meant that a re-conception of the research was needed. Ultimately, the focus of the original questionnaire on memorability issues was not the major problem with passwords as an authentication mechanism. The follow-on interviews took a more flexible approach to data gathering with a focus on themes identified from the open-ended sections of the questionnaire. The interviews were able to identify a whole range of security issues centring on users complying with or circumventing password mechanisms. These password behaviours were found to relate to perceptions of 'security levels', 'information sensitivity' and 'compatibility with work practices'. The qualitative analysis chapter (see Chapter 7) will highlight how different stages of the analysis revealed more detailed unpacking of these issues.

The interviews uncovered an array of interesting issues that, because of their sensitive nature, would never have been identified through a questionnaire. The respondents needed assurance that exact details of their passwords would not be required. They also needed continual declarations that the data would be confidential and only used in an aggregated form. Respondents' motivation to complete the study was increased greatly by the knowledge that the findings would be relayed back to the organisation's security department to improve systems. Through these assertions, participants felt at ease to reveal negative as well as positive password behaviours (e.g. putting passwords on post-it notes, sharing passwords, using other people's passwords to circumvent organisational procedures). The interviews were conducted at the participants' place of work with a semi-structured flow to them and a student–tutor style of interaction. All these approaches worked to put the participants at their ease and uncover sensitive yet very valuable information.

2.3.2 Interview and focus group study

The following series of studies were closely interlinked with an iterative development of questions and style closely interwoven with the analysis procedure. Computer technology and the 'knowledge society' have inspired speculation about their effects on society and its organisations (Gallivan, 2000). Social contexts and work practices can have a significant impact on a community's engagement with new technology systems (Duncker, 2002). Lave and Wenger (1991) argue that social practices shape how we learn and, in turn, who we become. However, those social practices grow from and interlink with organisational structures.

Technology as 'boundary objects' often traverses these structures and knowledge domains, supporting communication and collaboration (Star and Griesemer, 1989). However, the empowering or excluding nature of these technologies is rarely related back to specific HCI issues. In this set of studies (Adams *et al.*, 2005) we sought to review these issues in relation to interactions between social context, system design and implementation.

Method

A series of studies was conducted, over a four-year period, based around the introduction and use of digital libraries in a clinical and academic domain. Across four different settings (within these two domains) in-depth interview and focus group data were collected from 144 users: end-users, librarians, designers and management. The data were analysed with reference to 'communities of practice' to identify socially relevant issues, both specific to each domain and generic (see Chapter 7 for more details). The studies each had different influences but two themes focused the research throughout: work practices (both current and those changing) and the impact of digital resources on those practices. It was decided that, throughout all the studies, a pre-defined concept of a 'digital library' would not be employed. This approach was taken so as to allow the users to explore what they perceived as comprising a digital library.

As this research was qualitative in nature, a detailed analysis of the context for each of the studies was essential. This analysis of the context of study provided a background to previous change initiatives, implementation strategies and usage practices within each organisational structure. This in turn provided a backdrop to user technology expectations which proved invaluable. After each study was completed an analysis of how it related to the other contexts (similarities and differences) was undertaken. This analysis helped to contextualise each study at a generic level (see Chapter 7).

The academic domain data were gathered from a London-based university that is split over several geographically distributed campuses. Computers with web-accessible digital libraries were placed within the library and in computer suites. Focus groups and in-depth interviews were used to gather data from 25 academics and librarians (with a 50/50 split) from 4 different campuses within the university (10 from humanities, 10 from computer science, 4 from business and 1 with a library managerial role). The first clinical setting studied was a London teaching hospital. In this hospital, computers had been placed on the wards, with web-accessible digital libraries. Focus groups and in-depth interviews were used to gather data from 73 hospital clinicians. Fifty per cent of the respondents were nurses while the other fifty per cent were junior doctors, consultants, surgeons, Allied Health Professionals (AHPs; e.g. occupational therapists), managers and IT department members. A further comparative clinical domain study was conducted in a provincial teaching hospital. In this hospital, although all computers allowed access to web-accessible digital libraries, they were not placed on the wards, but within specified offices and the library. Twenty in-depth interviews were used to gather data from management, library, IT, consultant and nursing employees. Finally, an evaluation of an information intermediary's role within clinical communities of practice was undertaken. Twenty in-depth interviews were conducted across eight different clinical teams over a six-month period, as well as an observational study of one team and an information intermediary collaborating during a drop-in session.

Between the two domains a wide variety of electronic resources were used and a good spread of computer literacy and digital library usage was obtained. On average the level of literacy within the academic setting was higher than within the health service. However, within both domains usage patterns were similarly biased towards usage for research purposes. Finally, four broad issues guided the focus of interview and focus group questions within all the studies:

- perceptions of participants' role within the organisation and their information requirements
- perceptions of current information practices, social structures and organisational norms
- the impact of current practices, structures and norms on information resource awareness, acceptance and use
- technology perceptions (specifically of digital libraries) and how these affect other issues already identified.

Findings and re-design

The choice between in-depth interviews and focus groups was made primarily for logistical reasons and was adapted for the needs of each study. It was difficult to arrange interviews with high-level clinicians, for example, so focus groups with these participants would have been impossible to organise. In contrast, some focus groups were organised with the nursing staff and allied health professionals at the end of regular meetings. This meant that a homogeneous group of appropriate respondents was already gathered and focused on practice-based behaviours. The advantage of these sessions was that often one participant would bring up an account of the technology that would spark off a memory or a contradictory opinion from another participant. The richness of this data for socially relevant practices was evident.

To ensure interviews and focus groups were retained and not cancelled it became imperative to be extremely flexible. Some interviews were held in the lunch halls, others on the wards, while one interview with a surgeon was held in the surgery common room in between operations. A good recording device was essential for these varied and often noisy environments. Often the interviews had to stop because an urgent issue had come up or support for a tricky procedure was needed. It was essential to keep the momentum going so that time wasn't wasted when the interview resumed. It was useful, both during the interviews and afterwards, to make a set of notes summarising key points as a reminder for the participant of the previous discussion (e.g. 'You were telling me about when the

****** system was implemented ...'). It is important, though, not to let these kinds of notes take the interviewer's focus away from the interview (i.e. they should only be supplemental to the recording).

Although the interviews often contained sensitive discussions everyone agreed to the sessions being recorded. There was one participant, however, who asked for the tape to be turned off at one particular point in the interview. When the tape was turned off this participant went on to relay some of his opinions that he knew were rather contentious. The respondent, however, noted vehemently that he wanted these opinions noted and 'on-record' but that he simply did not want to have his voice recorded saying them. This highlights again the importance of being flexible in an interview and having a pen and pad available to make notes when required.

In contrast to the previous study, a grounded theory approach was taken from the outset of the research. As this approach to analysis was taken, a change in questioning evolved in conjunction with the ongoing analysis. It is interesting to note, then, that as the data collection proceeded there was a shift in the interviewing focus towards perceptions of organisational change and different approaches to the implementation of technologies.

Through the analysis and interviewing, it was identified that the four settings represented three different approaches to digital library implementation: making digital library resources available from existing computer systems in people's offices and the library (a traditional approach); making computer systems, and hence digital libraries, available in shared spaces (in this case, hospital wards); and employing information intermediaries to work with staff and library resources. These different approaches engendered different perceptions of the technology. Further analysis was undertaken to draw out these differences through a community of practice perspective (see Chapter 7). The traditional approach produced perceptions of technology as being irrelevant for current needs and community practices. Making technology available within shared physical space, but with poor design, support and implementation procedures, was widely perceived as a threat to current organisational structures. In contrast, technology implemented within the community, which could adapt to and change practices according to individual and group needs, supported by an information intermediary, was seen as empowering to both the community and the individual. Finally these findings were reviewed in light of the contextual details gathered during the data collection. See Chapter 7 for the details of how the anslysis developed as an integral part of the data collecting process.

2.4   Critique

Questionnaires can be an invaluable tool when usability data is needed from large numbers of disparate users. They can be both cost-effective and easier to analyse than other methods. However, it must be understood that they suit some research questions better than others. As mentioned above, they are reasonably effective at obtaining data about what issues are of increased importance (e.g. 95 per cent of respondents didn't use the help pages). It must be remembered, however, that these rely on respondents' subjective memories as opposed to objective measures that can be made in experiments and some user trials (see Chapter 1). Questionnaires that deal with opinions or attitudes will require a lot more time and effort in design, construction and piloting, thus increasing their cost.

It is also worth mentioning that all questionnaire designers must consider potential biases from subject sampling, fatigue and misinterpreting questions. Although many of these problems can be overcome through careful questionnaire design and standardisation, this takes a great deal of skill. Finally, it is important to understand that questionnaires are limited to the questions asked. If you miss out important issues in your questionnaire design they will not appear in the analysis. However, as identified in the questionnaire example above, open-ended questions can sometimes allow these issues to surface. Ultimately, though, the importance of situational or contextual issues will be missed if this is the only research approach taken.

In-depth interview and focus groups can provide a flexible and participatory method that contextualises users' perceptions and experiences. As noted in the example above, participants are far more likely to release sensitive data (e.g. related to privacy and trust) when they have formed some rapport with the researcher in question. It is interesting to note that both these approaches allow the participant to sequence their responses themselves. As seen in the qualitative analysis in Chapter 7, these sequencings can be enlightening in themselves. However, it must be remembered that each methodology has its own limitations. Qualitative approaches are frequently criticised for being subjective and subject to the researcher's own biases. These issues are often dealt with through a series of researcher quality and inter-rater validity checks (see Chapter 7). What cannot be disputed is the time-consuming nature of these approaches reducing effective timely input into the design process. Findings will also be reduced to lower numbers than can be produced by questionnaires, although focus groups can increase numbers with similar time outlays.

Additional literature

There has been little research into the HCI application of questionnaires, in-depth interviews and focus groups. Further detailed explanations of these methods can be found within the social science literature (e.g. Strauss and Corbin, 1990; Aiken, 1996; Lunt and Livingstone, 1996; Czaja and Blair, 1996; Aldridge and Levine, 2001; and Creswell, 2003). There has, however, been some usage of these methods within the domain. Pace (2004) details the use of in-depth interviews to identify a grounded theory analysis of online flow experiences. Folstad, Bark and Gulliksen (2006) describe the use of questionnaires to assess HCI practitioners' evaluation practices. This paper presents a simple yet ideal approach to questionnaires as a means of ascertaining a broad simple picture of what is happening within the field. Focus groups are less used within HCI but are beginning to be more readily used in the design domain as a whole. Bruseberg and McDonagh-Philp (2002) describe how the use of focus groups can effectively support the industrial/product designer in design decisions. Ultimately there is a growing appreciation for these methods and for how, through appropriate application, they can strengthen the quality of HCI research.

3 Eyetracking in HCI

NATALIE WEBB AND TONY RENSHAW

3.1 Overview

Eyetracking records eye movement and provides information on what people look at. Understanding how people look gives researchers an insight into how people think, especially in areas of cognition such as attention. The advantage of eyetracking is that it also gathers this information in real time and to a high level of detail.

The eye movement recorded by eyetrackers is a combination of two main behaviours: first, fixations, where the eye is relatively still; second, saccades, where the eye moves rapidly between fixations (Rayner, 1998; Salvucci and Goldberg, 2000). Fixations are usually of more interest, since these are the times when the eye receives the most detailed information.

The academic world has investigated tracking eye behaviour for over 100 years. However it really started to flourish in the 1960s and 1970s, being used in the realms of cognitive sciences, language and advertising (Jacob and Karn, 2003; Rosbergen, 1998, cited by Radach *et al.*, 2003). In the past few years however, it has been used more widely in academia and commercially. Early eyetrackers were very expensive and used bespoke equipment and software. They were also cumbersome for participants as sensitivity to head motion meant equipment such as bite bars and chin rests were used to reduce movement (see Figure 3.1). Advances in technology have greatly decreased the cost of eyetracking equipment and improved its accessibility and marketability. Eyetrackers are now also more natural for participants as tolerance to head motion has increased and head stabilisation is no longer required for much work (see Figure 3.2; Henderson and Ferreira, 2004; Goldberg and Wichansky, 2003). Eyetracking is now used for a wide variety of purposes including designing websites, digital TV menus and games.

Eyetracking has been described as a technique that has been on the brink of offering great potential for some time (e.g. Jacob and Karn, 2003). However the potential of eyetracking is still constrained by the complexities of interpreting the data. When using eyetracking in a research project, it needs to be carefully thought through and requires a strong study design. Researchers need to think about how the eyetracker will help answer their research goals, what results may be expected and what might be their cause.

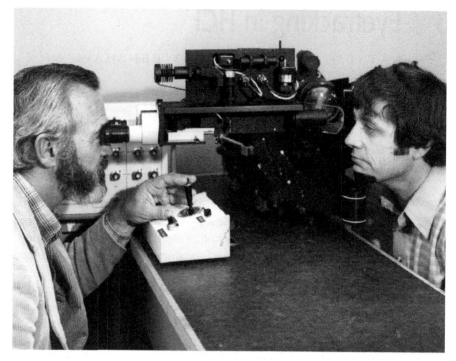

Fig 3.1 *1965 eyetracker showing chin rest (courtesy of SRI International)*

Infra-red diodes and camera are situated below the screen

Fig 3.2 *A remote eyetracker with integrated camera and infra-red LEDs. (A remote eyetracker is an eyetracker with no point of contact with a participant) (Tobii T60; courtesy of Tobii Technology AB)*

The purpose of this chapter is to give students, practitioners and researchers an introduction to using eyetracking in research and practice. In particular, this chapter will focus on designing, running and interpreting eyetracking studies. This chapter will not cover eyetracking in terms of gaze as input into systems. Neither will it cover in-depth visual processing nor the development of eyetracking technologies. However, references will be provided towards the end of this chapter for readers to find materials in these areas.

3.2   Methodology

3.2.1 Technical

In this section, we give an overview of how the visual system works and a brief outline of some aspects of eyetracking technology.

Vision

Eyetrackers measure aspects of vision and due to this there are some underlying basics any researcher using eyetracking should know. This section will briefly cover some key aspects of vision as they relate to eyetracking. For more detail, there are some references for further study later in this chapter

Vision dominates our perceptual systems and is estimated to use 50 per cent of the brain's cortex (Ware, 2003). Light enters the eye through the pupil, striking the receptors in the retina lining the back of the eye. This causes them to respond by emitting an electrical impulse. The brain processes these electrical signals and forms a representation (visual perception) of the colour, shape, movement properties and location of the objects seen (Palmer, 2002).

There are two basic types of receptors: rods and cones. These have different sensory properties. The cones can perceive finer detail than rods and are sensitive to colour. Most cones are tightly packed into an area called the fovea. This is found almost directly opposite the lens at the back of the eye (Gregory, 1998). The entire fovea covers an area of about 1.5 mm (5° of visual angle), but the area where both colour and spatial vision are most acute is about 2 degrees of visual angle (see Figure 3.3 for an illustration). A visual angle of 1.5–2.0° equates to around the size of your thumbnail viewed at arm's length (Duchowski, 2007).

This non-uniform distribution of receptors on the retina has a significant bearing on eye movement. People move their eye so that their cornea (transparent front part of the eye) and lens focus the image onto the fovea thereby getting the greatest level of detail about the object. It is this movement which is captured by an eyetracker system.

Eyetracking shows where the highest acuity of vision is deployed; people will still 'see' other parts of a scene, but with less detail (Henderson and Ferreira, 2004). Peripheral vision, which is vision outside our foveal gaze, is good at detecting movement and providing vision in low light conditions. Certain features

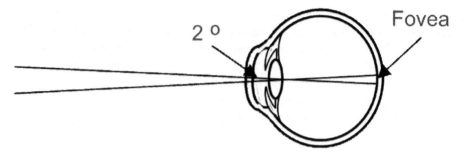

Fig 3.3 *Visual angle is the angle between light rays from two ends of a viewed object as they hit the eye. 2° of visual angle corresponds to the area of highest acuity on the retina*

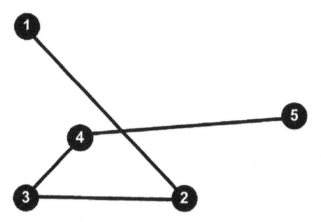

Fig 3.4 *Example scanpath which shows saccades (straight lines) between sequential fixations (circles)*

of a scene may be encoded by a massively parallel visual process (pre-attentive processing) which occurs before a fixation takes place, for example detecting line orientation and flicker. However, to build up a visual perception of a scene it is still necessary for the eye to scan the scene by moving from object to object (Ware, 2003; Palmer, 2002; Wickens, 1992).

Several types of eye movement are described in the literature (Palmer, 2002; Gregory, 1998; Duchowski, 2007), but the most significant one for our purpose is the saccade. A saccade is best described as a ballistic jump. Saccades are pre-planned and take 150–250 ms to plan and execute. They can reach speeds of up to 900° per second (angular speed) and it is thought that vision is greatly suppressed for their duration (Palmer, 2002).

A saccade ends with a fixation, where the eye is relatively stationary for a short period of time (200–300 ms). During a fixation all the visual detail made possible by the fovea can be encoded (Palmer, 2002). The sequence of saccade-fixation-saccade determines a scanpath (see Figure 3.4; Noton and Stark, 1971 cited in Duchowski, 2007). This sequence can be captured by eyetracking technology as eyetrackers record eye positions several times a second (usually at a frequency of 50 or 60 Hz in HCI studies). The recorded positions are then aggregated into fixations if they meet certain time and location thresholds determined by the eyetracker and operator. As well as fixations and saccades, eyetracking can record changes in pupil dilation and blinking.

The concept of a 'useful field of view' (UFOV) has been introduced by eye movement researchers in order to describe the dimensions of the area that can be seen in any one fixation (e.g. Mackworth, 1976, in Henderson and Ferreira, 2004; Drury and Clement, 1978). Its size is variable depending on many factors such as the individual and task, but is usually of the order of 5° (Henderson and Ferreira, 2004).

However, it would be wrong to always think that because a participant has fixated on an area it will influence their further actions or that the details are registered in memory. To ensure that eye movement reflects the mind's focus it is important that the participant is given a task. Under these circumstances the eye–mind hypothesis (Just and Carpenter, 1976, in Goldberg and Wichansky, 2003) is more likely to be valid.

The eye–mind hypothesis basically states that people look at what they are thinking about. In other words visual attention is the proxy for mental attention. Visual behaviour is influenced by both reactions to visual stimuli (bottom-up) and cognitive (top-down) processes. An example of a bottom-up influence is when a viewer's attention is drawn to an item that appears to 'pop out' from a display. For example, abrupt motion, flickering or strong contrasting colours all draw attention (e.g. Franconeri and Simons, 2003). In terms of top-down influences, it has long been known that fixations differ according to viewer goals (see Figure 3.5, Yarbus, 1967, cited in Duchowski, 2007). Certain visual elements are looked at and noticed based on what our intentions and our expectations are, for example browsing the BBC homepage for something interesting to read versus looking at the BBC homepage to try and find the weather forecast. For realistic tasks, both top-down and bottom-up processes are important (Burke et al., 2005; Palmer, 2002; Ware, 2003; Duchowski, 2007).

The influence of bottom-up and top-down factors means that although eyetracking can tell you what people looked at, when they looked and for how long, it will not necessarily tell you what they were thinking about. For example, if you asked 10 people to browse a site for 10 minutes it would be difficult to interpret the data afterwards because there are a variety of things the participants might have been trying to do. Were they looking for interesting articles? Were they trying to figure out where to find the contacts page? Did they look at the advertisement because it was annoying or because they loved it?

Technology

There are two main types of eyetracking: tracking the position of the eye relative to the head and tracking the position of the eye in space (called 'point of regard'). The first type of tracking includes approaches such as measuring the

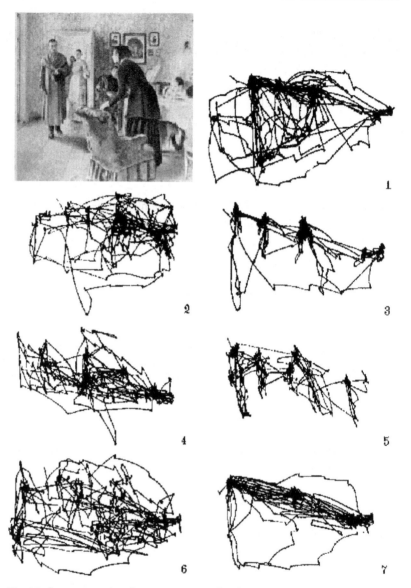

Fig 3.5 *Seven records of eye movements by the same subject looking at the painting 'Unexpected visitor' by Repin. Each record lasted 3 minutes (courtesy of Yarbus, 1967)*

Each gaze plot represents the eye movement after the viewer was given a particular task:

1 *Free examination.*
2 *Estimate the material circumstances of the family.*
3 *Give the ages of the people.*
4 *Surmise what the family had been doing before the arrival of the 'unexpected visitor'.*
5 *Remember the clothes worn by the people.*
6 *Remember the position of the people and objects in the room.*
7 *Estimate how long the 'unexpected visitor' had been away from the family.*

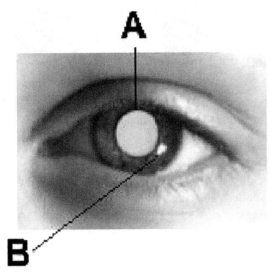

Fig 3.6 *Bright pupil method. Calculating gaze direction from the pupil reflection (A) and first Purkinje image (B) (courtesy of Slaviko Milekic www.archimuse. com/mw2003/papers/milekic/milekic.html)*

electric potential differences of skin around the eyes (electrical oculography), using a contact lens to mount a device on the eye (scleral contact lens/search coils) and measuring features of the eyes when the eye is in different positions, such as the apparent shape of the pupil (photo-oculography) (Duchowski, 2007). These methods can be very invasive however and are not commonly used in HCI studies.

Most commercial eyetracking systems are 'point of regard' systems which analyse the reflections of near infra-red light off the cornea and the pupil. A typical eyetracker set-up has LEDs shining infra-red light into a person's eyes and a camera mounted into the display to record the reflections. Near infra-red light will not be visible light to the participant and as such will not dazzle them. The remote eyetracker shown in Figure 3.2 uses this method.

Two methods are used to determine the gaze location in point of regard systems. The first, known as the dark pupil method, depends on the detection of the differing contrasts of the pupil, iris and sclera (the white of the eye). The second, known as the bright pupil method, uses light reflected from the retina back through the pupil; in this method the pupil looks like a bright grey-white disc (see Figures 3.6 and 3.7). Edge detection algorithms use this representation and an additional reflection of light from the cornea (aka first Purkinje image) to calculate where the eye(s) are looking. The eye positions can then be superimposed upon the scene being viewed either live or recorded for later playback. The time-stamped data can also be exported into spreadsheets or other data analysis software (Poole and Ball, 2005; Duchowski, 2007).

| Looking below the camera | Looking at the camera | Looking down and to the right of the camera |

Fig 3.7 *Position of corneal reflections changing according to point of regard (courtesy of Poole and Ball, 2005)*

The choice of eyetracking system depends on the budget available and the nature of what is being studied. The case studies in this chapter give an example of the use of both techniques (case study 1 uses the bright pupil method, case study 2 the dark pupil method). Some systems can switch between the two to provide the optimum means of catching eye movement. To the HCI practitioner, the method used to determine the eye's position is less important than the non-invasive nature of the equipment and its accuracy. The wearing of helmets and miniature cameras is likely to be more distracting than systems that rely on no physical contact with the participant (for example, Jakob and Karn, 2003). Other things to consider are the ease and speed of the calibration process, the robustness to movement of the eyetracker and the naturalness of the environment in which the evaluation is taking place.

3.2.2 Preparing a study

A good study design will ultimately help the researcher to clearly address their research questions. A study design needs to define the type of study being done, and how the data will be measured and analysed. The necessary steps in designing a study have been described in Chapter 1. Here the factors unique to eyetracking are considered. The first issue is of course to define a suitable research question. Eyetracking is particularly suited to research questions around attention. Examples of areas within HCI that have already been studied using eyetracking are listed in Table 3.1.

Qualitative and quantitative studies

An important factor to consider when creating your study design is whether you want to do a qualitative or quantitative study. In some studies, particularly commercial usability testing, eyetracking can be used in a qualitative way. Here the eyetracking recordings, particularly pictures of scanpaths and gaze replay movies, are viewed to get a better sense of what occurred or to look at patterns of behaviour which can be further explored in later test sessions. An example might be a usability test for a registration form. Participants appear to hesitate at a

Table 3.1 *Example areas of research suitable for using eyetracking*

Process	Areas	Example questions
Top-down and bottom-up	Search	• Where do people search for the correct navigation link? • What factors disrupt or aid search, e.g. effect of web banner ads (Burke *et al.*, 2005)?
	Comprehension	• What do people look at and for how long in order to make sense of the stimulus? • Do people find the correct navigation link but choose not to use it because the label is hard to understand?
	Making decisions and solving problems	• In what sequence do people look at visual elements in order to come to a decision, e.g. determining the best result from a search engine query (Silva and Cox, 2006)? • Do different user groups show different visual behaviours when solving a problem?
	Reading and scanning	• What parts of a web page were read versus scanned?
	Efficiency of task completion	• Do experts have a visual strategy that can be taught to novices (e.g. Yang, Gillies and Hansell, 2004)?
Bottom-up	Visual elements capturing attention	• Do people notice banner ads when using websites? • Does the rolling textual newsfeed on a TV screen distract viewers?
Methodological	Recording visual attention when attention cannot be articulated through other means	• Why did participants fail at a task? E.g. a participant reasons aloud that there is a technical fault when a system appears unresponsive, however the eyetracking recording shows the participants did not notice the status indicator showing the system was in a state of processing (e.g. Duchowski, 2006).

particular part of the process and examination of the eyetracking recording shows they are consistently going to an incorrect part of the form. Further sessions can be used to probe more on why this area is problematic and alternative designs could be tried to see if this removes the problem.

Eyetracking can produce large volumes of objective data, ideal for quantitative studies in which the effect of changes of an independent variable upon a dependent variable is measured and tested for significance (see Chapter 6). Attribution of cause and effect is very much dependent on the experimental conditions being controlled so that the eye–mind hypothesis is maintained for the duration of the experiment. This can be done by defining the task and context and confirming the results through triangulation (applying several research methodologies to study the same phenomenon).

An example of controlling the task and context tightly is Granka, Joachims and Gay's (2004) study of Google search results. The participants were given the specific task to view search results and click the most relevant link. Granka and colleagues found a pattern of eye movement behaviour where users would spend most of their time viewing the first and second result, and then select the first result. Participants did not use a strategy of scanning the entire list and then selecting a link.

However, defining the task and the context too tightly may reduce a study's ecological validity (realism). For example, if the task is to purchase shoes on an online store and go through checkout, there will be different sub-goals and sub-tasks within the main task. One way to separate out the eye movements for each task is to break the recording session into sections. The disadvantage of this, however, is that it is likely to disrupt the flow of the experience for the participant.

Using self-report

Self-report is a common triangulation method used to help interpretation of eye-tracking and can be done using the 'think aloud' technique either during or after the recording. In the former, the participant's eyes are tracked as they talk through their task, explaining their motivations and behaviour as they are doing the activity. In the latter, a participant completes the task then explains their behaviour while watching a recording of their eye movements. For example, a participant who is seen examining certain menu structures repeatedly can then explain what caused their confusion.

Think aloud protocol during eyetracking is a frequently used technique, but asking the participants to describe what they are doing as they do it affects the realism of the eye movements (Bojko, 2005; Guan, 2006). The alternative as described is to allow the tests to proceed without interruption and ask participants to explain their decisions after the eyetracking session has ended. Some eyetrackers have the facility to replay the recorded eye movements over the scene after the completion of the tasks and Eger et al. (2007) argue that such an approach can have benefits. An alternative is to show a gaze plot as a summary of the session (Bunnyfoot, personal communication). One additional benefit from showing participants their eye movements is that they can share in the excitement of seeing their own recordings. However, this approach has downsides as well. There may be a risk of post-hoc justification of behaviour or the participants may forget some of the problems experienced once the task is completed. On a practical level, replaying all the recording also doubles the session time. Finally, there may be a risk that it makes participants more conscious of their eye behaviour in the subsequent recordings within the session.

Questionnaires and surveys are additional self-report methods which can be usefully combined with eye movement metrics. For example, Renshaw *et al.* (2005) found ratings of satisfaction from post test questionnaires correlated with visual back-tracking when participants were interpreting a graph.

What measures to use?

One of the important tasks when creating a study design is deciding upon what metrics to use. The research question itself is likely to suggest appropriate metrics. For example, for a time critical application a good metric might be the time taken until the first fixation on the correct interface element.

A common practice is to aggregate fixations into 'Areas of Interest' (AOIs), also called 'Regions of Interest' (ROIs; see Figure 3.12). A typical one-minute eyetracking could have up to 50 fixations recorded. Aggregating individual fixations into AOIs is one way to reduce the amount and complexity of data. It also often corresponds to study questions; e.g. on a website do people look at the top advertising banner or left-hand side menu? Typically AOIs are defined by the researcher, however there is some work where automated AOIs have been created by clustering fixations into groups according to algorithms (e.g. Santella and DeCarlo, 2004). There are some cautions when using AOIs. Eyetracking on remote eyetrackers measures at typically $+/-0.5 - 1°$ visual angle and the 'useful field of view' is about $5°$. This blurring of recorded fixation and what is 'seen' needs to be considered especially when examining two adjacent AOIs or very thin AOIs (e.g. streets on maps). Another factor to consider is whether participants need to look around the area of interest in order to fulfil a task; for example, confirming the type of building seen on an aerial photograph through looking at its surrounding buildings and layout (C. Davies, personal communication).

As well as measuring the number and duration of fixations, scanpaths are also interesting to measure. Scanpaths are straight lines drawn between consecutive fixations (see Figure 3.4). Regression or back tracks are a particular type of scanpath in which a previously fixated point is revisited. This is typically seen in reading but is evident in other contexts too, such as interpreting graphs (Renshaw *et al.*, 2004a). Regressions are associated with uncertainty and changes in goals (Goldberg and Kotval, 1999).

Scanpath analysis is a very promising method of data analysis and can be particularly useful when examining efficiency in certain interfaces. For example, where an optimal scanpath is a straight line to a target, less efficient designs will show longer scanpaths as non-targets are fixated on (Kasarkis *et al.*, 2001). Scanpaths can also be used to infer cognitive strategies or level of expertise (Yarbus, 1967; Sadasivan *et al.*, 2005; Nodine *et al.*, 1996 in Yang *et al.*, 2004; Josephson and Holmes, 2002; Yoon and Narayanan, 2004; Underwood, 2005;

West *et al.*, 2006). However, inferring strategy from scanpaths is not straight-forward as many factors influence eye behaviour. For example, Yang *et al.* (2004) found that radiologists will examine key areas in images of lungs when deter-mining whether they are diseased. However, diseases can sometimes manifest in distributed areas, meaning the same expert strategy will result in very different scanpaths. This shows that though experts have an effective strategy for identi-fying diseases, the same strategy has different visual patterns depending on the stimulus viewed. Methodology may also influence strategies taken. For exam-ple, if a participant is asked to discuss what they are doing as they do a task, is the strategy the same even if the scanpaths alter? Or does the strategy alter too?

Determining differences in scanpaths has been done through 'eyeballing' the visualisations (e.g. Aula, Majaranta and Rih, 2005; Yoon and Narayanan, 2004), however the literature cites two principal techniques of determining patterns in scanpaths in a more methodical manner (West *et al.*, 2006). Both techniques are dependent upon splitting the scene up into AOIs, labelling them and determining the sequence of transitions between the AOIs over time. The two methods are known as the string edit method and the Markov chain method (Rayner and Liversedge in Henderson and Ferreira, 2004). In the string edit method a string of letters is created to represent the scanpath. Each letter represents a specific AOI that was fixated on. The string edit method then involves counting the changes required to make one string identical to a second string. This method is complex and requires specialist software for its execution (West *et al.*, 2006). The Markov chain method considers the frequencies of transitions between two consecutive AOIs; e.g. B to F, or G to A. It assumes that all transitions occur independently of each other and so looks at individual transitions rather than an entire scanpath. The frequency of the various transitions can then be compared between groups. The advantage of the Markov chain method over the string edit method is that it is simpler to apply to the data. The necessary transition data can be derived from the *x, y* co-ordinates and/or AOI data collected by an eyetracker. Underwood (2005) used it to analyse eye movements of players of the game Tetris.

Both the string edit method and the Markov chain method make use of transition matrices (Goldberg and Kotval, 1999). A transition matrix is constructed from scanpaths (see Figure 3.8). Movements from one AOI to the next are recorded in a two-dimensional matrix. For example, a movement from AOI 'A' to AOI 'F' would be recorded as one instance in cell AF. Once a complete scanpath has been processed in this way assessments can be made as to how many cells in the matrix contain such transitions and the proportion that such transitions comprise of the total number of possible transitions in the matrix. You can also characterise a matrix with a single number by dividing total transition cells by the total number of cells. For a search task, a large number means a dispersed and lengthy search, a smaller number a more direct or efficient search.

The standard measures of fixations and scanpaths can be evaluated in different ways depending what you are examining. See examples in Table 3.2.

Scan path over Areas of Interest

Transition Matrix

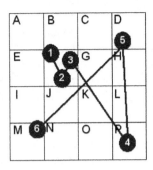

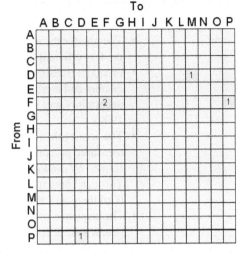

To

	A	B	C	D	E	F	G	H	I	J	K	L	M	N	O	P
A																
B																
C																
D												1				
E																
F				2												1
G																
H																
I																
J																
K																
L																
M																
N																
O																
P		1														

From

Transition Density:
4 filled cells / 256 cells = 0.16

Fig 3.8 *From a scanpath the transition of fixations across different AOIs can be recorded in a transition matrix. From this matrix the transition density can be calculated. A high transition density indicates that lots of transitions were done. For a search task this means extensive search was required before the target was found. A low transition density for a search task indicates a more direct and efficient search (from Goldberg and Kotval, 1999)*

Pupil dilation and blink rate have also been explored as measures of cognitive load and/or stress (Marshall, 2002; Iqbal, Zheng and Bailey, 2004). Marshall (2002) claims to have developed a technique that can distinguish between the dilation cause by luminance and that caused by cognitive workload. However there are other issues. Pupil dilation occurs over time, hence when a measurement is taken is important, as well as clearly identifying to which external stimulus the pupil is responding (Carbon *et al.*, 2006). These issues appear to be less well addressed in the literature. Another issue with using pupil dilation is how much response indicates a significant change in workload (Iqbal *et al.*, 2005; Partala, Jokiniemi and Surakka, 2000).

There are limitations on the use of metrics given the current knowledge of cognitive processing and vision. For example, what are you comparing when the total fixation duration is the same but one gaze pattern is marked by lots of small fixations but another is marked by few but long fixations? Renshaw *et al.* (2004b) suggested a matrix of interpretations that could be applied in certain circumstances, but the maxim must be to always triangulate your results with some other measure to support your conclusions. There is some exploratory work looking at correlating eyetracking patterns to higher-level measures such as usability problems, for example eyetracking patterns seen when a web page is too crowded

Table 3.2 *Example eyetracking metrics in different areas of research interest*

Process	Areas	Examples of measures
Top-down and bottom-up	Search	• The greater the number of fixations before locating a target, the less efficient the layout is (Goldberg and Kotval, 1999). • Frequent transitions back and forth between regions of a display and a greater number of saccades indicate uncertainty and inefficient searching (Goldberg and Kotval, 1999). • The area of the interface covered by scanning can be measured by convex hull area, which outlines the shape formed by drawing around a gaze path (see Figure 3.9). This can show if the area searched was large or small (Goldberg and Kotval, 1999). • The sequence of fixations in a scanpath shows the direction people take when locating a target (e.g. Granka *et al.*, 2004).
	Comprehension	• Fixations elsewhere on an image, after the participant has already fixated on the task target, can indicate the target lacked meaningfulness (Goldberg and Kotval, 1999). • Fixations on previously fixated areas of interest (regressions) indicate these areas are difficult to understand (Renshaw *et al.*, 2004a). • Longer fixations indicate greater processing of this area. This may be due to the area being more engaging or requiring more effort to process (DeGraef, Christiaens and D'Ydewalle, 1990; Friedman, 1979; Henderson *et al.*, 1999, cited in Henderson and Ferreira, 2004).
	Making decisions and solving problems	• Time to fixation and percentage of people fixating on an area can indicate how salient an area is given participants' expectations and interests. • Grouping scanpaths according to different user strategies; e.g. Yoon and Narayanan (2004) found some participants used eye movements to 'redraw' diagrams from memory. • Subtracting heat maps between two participant groups in order to bring out differences.
	Reading and scanning	• Words that are infrequently used or ambiguous in terms of their context are fixated on for longer (Rayner and Liversedge, in Henderson and Ferreira, 2004). • Examining the distance between fixations one can tell which parts of a webpage's copy were read versus scanned (Rayner and Liversedge, in Hendersen and Ferreira, 2004; Holmqvist *et al.*, 2003).
	Efficiency of task completion	• Deviation from an optimal scanpath can show how an interface is hindering a participant from completing a task, or may reflect individual differences such as between novice users and expert users (Kasarskis *et al.*, 2001).
Bottom-up	Visual elements capturing attention	• Fixations on areas of interest that are not required for task completion.

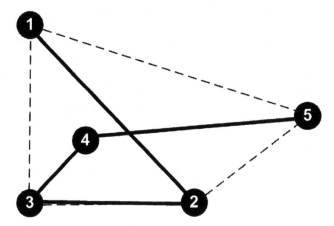

Fig 3.9 *The dotted black line outlines the scanpath and the area within is the convex hull area (from Goldberg and Kotval, 1999)*

with information (Ehmke and Wilson, 2007). However most eyetracking metrics are used at a lower level of granularity, for example, processing effect indicated by fixation duration.

A final note about metrics in eyetracking is that definitions can vary across research depending on the type of study and the stimulus. For example, for the purposes of reading, shorter durations of motionless gaze can be defined as a fixation (Rayner, 1998). Also different eyetrackers will be sensitive to different metrics, for example focusing on finding fixations (i.e. 'fixation pickers') vs. finding saccades ('saccade pickers'). Fixation pickers tend to have lower rates of data sampling and are typically set at 50–60 Hz (Karn, 2000). Currently not all studies give details on the study set-up making cross-study comparisons difficult. It is important that published work in eyetracking fully describes the metrics, equipment and sampling rate (Webb and Renshaw, 2006a; 2006b).

The number of participants required

The numbers of participants required depends on whether you are doing a qualitative or quantitative study. For qualitative work, like usability testing, there are the usual considerations of the number of users needed to find interface problems. In usability testing, eight participants are typically used (Nielsen, 1994b). This number will increase if the product to be reviewed is too large to be completely evaluated by a single user within a session, or if there are different user groups with different behaviours that are the targets for the product. Quantitative studies need enough participants to achieve power to detect statistical differences. In a review of quantitative eyetracking studies, Goldberg and Wichansky (2003) found the number of participants used by researchers in studies ranged between 6 and 30 people.

Analysis of data

A common concern with analysing eyetracking data is dealing with the large amount of data that can be generated. Undertaking an eyetracking study with little focus can generate a large volume of data, forcing the researcher to 'boil the ocean' to find useful answers. Planning up-front what your focus will be reduces the volume of data and makes your analysis more manageable and robust.

Most eyetrackers will provide you with the following types of data:

- Real time movies of the gaze trails
- Gaze plots showing location, order and duration of fixations (see Figure 3.10)
- Heat maps showing aggregated data on the same stimulus across participants (see Figure 3.11)
- Raw data such as location and duration of fixations and events (e.g. keystrokes)
- Raw data aggregated by AOI (see Figure 3.12).

For qualitative work, visualisations are useful starting points. However, care needs to be taken not to rely overly on aggregations, such as heat maps, which may hide detail or patterns of eye movement (Kara Pernice Coyne, personal communication). Watching entire gaze movies is recommended. In particular, if this is done during a series of usability sessions, it can provide guidance as to what should be focused on in later sessions.

When analysing data, a researcher needs to consider visual angle error and the useful field of view. Most remote eyetrackers have an error of 0.5–1° of visual angle. This equates to around plus or minus 1 cm at a sitting distance of 50 cm to the viewed object. As discussed previously the 'useful field of view' is where people can do a degree of semantic processing around a fixation point (Henderson and Ferreira, 2004). Both these factors mean that perceived visual areas may be larger than the fixation points may indicate. To counter for visual angle error you can define the AOIs for analysis to be slightly larger than the actual area of interest. This buffer zone of 1° corresponds to a 30-pixel buffer in a 1024 × 768 screen resolution (Tobii User Manual, 2006).

Eyetrackers have difficulty dealing with dynamic data on the web such as Java. For example, if a travel booking site has a pop-up calendar, the gaze plot will not show you if a fixation was on the calendar or on the page beneath. New tools such as the Scene Cutter within Clearview 2.7 (Tobii, 2006) allow you to cut up the recording into pieces, but it takes more time for analysis than using the automated outputs showing web page frames.

An important factor when making conclusions from analysis is generalising results. For example, if a newspaper website is found to have greater viewing of pictures than an entertainment site, can we generalise to other newspaper websites? To other participants? Because eyetracking combines both 'bottom-up' stimulus effects and 'top-down' motivations, care needs to be taken about what is affecting the response; for instance, colour, position, animation, motivations, instructions to participant (see also Henderson and Ferreira, 2004).

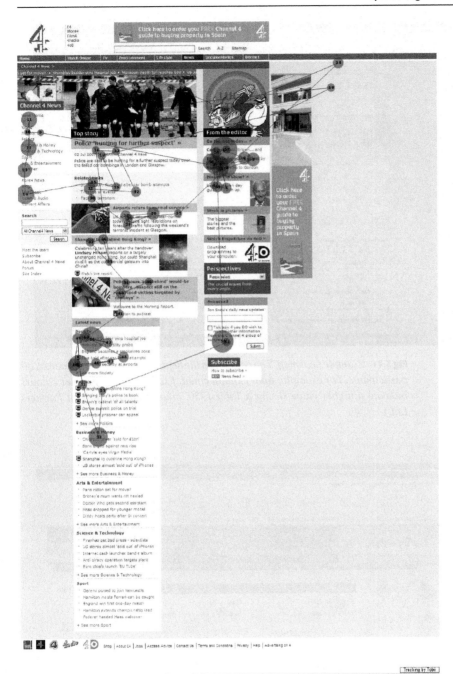

Fig 3.10 *Example gaze trail. The size of the fixation circles indicates the duration of the fixation. The number indicates the order of fixation within the scanpath (using a Tobii 1750, courtesy of Channel Four and Amberlight Partners Ltd.)*

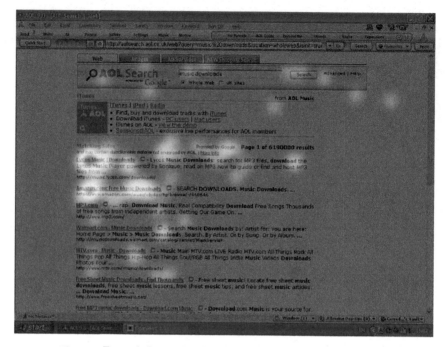

Fig 3.11 *Example heat map. The colours on the heat map represent data across all participants. For example; total fixation count, fixation length. Warmer colours indicate a higher value (using a Tobii 1750, courtesy of Amberlight Partners Ltd.)*

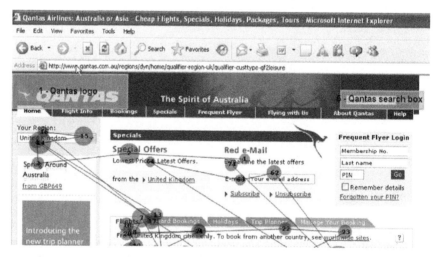

Fig 3.12 *Example web page showing AOIs; Company Logo and Search box (using a Tobii, 1750, courtesy of Amberlight Partners Ltd.)*

From analysis to design

In the context of interface design, a key question is how to move from analysis to design recommendations. Eyetracking can help in a number of ways including:

- Assisting finding and removing design problems, e.g., inefficient search, labelling
- Highlighting internal participant expectations, e.g., where people expect something to be
- Helping participant visual strategies, such as how a design supports an optimal scanpath for situational awareness
- Demonstrating which alternative design supports the right behaviour, e.g., search, the visibility of different elements, efficient reading performance (Yamamoto and Kuto, 1992 in Goldberg and Kotval, 1999).

In summary, a good study design will help a researcher address their research questions. In eyetracking this means thinking through the context of the task, the type of study (quantitative or qualitative), the metrics, your approach to analysis and design implications.

3.2.3 Running a study

In this section, we discuss logistical hints and tips derived from practical experience over many years.

Things to do before the day

Ethical clearance: Researchers have to be concerned about the ethics of what they are about to do and ethical considerations are also discussed in detail in Chapter 1. Once you are happy that you have a clear idea as to what you are testing, why you are testing it and how you are going about it, you are in a position to approach the Ethics Committee – your institution should have one and each body will have its own policies procedures and pace of progressing things. As the process can often be slow, it is a good idea to get ethical approval underway as soon as possible whilst you get on with other activities.

    Recruitment of participants: How many participants should be recruited? As discussed previously, this depends on a number of factors including study design. It also depends on the strength of differences observed. Conducting a pilot study with five or six participants will help you to get an idea of the strength of the effect you are measuring (for more information on experimental design and participant numbers see Chapter 1).

    You should also allow for the following in your recruitment plans:

- The budget for paying participants
- A number of 'no shows' on the day
- Data loss associated with loss of eye contact and other technical problems; this ranges between 5 and 10 per cent in our experience (data loss is defined as percentage of eyetracked time not accounted for by either fixations or saccades)
- The availability of resources such as laboratories and the eyetracker itself.

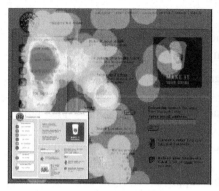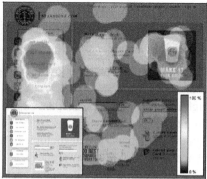

Fig 3.13 *Starbucks homepage. The inserts in the lower left-hand side were the two stimuli shown to the participants. The larger background images are heat maps showing the combined gaze of participants looking for a store locator. Thirteen users were shown the black and white version of the homepage on the left. Twelve users were shown the colour version on the right. Two users looked at the black and white image of the cup but almost all users on the colour version looked at the purple cup (courtesy of Agnieszka Bojko, User Centric, Inc., 2005)*

Your institute might have a policy and sets of procedures of which you need to be aware when recruiting participants. However, in practice the biggest problem you may face, particularly if you are a researcher within an academic institution, is getting sufficient numbers of volunteers. Friends, fellow researchers, students recruited through advertising on display notice boards are all possible sources of recruits. Once recruited you may be tempted to cultivate a group of people and use them in a series of studies. However, beware of introducing unintentional biases by doing so. The group might get insights into what you are trying to do and go out of their way to help you get the answers you want. To be safe, recruit another set of naïve participants. The number of volunteers may be increased if you can reward them in some way, e.g. through cash incentives.

Preparing the stimuli: Examples of stimuli used in eyetracking studies include websites, films, games, spreadsheets and pictures. You need to check what stimuli types your eyetracker can display. There are some instances where the eyetracker cannot record the stimuli rendered in a particular way (pop-ups or Flash images for example). If so you need to redesign the test or find a technical solution (e.g. render the visual image without pop-ups). Bojko (2005) provides some pictorial evidence of the variability of eye movements caused by differing standards of image rendering. This indicates that the higher the visual realism of the stimulus the more realistic the data will be; e.g. provide colour if colour would be in the final interface (see Figure 3.13). For similar reasons, in comparative studies the stimuli must be produced to the same standards. A website page may have different page elements downloading at different speeds, such as graphics and advertisements. If the study's focus does not include looking at this effect, the page elements can be downloaded in the background before the page is displayed.

Designing the tasks: We have previously described the requirements of the eye–mind hypothesis when designing tasks. However, in addition to those requirements the tasks have to be as realistic as possible and critically reviewed in advance to ensure their completion will give answers which will address the research question(s). The tasks have to be communicated effectively to the participant, in circumstances in which the participant may feel, despite your best efforts, self-conscious or stressed. This means tasks may need to be written down and not unduly complex. Importantly, they need to be rehearsed by the researcher to make sure that they can actually be performed and to remove any operational glitches (e.g. invalid urls or commands, the omission of some vital instruction). It is a good idea to get somebody, who will not be part of the formal study, to go through and rehearse the tasks so that ambiguities and incompleteness of instructions can be removed.

Questionnaires and other documents: The following documents need to be prepared in advance:

- The participant briefing. This describes the broad nature of the experiment and processes to be gone through.
- An informed consent form. This is signed by each participant and gives them the right to withdraw at any time. It gives you the right to publish the data and/or use any video recordings.

If required you may also need to prepare:

- A participant profile questionnaire.
- A post evaluation questionnaire or interview script.

Participant profile questionnaires should be used to capture the skills, experiences, attitudes, age and gender of your participants. You may want to filter out those participants with attributes you do not want in your data set by using a participant profile questionnaire or interview before the test. However, you do not necessarily have to filter participants on the basis of corrective eyeware (such as glasses) or eye colour, as modern eyetrackers can usually cope with a range of these factors. Because the causes of eye movements can never be absolutely attributed and have to be inferred it is always advisable to capture participants' experiences through the use of post test questionnaires and/or interviews. These need to be planned in advance. It is beyond the scope of this chapter to describe how to design questionnaires or interview scripts; see Chapter 2 for more detail.

Scheduling the day

Participants will need reasonable notice of the date and time at which they are required and be told the duration of the tests. The length of time an eyetracking session should last needs to be predetermined. Too long a session and there is a risk of participant boredom, technical failure and data analysis overload. There are also ethical issues around the amount of stress participants should be expected to undergo and how much work they should be expected to do. Also time should be allowed for the completion of any questionnaires.

In preparing for your study the authors make the following suggestions:

- Plan for no more than four to eight participants a day (though this will be dependent upon how much you ask them to do).
- There should be a daily time limit to a participant's involvement in a single session: we recommend up to 90 minutes maximum.
- The eyetracking element should last no longer that 30 minutes – 15 minutes is usually sufficient. These time periods help create more manageable amounts of data for analysis.
- Schedule breaks into the sessions for you and your participants.

On the day

Upon arrival, participants need to be made to feel at home. They should be asked to read a brief which outlines what is going to happen and what is expected of them during the test. They can then sign the informed consent form. They should be briefed as to how the equipment works and what the tasks are (in writing or verbally or both). If at all possible, they should be seated in a high-back, wheel-less, height adjustable chair. This will help position the participant in the right place for the eyetracker's camera. They should be asked if they understand what they are to do, if they have any questions and if they are willing to proceed.

The next essential and really important step is to calibrate the equipment to each participant. In this process participants are asked to look at a series of stimuli on the eyetracker screen whose position is known precisely. The tracker detects where their eyes are looking and makes the necessary adjustments to align the detected eye position to the known target positions. It can take as little as 30 seconds to do this vitally important task. Modern eyetrackers can tolerate normal head movements as people look at the screen, look down at the keyboard and back again, or from left or right to the edges of the display screen. However, it is important that the participant is sitting comfortably in a position they can hold for the duration of the eyetracking session as radical changes in position during the study could result in loss of eye movement recording and invalidate the results. If your eyetracker configuration allows the simultaneous display of eye movements on a separate monitor to that being viewed by the participant this loss will become immediately apparent when it occurs. If it does happen note the time the event occurred and remove any spurious data prior to analysis. Losses post-evaluation may be picked up by reviewing the data collected and investigating any unusual results, for example, a small number of fixations or large time periods between fixations. The question as to whether to include these data in the analysis depends upon what metrics are being considered and the distortion such inclusion may introduce.

At this point, it is advisable to take the participant through a rehearsal of the process they will encounter in the test. One option is to give the participant practice tasks similar to the ones in the study. This helps to decrease participants' stress, eliminate potential 'noise' in the results arising from participants' unfamiliarity with the experimental design and ensures the equipment is working properly. Depending upon the experimental design, now is the time for the test supervisor to leave the participant to it, or sit behind or next to the participant during the session. If the facilitator remains, you need to be aware your presence may be distracting, for instance, the participant may want to turn to talk to you. However correctly briefing the participant can reduce the likelihood of this. Other interruptions such as people moving around or in and out of the laboratory are also likely to be distracting and should therefore be minimised.

Finally at the end of the session the participant should be thanked, reimbursed if this hasn't been done already, data backed up and documents filed safely.

3.3   Two case studies

3.3.1 Case study 1: How do people view line graphs?

The following is based on work reported in Renshaw *et al.* (2003).

Overview and research goal

How do people view graphs? What elements of a graph do people look at to help them answer questions about the information shown in the graph? Traditional performance measures were used in conjunction with eyetracking metrics to evaluate the usability of two contrasting formats of line graphs (see Figures 3.14 and 3.15). One style of graph followed established design guidelines for facilitating efficient visual processing, the other flouted them.

The hypothesis was that the specially designed legend area of Graph Type 1 would enhance the usability of the graph's design. In addition, eye movements extended the study to demonstrate how different areas of the graph were used in assimilation of the data and to demonstrate that eye movements can be influenced by design features.

Metrics

Usability was gauged in three ways:

1 Timing and accuracy of task completion
2 Participant assessment: the participants rated the graphs on a Likert scale from 5 (very usable) to 1 (low usability)
3 Eyetracking: graph legend areas were defined as AOIs. Metrics used were number of fixations, their duration, the scanpath length and the number of regressions. Eye movement behaviour in the legend areas was calculated as vertical or horizontal using the gaze orientation ratio.[1] The amount of fixating within legend areas was used as an indication of interest or difficulty understanding the legend.

---

[1] The gaze orientation ratio is derived by dividing the vertical distance between consecutive fixations by their horizontal separation. The resultant measure is then used to categorise the movement as vertical or horizontal.

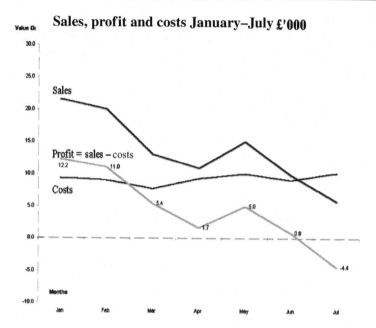

Fig 3.14 *Example of graph design style 1 – follows design guidelines for line graphs. The legend is incorporated as labels on the graph*

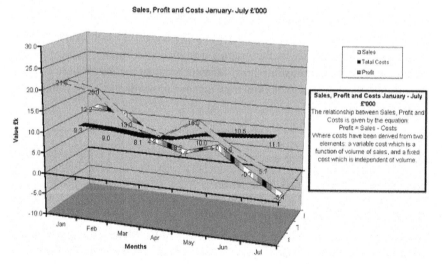

Fig 3.15 *Example of graph design style 2 – flouts design guidelines for line graphs, incorporates a superfluous third dimension and a more complex legend remote from the variables to which it is related*

Graph Type 1 was predicted to be the most usable graph as it follows established design guidelines. Two specific behaviours associated with the Graph Type 1 legend were also anticipated: first, a larger proportion of vertically orientated gazes due to the vertical legend area; second, the location of the first fixation would be near this specially designed legend (the 'emergent feature', see Pomerantz, 1986).

Method

Twenty-four volunteer participants (15 male, 9 female) took part in the experiment. The experiment was a repeated measures design with each participant viewing 8 graphs of each type of design format. Graphs were viewed one at a time in a random sequence until all 16 graphs had been displayed.

Eye movement is task dependent and so participants were asked to visually and physically locate (by means of a mouse pointer) the answer to one unique question associated with each particular graph, e.g. 'What sales were achieved in March?' The questions varied for each graph displayed.

Apparatus and Materials

The experiment used an ASL 504 pan/tilt eyetracker system capable of detecting a bright backlit pupil image. The resolution of the eyetracker is better than 1° of visual angle and uses a sampling rate of 50 Hz. It was positioned immediately below a 17 in. PC colour monitor with a screen resolution of 1024×768 pixels. The graphs were created in Excel XP and commercially available software was used to select the images at random and control the timed presentation of the visual prompt for the facilitator to ask the task question.

Procedure

All 24 participants were volunteers, recruited without vetting. Upon arrival the participants were encouraged to relax and become familiar with their surroundings. They were briefed on the equipment and the principles of its operation. The participants were asked to read and then sign a consent form. They were advised they could abandon the test at any time. A pre-experiment briefing involved the display and rehearsal of responses to a hybrid graph, containing features of the two designs.

During the running of the experiment participants were asked to keep their heads as still as possible whilst looking at the screen. (The ASL 504 is less tolerant of head motion than other eyetrackers.) The first of a randomised sequence of graphs was displayed and the participant was allowed to look at it for 15 seconds after which the researcher, cued by the disappearance of a coloured box placed at the lower edge of the graph display, asked a graph-related question (the task). The graph remained until the participant indicated the answer by clicking over a point on the display. This cycle was repeated for all 16 graphs. When the final question had been answered, the system displayed the answers recorded and the participant was asked to rate the graph formats for ease of use on a scale of 1 (low)

Table 3.3 *Results from metrics of timing and accuracy, participant assessment and eyetracking*

Metric	Test	Graph Type 1	Graph Type 2
Timing and accuracy	Error rate for first question (%)	7.30	14.60
	Time taken to answer first question* (s)	22.88	24.60
	Error rate for second question*	27.70	49.50
Participant assessment	Ease of use ratings*	4.46	1.71
Eyetracking	Number of fixations	38.75	39.77
	Total fixation duration (s)	14.94	17.05
	Proportion of regressions (number of regression/total fixations)* (%)	14.60	17.30
	Proportion of vertically orientated gazes*	0.46	0.20
	Scanpath length*†	5929 units	*7856 units

* Significant to $p < 0.05$ (two-tailed).
† The ASL 504 screen is divided into an area of 950×840 units which does not have physical measurements associated with the units, such as millimeters or pixels.

to 5 (high). The location and temporal distribution of all the fixations together with the mouse clicks were collated for analysis.

Results

All usability measures (timing and accuracy, participant assessment and those based on eye movement metrics) consistently indicated that Graph Type 1 was more usable compared to Graph Type 2 (see Table 3.3).

Eye behaviour anticipated with the Graph Type 1 legend was also apparent. There were significantly more vertically aligned gazes in the legend of Graph Type 1 than in Graph Type 2 (see Table 3.3).

As also predicted, the first fixations for Graph Type 1 were found to be in or very near to the legend area – an area which was accessed frequently throughout the experiment. This differed from Graph Type 2 where the first fixations were found in a predominantly central position on the display. This indicates that important information on Graph Type 1 was more easily located than on Graph Type 2.

Conclusion

This study demonstrated the importance of the legend and data areas for the comprehension and usability of graphs. Eye movement data were found to be consistent with more traditional performance measures and helped establish that graphs constructed in line with design criteria have a statistically significant advantage over other designs in terms of time taken to complete tasks, accuracy and user appeal.

The use of eyetracking in a related study (Peebles and Cheng, 2003) is reported in Chapter 4. Peebles and Cheng made use of scanpaths to infer attention on the different parts of the display when people were trying to extract data from a graph in order to answer a question. They were able to compare the scanpaths to the output from a cognitive model in order to test their theory about what people do to solve these types of problems.

3.3.2 Case study 2: The use of eyetracking in the study of computer games

Overview

Renshaw, Stevens and Finlay (2006) undertook a series of eyetracking studies using a third person action game as the stimulus. Applications such as video games, video and film are an interesting challenge for eyetracking as they contain dynamic moving images. Dynamic stimuli present additional and relatively unexplored challenges to eyetracking technology over and above those posed by static images. A principal challenge is determining the viewer's object of interest. Some eyetracker manufacturers provide software development kits which may facilitate this (e.g. LC Technologies, ASL). Brumby, Cutrell and Sarin (2006) state that they have used a software development kit to send 'events' to an eyetracker enabling them to map fixations to application interface features. A similar approach could in principle be used in games to enable the linking of objects to fixations. However, the method also requires access to the game's source code. At the time of writing, little work has been found describing such an approach in games (an exception being Sennersten *et al.*, 2007).

The case study below is based on the study by Renshaw *et al.* (2006) and shows what can be achieved by way of analysis using only a conventional eyetracking system and basic fixation analysis software.

Research goal of the study

The objectives of the study were to determine whether eyetracking would:

- provide an explanation as to why even experienced players became stuck at particular levels within games
- whether any changes in eye movement characteristics could be related to the players' stress, frustration or boredom with a game
- whether different game levels would induce significant variations in the distribution of eye movements over the screen surface (this could inform where supporting feedback or information for players should be located or where in-game advertisements could be best located).

Method

Tomb Raider Levels 'Peru: Ball Puzzle' and 'England: Pool Area' were selected for comparison. Each player played the same game in the same order on a

Pentium 4 PC using a Playstation 2 Dualshock game controller. The images were displayed on a Tobii 1750 eyetracker which can capture eye positions at 50 Hz. The eyetracking data were collected on a PC with a high specification graphics card and powerful enough to handle the simultaneous playing of the game and the collection of eyetracking data. The eyetracking software was configured such that eye positions were aggregated into fixations if they occurred within 40 pixels of each other within 100 ms. The eyetracker was configured to accept external video as the stimulus.

Procedure

Seven male participants aged 20–29 were selected on the basis of their gaming skills and experience. Upon arrival, the participants were briefed in a general way as to the nature of the experiment and the experimental process to be deployed. They all completed a profile questionnaire giving details of themselves and their gaming experience. The eyetracker was then calibrated to each participant's eyes. Each participant was allowed a brief period of familiarisation with the game console using an excerpt from another level of the game.

Prior to each game the participants were informed that they had to solve the puzzle presented by that level. They were not told that the time to solve the puzzle was strictly limited to five minutes. They were also told that they would be asked how they felt at regular intervals during the course of the experiment and that they were to reply using single-word expressions such as, 'fine', 'great', 'frustrated', etc. These responses were recorded manually.

After both games had been completed the participants were asked to complete a questionnaire giving details of their feelings about the last game played. Finally, an interview was conducted with each player about their experience of playing the second game. (Note, the interview was only after the second game in order to safeguard against memory degradation.)

Results

The first question addressed by the study was to determine whether the eyetracking technique could be used to determine why players get stuck at certain levels within a game/level. In the Peru game the players had to manoeuvre several stone balls into indentations in the floor. A replay of the recorded eye movements superimposed over each individual's game showed that within the first minute of play all players had identified the indentations in the floor into which the balls should be placed and the location of two out of the three balls. The third was too well hidden and the appropriate area was not fixated upon by any of the players, consequently the puzzle remained unsolved.

In the England pool game level the benefits of being able to replay eye movements and re-live the game as played were even more apparent. A review of the recorded eyetracking data revealed that a verbal cue was given as to the where-abouts of a target when Lara (the main character in the game) crossed a specific area. However, for the verbal cue to have any meaning the player had to be looking in the right direction with the correct camera attitude. Only one player did this. So from the majority of players' point of view the audio cue, although obtrusive, was irrelevant.

The second research question posed by the study concerned the response of the eyes to experience of frustration during a game. Fixation duration was examined in detail principally because of the measure's association with cognitive effort (Goldberg and Kotval, 1999). There was no correlation with either the participants' self-reported increase in frustration or with the increased time pressure incorporated into the experiments. There may well be several interrelated reasons for this – was the eye metric appropriate to measure frustration? Did the verbal prompts elicit an accurate response?

The third and final question asked if there were differences in fixation distribution and transitional movements across the screen between different game levels which demanded different types of player activity. A replay of the eye movements appeared to show them to be predominantly confined to the centre of the screen for both game levels. However, despite their apparent similarity there were some significant differences in fixation distribution and transition pattern. The Peru game level was fixated more intensely and within a more confined area than was the England pool game level, which demanded more searching for objects. This is an important distinction; for example, advertisers may want to know the extent and frequency with which specific areas of a screen are fixated upon during the conduct of a game to inform the placement of advertising.

Discussion

The study confirms that eyetracking has some applications in investigating problematic game design issues such as confirming the player's identification of particular interactive objects. In this study of a third person action game, the majority of fixations seem to fall in the centre of the screen, but it is possible to detect differences in the spread and in the nature of transitions between areas on the screen as gamers undertake different tasks. This may be of importance to advertisers wishing to incorporate such things as advertising messages into games design.

The capturing of the players' emotional reaction to the games seems to have been problematic and the authors conclude that there may have to be a re-think/exploration as to what eye metrics are most appropriate to measure players' emotional responses.

3.4   Summary and critique

The case studies provided in this chapter help to demonstrate the variety of areas in which eyetracking can be applied. (For further references on other areas in which eyetracking has been used see Section 3.5 of this chapter.) In addition, they show both the strengths and weaknesses of the method. Its strengths lie with it being unobtrusive, objective, detailed and offering compelling visualisations. It provides a way to investigate visual attention that is unavailable by many methods. In terms of practicalities, the technology has become much more accessible for researchers and is continuing to improve. However, eyetracking requires good study design and, due to assumptions of the eye–mind hypothesis, researchers need to be careful in their conclusions about the cognition behind behaviour.

One of the strengths of eyetracking is that it seductively offers a way to get detailed realistic data in real time. Most commercial eyetrackers sample at 50–60 Hz, which provides thousands of data points from a typical task. Remote eyetracking is unobtrusive and the physical set-up interferes very little with realistic behaviour. However, mobile eyetracking, where people wear eyetrackers when undertaking real-life tasks, such as shopping, may be less natural an experience than studies where the tasks are computer based.

Eyetracking provides a way to examine visual attention which has been difficult to investigate with other methods. Visual attention can be difficult to establish with self-report, as much of it can be unconscious or too rapid to report in great granularity. In certain situations, self-report is also influenced by bias, where a person may be uncomfortable reporting where they were looking, e.g. sexual content or advertising. Though there appear to be no studies in this area, visual attention would seem difficult to consciously falsify. Eyetracking may also be useful for children where they may have more trouble articulating their thoughts or may tend to give uniformly positive reports (Read, MacFarlane and Casey, 2002).

Eyetracking does not require the participant to do any additional tasks in order for data to be recorded, e.g. recording a diary, mouse clicks. This offers an advantage in situations where using common HCI methods such as think aloud may be inappropriate; for example, in a time-critical piece of software, or an application that requires high cognitive load. As discussed, there is some evidence that retrospective feedback prompted by eye movement recordings trigger more reporting of problems with less interference in the task than when using concurrent think aloud (Eger et al., 2007).

Lastly, another attraction of eyetracking is that the software can easily create compelling data visualisations. Visualisations such as gaze plots and heat maps are a good tool for visual inspection of data and also are great ways to visualise findings especially for commercial HCI work. Eyetracking also allows live visualisation of data through eye positions being shown simultaneously on a separate monitor.

Eyetracking has a number of constraints as a technique, primarily around the eye–mind hypothesis. As discussed previously, visual attention can mean many things, from searching, to reading, to indicating confusion. The role of the researcher is to define the study so that the behaviour can be interpreted. Generalising from studies also needs to be done carefully. For example, generalising results from one website to other sites is poor practice unless the sites are very similar in terms of who their users are and visual design.

Researchers also need to keep in mind the complexities of vision and that vision cannot be reduced to only fixations, saccades and pupil dilation. For example, as discussed, 'useful field of view', peripheral vision and pre-attentive processing need to be considered. Eyetracking data do not show a complete summary of what people see; they show where the highest acuity of vision was deployed (Henderson and Ferreira, 2004).

Relating eyetracking to the wider HCI picture needs to be considered. HCI practionners regularly think of behaviour in terms of efficiency, effectiveness and satisfaction. These are fairly high-level measures and as discussed the researcher needs to think about the connection between research goals, metrics for analysis and how eyetracking data of fixations, saccades and pupil dilation relate to these measures.

Technically there are still limitations with eyetracking. Some analysis has not yet been greatly automated; for example, you cannot easily show gaze plots with dynamic elements such as pop-up calendars. Also there is no commercially available software to help speed up gaze path analysis, though some software is in development (West *et al.*, 2006).

Investment in eyetracking also needs to be considered. Eyetrackers are expensive pieces of technology, ranging from about £16,000 to £20,000 including software. Eyetracking data can also take more time to analyse and interpret in comparison to traditional user testing.

In summary, eyetracking can offer a unique window into visual attention. Eyetracking collects detailed behaviour in real time that is not influenced by self-report and interferes little with undertaking of activities. However, eyetracking data need to be carefully interpreted with regard to the eye–mind hypothesis and the visual system. The researcher also needs to think through how patterns of fixations and saccades relate to study goals.

3.5 Further reading

Rayner, K. 1998. 'Eye movements in reading and information processing: 20 years of research.' *Psychological Bulletin* 124(3):372–422. Published in 1998 this is perhaps a bit dated now. However it is a very comprehensive review of the research done up to that point of eyetracking in reading and visual information processing. It contains a very comprehensive bibliography.

Goldberg, J. H. and Kotval, X. P. 1999. 'Eye movement based evaluation of the computer interface – Its psychological foundation and relevance to display design.' *Int. J. of Industrial Ergonomics* (24)6: 631–45. Goldberg and Kotval have authored several papers on eyetracking. This paper however is a cornerstone for modern quantitative eyetracking in usability evaluation. It is a very readable paper with its main contribution the definition and description of various eye movement metrics. The metrics are then evaluated through seeing if they correlate with the findings of expert reviews.

Cowen, L., Ball, L. J. and Delin, J. 2002. 'An eye movement analysis of web page usability.' In Faulkner, X., Finlay, J. and Detienee, F. (eds.) *People and Computers XVI: Memorable Yet Invisible*, Berlin: Springer, pp. 317–35. The appeal of this work is that, unlike Goldberg and Kotval's work, it uses realistic website designs as stimuli for a usability evaluation study. This paper established the use of eyetracking as a useful adjunct to conventional usability evaluation techniques. It gives a description of how to design an evaluation and is thorough in its statistical treatment of the eyetracking measures used. It suggests that the mechanisms driving eye movements might be numerous, complex and compete one with the other. It sets the standard to which all would-be eyetracking researchers ought to aspire.

Goldberg, J. H., Stimson, M. J., Lewenstein, M., Scott, N. and Wichansky, A.M. 2002. 'Eyetracking in web search tasks: Design implications.' In *Proc. of Eye Tracking Research and Applications 2002*, New York: ACM Press, pp. 51–8. This work describes a multi-task eyetracking study which uses pages from a multi-screen web interface development tool in which there are numerous portals. The paper carefully describes the rationale for the study, its execution, and the collection and analysis of the large volume of data. The study results are presented at various levels starting with standard usability measures such as task completion times, then eye movement characteristics at the page level and finally between objects on a page. They look for, but cannot find, evidence that searches become more directed as users become more familiar with the site. They do find, however, that there was a tendency for users to adopt a between-column horizontal search rather than a vertically orientated within-column search. They also detect that the optimum position for links is to be amongst those at the top left of a screen. They conclude that eyetracking has the potential to inform design decisions.

Goldberg, J. H. and Wichansky, A. M. 2003. 'Eyetracking in usability evaluation: A practitioner's guide.' In Hyönä, J., Radach, R. and Deubel, H. *The Mind's Eye: Cognitive and Applied Aspects of Eye Movement Research*, Oxford: Elsevier Science, pp. 493–516. This paper is a chapter in a comprehensive but relatively expensive book. The chapter title describes precisely what the chapter contents cover and is a must read for those contemplating using eyetracking as a usability evaluation tool. It reviews usability evaluation techniques generally then goes on to describe eyetracking technology, the role eyetracking can play in evaluations and the issues involved in setting up and conducting an eyetracking study. Finally, it outlines areas requiring further research.

Jacob, R. J. K. and Karn, S. K. 2003. 'Eyetracking in Human-Computer Interaction and usability research: Ready to deliver the promises.' In Hyönä, J., Radach, R. and Deubel, H. *The Mind's Eye: Cognitive and Applied Aspects of Eye Movement Research*, Oxford: Elsevier Science, pp. 573–606. This is a commentary in the same book as the Goldberg and Wichansky paper. This too is a really excellent introduction to eyetracking. It discusses not only eyetracking as a tool for usability evaluation but its contribution to the study of HCI using the eye as an input mechanism. The authors discuss why eyetracking is not more popular than it is, given its seemingly rich potential to provide insights into cognitive processes. Their view is naturally coloured by the technologies available at the time of writing. They have not had the advantages of technological advances that have made current eyetrackers more reliable, robust and easier to use. Nonetheless the paper is essential reading for those that want an introduction to eyetracking issues within the context of HCI now and in the future.

McCarthy, J., Sasse, M. A. and Riegelsberger, J. (2003). 'Could I have the menu please? An eyetracking study of design conventions.' In O'Neill, E., Palanque, P. and Johnson, P. (eds.) *People and Computers XVII: Designing for Society*, Berlin: Springer Verlag, pp. 401–14. In this paper, the authors explore the importance of keeping to conventions in respect of menu position when designing web pages. They argue that whilst site complexity does impact task completion times, users can rapidly adapt to changing menu locations.

Granka, L., Joachims, T. and Gay, G. 2004. 'Eyetracking analysis of user behaviour in www search.' *Proc. of SIGIR 2004*, New York: ACM Press, pp. 478–9. This is a short paper describing how users browse search engine results and select the most relevant link. The research used eyetracking to gain a more comprehensive understanding of what the searcher is doing, and what they are reading, for how long, and in what order. The paper is a good example of how eyetracking can add unique insight.

Poole, A. and Ball, L. J. 2005. 'Eyetracking in Human-Computer Interaction and usability research: Current status and future prospects.' In Ghaoui, C. (ed.) *Encyclopedia of Human Computer Interaction*. Hersley, USA: Idea Group, pp. 211–19. A good clear introductory chapter to the basics of eyetracking. It also collates a large number of different metrics used for measuring interface usability.

Burke, M., Hornhof, A., Nilsen, E. and Gorman, N. 2005. 'High-cost banner blindness: Ads increase perceived workload, hinder visual search and are forgotten.' *ACM Trans. on Computer–Human Interaction* 12(4): 423–45. This paper brings together two main experiments looking at the effect of banner ads on visual search on the web. The authors recap nicely the interactions between top-down and bottom-up factors on attention and have a good synopsis and critique of prior work looking at visual search and banner ads. They detail the lengths they go to to remove confounds from their study design. Overall the paper is a good example of bringing together different approaches and methods (e.g. workload, recall, speed) as well as showing the unique contribution that eyetracking provided to help answer the research question.

Bojko, A. 2006. 'Using eyetracking to compare web page designs: A case study.' *J. of Usability Studies* 3(1): 112–20. Well and clearly written, this study shows powerfully how eyetracking can augment conventional usability metrics. In the study, two different designs of the same website are compared. The eyetracking results demonstrated that a search and locate task can be viewed as a two-stage process. The first stage is to locate the relevant area of the web page and the second stage is to recognise and process its content and meaning. Eyetracking showed behavioural differences arising from design variations, when these differences were not apparent from task completion times or accuracy rates.

Duchowski, A. 2007. *Eye Tracking Methodology Theory and Practice* (2nd edn). London: Springer-Verlag. This book has a very appealing title promising answers to many questions in eyetracking and, being a paperback, is not too expensive even for the most modest of budgets. However, it may be too detailed in certain areas for usability practitioners wanting a quick introduction to eyetracking. It details the neurological paths and mechanisms associated with perception and eye movement. For those wanting to develop their own eyetracker or with an interest in eye movement outside the context of usability this book is a good starting place.

For example, there are details on what factors contribute to the mathematical determination of eye positions. For the non-technical this is most probably the most detailed scientific exploration of eye movement cited in this chapter; perhaps more a book to dip into in search of an authoritative, comprehensive answer to a specific problem than a book to be read cover to cover.

3.5.1 Further references

These are some additional references for areas not covered in depth in this chapter.

Eyetracking as input

Jacob, R. J. K. 1991. 'The use of eye movements in human–computer interaction techniques: What you look at is what you get.' *ACM Trans. on Information Systems* 9(3): 152–69.

Sibert, L. E. and Jacob, R.J.K. 2000. 'Evaluation of eye gaze interaction.' In *Proc. of CHI 2000*, New York: ACM Press, pp. 281–8.

Visual system

Gregory, R. L. 1998. *Eye and Brain: The Psychology of Seeing*. Oxford: Oxford University Press.

Palmer, S. E. 2002. *Vision Science: Photons to Phenomenology*. Cambridge, MA: MIT Press.

3.6   Organisations and conferences

Cogain.org: COGAIN stands for Communication by Gaze Interaction. COGAIN brings together expertise to develop assistive technologies for citizens with motor impairments.

ETRA (www.e-t-r-a.org): ETRA stands for Eye Tracking Research and Applications. ETRA is a biennial symposium focused on all aspects of eye movement research across a wide range of disciplines. The goal of ETRA is to bring together computer scientists, engineers and behavioural scientists in support of a common vision of enhancing eyetracking research and applications.

OpenEyes (http://hcvl.hci.iastate.edu/cgi-bin/openEyes.cgi): OpenEyes is an open-source open-hardware tool kit for low-cost eyetracking. The development of OpenEyes rose from the lack of freely available software to implement eyetracking methods. The tools available for this platform include algorithms to measure eye movements from digital videos, techniques to calibrate eyetracking systems and example software to facilitate eyetracking application development.

Scanpaths.org: This organization and website aim to provide the research community with a central online repository of eye-movement data gathered from laboratories and companies around the world. These data are available for researchers to develop new gaze-tracking and visual information analysis algorithms and systems, without needing to recreate the experiments carried out to collect the data.

3.7   Acknowledgements

The authors would like to warmly thank the following for their support and feedback: Amberlight Partners Ltd (United Kingdom), Dr Linden Ball (Lancaster University, United Kingdom), Dr Anna L. Cox (UCL Interaction Centre, United Kingdom), Nikki Bristol (Optimal Usability, New Zealand), Prof. Andrew Duchowski (School of Computing, Clemson University, USA), Prof. Janet Finlay (Leeds Metropolitan University, United Kingdom), Leeds Metropolitan University (United Kingdom), Trent Mankelow (Optimal Usability, New Zealand).

4 Cognitive modelling in HCI research

ANNA L. COX AND DAVID PEEBLES

4.1 Overview

Over the last 30 years or so, computers have evolved rapidly into powerful and complex systems that underlie virtually every aspect of modern life and, if current trends continue, it is likely that they will be even more pervasive in the future. With the increased embeddedness of computer technology into our society, the characteristics of users have diversified rapidly from a situation where the average user was often a white, middle-aged male with a particular educational and socio-economic background to one in which users of all ages, sexes, social and ethnic backgrounds, levels of education and computer knowledge are interacting with complex interfaces to computer systems. The range and complexity of people's interactions with computers have also grown rapidly over recent years, so that we now do many things via a computer (e.g., managing a bank account, paying household bills, shopping, organising a holiday) that would have been done in the high street just a few years ago.

These rapid developments present significant challenges to interface designers. As the range and sophistication of computer-based tasks have increased so have the interfaces that people are required to use, and so the issue of how people perceive and process complex displays of information when carrying out tasks becomes ever more important. In order to understand these processes more closely, analysts have utilised the theories and methods of cognitive psychology – the study of human perception and information processing – to construct *cognitive models*: specifications of the mental representations, operations and problem-solving strategies that occur during the execution of computer-based tasks. These models can take several forms, from relatively general descriptions of the steps required to complete a task, to sophisticated computer simulations of users performing a task with an interface. Whatever the form, the process of cognitive modelling can benefit interface design by enabling analysts to develop a more precise and detailed understanding of human–computer interactions and in some cases to predict how users will behave. Much of the benefit of cognitive models, therefore, is that they can be used early on in the design process as well as in the evaluation of existing designs. Cognitive models can also allow designers to identify and explain the nature of problems that users encounter and provide information concerning the cognitive and perceptual constraints on human performance. This would assist in designing systems that do not place excessive processing demands on users or that can take advantage of particular aspects of users' skills and abilities.

In this chapter, we describe two of the most commonly used cognitive modelling techniques and illustrate both with examples of their use to show the insights into human–computer interaction that each provides. The first approach consists of a family of analysis techniques based on a model of human information processing and a related task analysis method proposed by Card, Moran and Newell (1983). The second, more recent approach employs *embodied cognitive architectures* – theories of cognition, perception and motor control implemented as software systems – to understand human–computer interaction by simulating it. Finally, we point the reader towards a number of recent attempts to develop tools to integrate both of these approaches with the aim of facilitating the modelling process and making cognitive modelling techniques more accessible to a wider range of HCI practitioners.

4.2　Engineering models

4.2.1　GOMS

The oldest and still arguably most widely used approach to modelling human–computer interaction is based on a model of human information processing and a task analysis method proposed by Card *et al.* (1983). The models produced using this method are often called *engineering, predictive* or *zero-parameter* models because they are used to predict aspects of human performance with an interface or device *before* users are actually introduced to it. One benefit of such models is that they allow designers to evaluate different interface designs in terms of the speed and number of operations required to perform different tasks without actually having to build complete systems and get people to test them. This process differs from the cognitive modelling traditionally conducted in psychology which typically develops models with free parameters that can be adjusted to optimise the fit between the models' output and human data previously collected in experiments.

A core feature of this approach is the GOMS task analysis method. GOMS is an acronym formed from the four elements of the analysis: *Goals* (the aims of the user when interacting with the computer), *Operators* (the possible interactions that the interface allows, for example clicking and dragging with a mouse cursor, opening a text editor window, pressing a key on the keyboard etc.), *Methods* (sequences of sub-goals and operators that can be used to achieve a particular goal) and *Selection rules* (the rules by which a user chooses a particular method from a number of alternatives for achieving a goal). The primary method for producing a GOMS task analysis is to break down tasks into a hierarchy of goals, *unit tasks* (basic learned sequences of integrated actions) and sub-tasks using the four elements outlined above. To illustrate the approach, below is a GOMS analysis (adapted from Kieras, 1994) of the common task of deleting an object (e.g., a file or directory) using a graphical user interface such as Microsoft Windows or the K desktop environment (KDE) on Linux. All of the most commonly used graphical user interfaces use the 'trash-can' metaphor for deleting objects, according to which objects must be placed into a specific location in order to be deleted. All of the popular desktop environments also generally provide multiple ways for this goal to be achieved.

Method for goal: **delete object**

1 Accomplish goal: move object to trash
2 Return with goal accomplished

Method for goal: **move object [destination]**

1 Accomplish goal: drag object [destination]
2 Return with goal accomplished

Method for goal: **move object [destination]**

1 Accomplish goal: send object [destination]
2 Return with goal accomplished

Method for goal: **drag object [destination]**

1 Locate icon for object on screen
2 Move cursor to object icon location
3 Hold left mouse button down
4 Locate destination icon on screen
5 Move cursor to destination icon
6 Verify that destination icon indicates activation
7 Release mouse button
8 Return with goal accomplished

Method for goal: **send object [trash]**

1 Locate icon for object on screen
2 Move cursor to object icon location
3 Hold right mouse button down
4 Locate 'Move to Trash' item on pop-up menu
5 Move mouse cursor to 'Move to Trash' item on pop-up menu
6 Release mouse button
7 Return with goal accomplished

The five methods above specify two ways to place objects in the trash: by dragging them there with the mouse or by sending the object there using a pop-up menu. There are alternative methods for doing this, for example by selecting the object and pressing the 'Delete' key (KDE) or 'Ctrl' and 'D' keys together (Windows) but these are not included in this example. The first method defined above states that in order to delete an object the user must move the object to the 'Trash' (KDE) or 'Recycle Bin' (Windows). The next two methods then define two ways in which an object can be moved to destinations, the first by dragging it there with the mouse, the second by sending the object using a pop-up menu. The last two methods then describe the step-by-step actions (or 'operators') that the user must perform in order to drag an object to a destination or send an object to the trash. Users may decide to use different ways to delete objects depending on specific internal or external factors, and these factors can be defined as selection rules, which typically are represented as conditional statements. For example, users may choose to drag an object to the trash if the trash-can is clearly visible, but send it to the trash if the desktop is cluttered with windows and the trash-can is obscured from view. This situation may be represented by the following two rules:

IF   the goal is to delete an object
AND   the trash-can is visible
THEN   use the *drag object* method

IF   the goal is to delete an object
AND   the trash-can is not visible
THEN   use the *send object* method

Over the years GOMS has evolved into several variants that provide different analyses. Two widely used variants, KLM and CPM-GOMS, are discussed below.

4.2.2 KLM

The Keystroke-Level Model (KLM) is a restricted version of GOMS that does not include goals or selection rules but simply specifies the sequence of operators and methods required to perform a task. The main function of a KLM analysis is to predict the execution time of interactive tasks. All of the operators have a specific execution time and task completion time is calculated by summing the times spent executing the different operators. The eight standard operators with their associated estimated execution times (Kieras, 2001) are listed below:

K Press a key on the keyboard (0.28 s).
T(n) Type a sequence of n characters on the keyboard ($n \times$ K s).
P Point the mouse to a target on the display (1.1 s).
B Press or release the mouse button (0.1 s).
BB Click mouse button (0.2 s).
H Move hands between mouse and keyboard (or vice versa) (0.4 s).
M Mental act of routine thinking or perception (1.2 s).
W(t) Wait time for system response (t s).

For many of these operators estimated times depend on specific attributes of the user or environment. For example the 0.28 s estimate for entering a keystroke is for a 'typical' user and other estimates exist for expert typists (0.12 s) and novices (1.2 s). A KLM analysis of the two methods for deleting a file in the previous example (adapted from Kieras, 2001) is shown below.

> Operator sequence: **drag object [trash]**
> 1 Point to file icon (**P**)
> 2 Press and hold mouse button (**B**)
> 3 Drag file icon to 'Trash-can' icon (**P**)
> 4 Release mouse button (**B**)
> 5 Point to original window (**P**)

> Operator sequence: **send object [trash]**
> 1 Point to file icon (**P**)
> 2 Press and hold mouse button (**B**)
> 3 Point to 'Move to Trash' item on pop-up menu (**P**)
> 4 Release mouse button (**B**)
> 5 Point to original window (**P**)

According to these analyses, both methods require three **P** and two **B** operators and so both should take $3\mathbf{P} + 2\mathbf{B} = 3 \times 1.1 + 2 \times 0.1 = 3.5$ s to complete.

In the statistics and experimental design chapters of this book we have used an example of a study that compares a number of different interaction methods for composing a text message on a mobile phone. In this study, a KLM model is used to create a set of predictions of the time it would take a user to perform a task using each of the different interaction methods. These predictions (shown in Table 6.5 of Chapter 6) are used to form a hypothesis for the experimental study. The model enabled Cox *et al.* (in press) to have confidence in their experimental results as they were able to explain both why the empirical data followed the pattern of their predictions, and where the KLM did not accurately reflect the behaviour of the human participants.

4.2.3 CPM-GOMS

The CPM in CPM-GOMS (John, 1988, 1996) can stand for either 'cognitive-perceptual-motor' or 'critical-path-method' and both alternative interpretations reveal a core assumption of the approach. The first indicates the theoretical basis of CPM-GOMS – the *model human processor* (MHP; Card *et al.*, 1983), a simplified model of the three core components of human information processing: cognition, perception and motor control, together with a set of memories that store task knowledge, information from the environment and the current contents of cognitive processing. The MHP is governed according to a set of *operating principles* which determine how the processors behave and define such things as the time to make decisions, move a mouse cursor to a target or how performance time reduces with practice. MHP assumes that cognitive, perceptual and motor operators are performed in parallel and CPM-GOMS represents these parallel processes in the

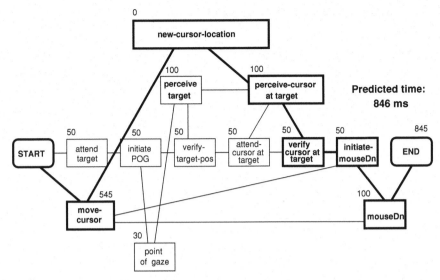

Fig 4.1 *A CPM-GOMS model of a micro-strategy to move the mouse cursor to a button and click on it. From Gray and Boehm-Davis (2000)*

form of a *schedule chart* (sometimes known as a 'PERT' chart). The second definition of CPM identifies a key feature of the analysis method – that of a *critical path* through the sequential dependencies between the three parallel processing streams that determines task execution time. A critical path is the sequence of processes with the longest overall duration, which consequently determines the shortest time possible in which the task can be completed. Figure 4.1 shows a CPM-GOMS model of the task of moving a mouse cursor to a button and clicking on it. The middle row depicts the cognitive operators with the perceptual and motor operators represented immediately above and below respectively. The number above each operator indicates the estimated execution time (in milliseconds) for that operator, with that of cognitive operators defaulting to 50 ms. According to the MHP, all operators within a processing module are performed sequentially and lines between operators indicate sequential dependence between operators. The critical path through the chart is indicated by the bold lines and represents the dependencies between the cognitive, perceptual and motor operators. It is the accumulated times of these operators on the critical path that constitute the predicted total execution time for the task. In the example shown in Figure 4.1, this is 545 + 0 + 100 + 50 + 50 + 100 = 845 ms. CPM-GOMS has been widely used to analyse a range of interactive behaviour, most famously when Gray, John and Atwood (1993) used CPM-GOMS in Project Ernestine to evaluate a new computer system for telephone operators at the NYNEX telephone company. The critical path produced by the CPM-GOMS analysis showed that the typical interaction when processing a call would actually take longer than with the existing system. Because of their predictions (which were subsequently validated by a field study), the new system was redesigned, thereby saving millions of dollars.

4.2.4 Limitations of the GOMS approach

Although the GOMS approach has been extremely useful in providing a range of techniques for analysing interactive behaviour and predicting execution times for a variety of tasks, it has a number of constraints (John and Kieras, 1996a). For example, analysts must assume that users are well practised, make no errors during the task or perform worse over repeated performance of a task due to fatigue. In addition, GOMS analyses require that reliable estimated times are available for all components in the task, which may not be the case for novel tasks or artefacts.

Cox *et al.*'s (in press) KLM model referred to above provides us with an example of both of these limitations. First, the existing literature did not provide all the necessary information required to build the model. As no one had used KLM previously to model these novel interaction methods, it was necessary to first conduct some small experiments to measure the average length of time it took to perform certain actions using the different interaction methods. Once gathered, these estimates could be used within the model. Second, as we have explained above, a KLM is a model of expert behaviour and as such does not model slips or mistakes. Of course, the performance of the participants in the experiment was not error free and as such was never going to match the predicted times exactly.

4.3 Cognitive architectures

In contrast to a cognitive model, a cognitive architecture aims to provide an explanation of all aspects of cognition. One way of studying a computer-based task in fine detail is to produce a computational model of the information and processes required to carry out the task that is built within a cognitive architecture. The architecture restricts the models that can be built within it thus ensuring that the model adheres to the psychological theories encapsulated by the architecture. Simulating interactions in this way is useful as it allows us to specify precisely the various perceptual, cognitive and motor processes involved in the interaction and to predict the effect of the human cognitive system (e.g. working memory) on behaviour. It is also useful to system designers as it has the potential to provide artificial users to allow us to test designs and judge whether one design is better in some way than another. This is possible because the models are themselves computer programs which can be run. The resulting behaviour can be compared to human behaviour.

In HCI, we characterise humans as information processors (see Card *et al.*, 1983) where information undergoes a series of ordered processes aimed at completion of a particular goal. This allows psychologists and cognitive scientists to view interaction with the computer as an information processing activity. Analysis of HCI in this way can support the work of interaction designers by helping them to understand what information requirements and resources are needed by human users when performing goal-based tasks.

Computational cognitive models are playing an increasingly important part in HCI research. Unlike the GOMS family of models which can model only expert performance, computational cognitive models allow researchers to show how users learn to use systems and also how users may perform in certain circumstances. Unlike artificial intelligence programmers, who aim to build programs that complete tasks faster and with fewer errors than humans, computational cognitive modellers try to write computer programs that complete tasks in exactly the same way as humans, that is, that make all the mistakes that humans make and take as much time as humans do to perform tasks.

Computational cognitive models are models which help designers to understand how the human mind works and how users learn and interpret information and how they interact with computers. They are used in HCI because they help to identify and explain the nature of problems which users encounter and provide knowledge about what users can and cannot be expected to do, as well as helping designers to understand what is going on when users use systems. This also benefits interactive systems design because it allows designers to apply the knowledge from these models to build better equipment and interfaces with improved usability and a design which users can understand with a shallower learning curve.

In recent years, cognitive modelling has grown in popularity as a research method in Cognitive Science generally and specifically in the area of HCI research. This can be seen by the increase in the number of published papers reporting results of modelling efforts, the number of textbooks on the subject (e.g. Boden, 1988; Cooper, 2002; Polk and Seifert, 2002; Gluck and Pew, 2005) and by the growth of the International Conference on Cognitive Modelling (ICCM) series (e.g. ICCM 2006, 2007).

There are too many architectures in existence for us to provide a comprehensive review here, therefore the reader is directed to Gray, Young and Kirschenbaum (1997) for a more detailed discussion of cognitive architectures and their use for HCI. As ACT-R is the architecture that has been used most in recent years to build computational models of HCI, we will outline its structure here and provide an example of its use in Section 4.4.

4.3.1 ACT-R

ACT is a theory of human cognition developed over a period of 30 years by John Anderson and his colleagues that builds on the theory of rational analysis. It is a principal effort in the attempt to develop a unified theory of cognition (Newell, 1990). Over the years, ACT has developed substantially and its name has varied to reflect these new developments (ACT*, ACT-R, ACT-R(PM), etc.). The current version is known as ACT-R 6.0 and this is the version that is outlined here (Anderson and Liebere, 1998).

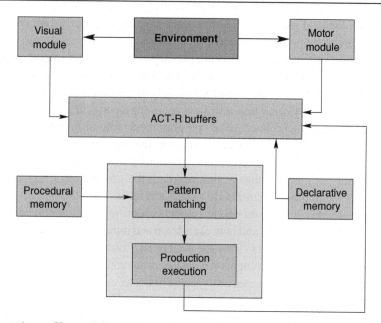

Fig 4.2 *The modular structure of ACT-R 6.0*

Figure 4.2 illustrates the components of the architecture relevant to our discussion. ACT-R consists of a set of independent modules that acquire information from the environment, process information and execute motor actions in the furtherance of particular goals. There are four modules that comprise the central cognitive components of ACT-R. Two of these are memory stores for two types of knowledge: a declarative memory module that stores factual knowledge about the domain, and a procedural memory module that stores the system's knowledge about how tasks are performed. The former consists of a network of knowledge chunks whereas the latter is a set of productions, rules of the form 'IF <condition> THEN <action>': the 'condition' specifying chunks that must be present for the rule to apply and the 'action' specifying the actions to be taken should this occur. There are a further two cognitive modules (not shown in the diagram) that represent information related to the execution of tasks. The first is a control state module that keeps track of the intentions of the system during problem solving and the second is a problem state module that maintains the current state of the task.

In addition to these cognitive modules there are four perceptual-motor modules for speech, audition, visual and motor processing (only the latter two are shown in Figure 4.2). The speech and audition modules are the least well developed and at present simply provide ACT-R with the capacity to simulate basic audio perception and vocal output for the purpose of modelling typical psychology experiments. The visual and motor modules are better developed and provide ACT-R with the ability to simulate visual attention shifts to objects on a computer display and manual interactions with a computer keyboard and mouse.

Each of ACT-R's modules has an associated buffer that can hold only one chunk of information from its module at a time and the contents of all of the buffers constitute the state of an ACT-R model at any one time. Cognition proceeds via a pattern matching process that attempts to find production rules with conditions that match the current contents of the buffers. When a match is found, the production 'fires' and the actions (visual or manual movements, requests for the retrieval of a knowledge chunk from declarative memory, or modifications to buffers) are performed. Then the matching process continues on the updated contents of the buffers so that tasks are performed through a succession of production rule firings. As an example, two production rules (written in English rather than in ACT-R code) that instantiate part of a search task may look something like this:

IF   the goal is to find the meaning of *eudaimonia* (control state module)
AND   there is nothing in declarative memory about *eudaimonia* (declarative module)
THEN   set the goal to search the WWW for *eudaimonia* (control state module)

IF   the goal is to search the WWW for *eudaimonia* (control state module)
AND   the web browser is open (problem state module)
THEN   look for the menu labelled *Bookmarks* (visual module)
AND   update the problem state to *looking for Google* (problem state module)

The processing in ACT-R's modules is serial but the modules run in parallel with each other so that the system can move visual attention while also moving the mouse and attempting to retrieve knowledge from declarative memory. ACT-R processes also have associated latency parameters taken from the psychology literature. For example, it typically takes 50 ms for a production to fire and the time taken to move the mouse cursor to an object on the computer screen is calculated using Fitts' Law (Fitts, 1954).

ACT-R implements rational analysis in two ways. The first is its mechanism for retrieving knowledge chunks from declarative memory which is based on the notion of activation. Each chunk in declarative memory has a level of activation which determines its availability for retrieval and the level of activation for a chunk reflects the recency and frequency of its use. This enables us to understand how rehearsal of items in a short-term memory task can boost the activation levels of these chunks and consequently increase the chances of recall/retrieval from the declarative memory store. The level of activation of a chunk falls gradually over time and without retrieval or spreading activation from cue chunks may fall below a threshold level which then results in retrieval failure. This enables models built within the ACT-R architecture to model forgetting without having to delete the item from the declarative memory store.

The second way that ACT-R implements rational analysis is in the mechanism for choosing between alternative production rules. According to rational analysis, people choose between a number of options to maximise their expected utility. Each option (production rule) has an expected probability, P, of achieving the goal and an expected cost, C. It is assumed that when carrying out computer-based tasks people interact with the task environment and choose actions that will optimise their efficiency (i.e. maximise the probability of achieving the goal while minimising the cost). At each point in time, therefore, all possible production rules that match against the current goal are proposed in a choice set and the one with the highest level of efficiency is chosen and executed.

4.4   Applying the method

4.4.1   Peebles and Cheng, 2003

Modern computer systems (e.g. statistical packages such as SPSS, spreadsheet packages such as Excel, and Geographical Information Systems) are able to manipulate large amounts of data very quickly and produce representations of different aspects of that data. These systems enable users to create different types of graphical representations in order to aid understanding of the data itself. However, little is currently known about how different aspects of the representations can influence people's abilities to extract information from the representations once they have been created. In order to address this, Peebles and Cheng (2003) conducted an experiment, eye movement study and cognitive modelling analysis to investigate the cognitive, perceptual and motor processes involved in a common graph-reading task using two different types of Cartesian graph. The purpose of the study was to determine how graph users' ability to retrieve information can be affected by presenting the same information in slightly different types of the same class of diagram. The two types of graph, shown in Figure 4.3, represent amounts of UK oil and gas production over two decades. The only difference between the two graph types is which variables are represented on the axes and which are plotted. In the function graphs, the argument variable (AV: time in years) is represented on the x-axis and the quantity variables (QV: oil and gas) on the y-axis, whereas in the parametric graphs, the quantity variables are represented on the x and y axes and time is plotted as a parameterising variable along the curve.

In the experiment, participants were presented with the value of a *given* variable and required to use the graph to find the corresponding value of a target variable – for example, when the value of oil is 3, what is the value of gas? This type of task has typically been analysed in terms of a minimum sequence of eye fixations required to reach the location of the given variable's value and then from there

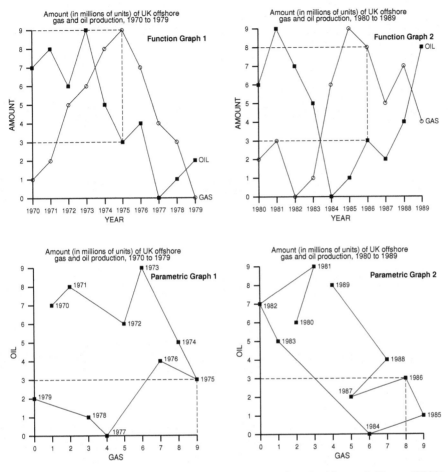

Fig 4.3 *Function and parametric graphs used in Peebles and Cheng (2003) depicting values of oil and gas production for each year. The graphs on the left (labelled 1) show years 1970 to 1979 while those on the right (labelled 2) show years 1980 to 1989. Dashed lines indicate the optimal scanpath required to answer the question 'When the value of oil is 3, what is the value of gas?'*

to the location of the corresponding value of the target variable (Lohse, 1993; Peebles *et al.*, 1999; Peebles and Cheng, 2001, 2002). Forty-nine participants (four of whom had their eye movements recorded) completed 120 trials, each participant using only one graph type. The 120 questions were coded into three classes (QV-QV, QV-AV and AV-QV) according to which variable's value was given and which was required (QV denotes a quantity variable, oil or gas, and AV denotes the argument variable, time). On each trial, a question (e.g., 'GAS = 6, OIL = ?') was presented above the graph and participants were required to read the question, find the answer using the graph on the screen and then enter their answer by clicking on an Answer button on the top right corner of the window which revealed a circle of buttons containing the digits 0–9. Reaction times (RTs)

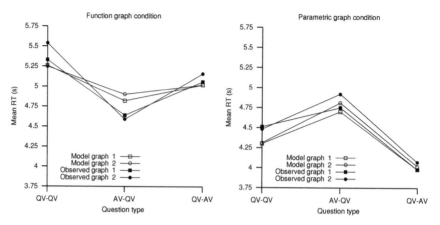

Fig 4.4 *Mean response times for experimental participants and ACT-R models for each question type (Peebles and Cheng, 2003)*

were recorded from the onset of a question to the mouse click on the answer button.

The RT data from the experiment, displayed in Figure 4.4, showed that the graph used and the type of question asked both had a significant effect on the time it took for participants to retrieve the answer. This was all the more surprising because, for two of the three question types, participants were faster using the less familiar parametric graphs by nearly a second.

The results of the eye movement study were also surprising. It was found that in 62.7 per cent of all trials (irrespective of the graph used or question type being attempted), after having read the question at the start of a trial, participants redirected their visual attention to elements of the question at least once during the process of problem solving with the graph. This was not predicted by the simple minimal fixation sequence account outlined above, but two possible explanations may be provided: (a) participants initially encode the three question elements but are unable to retain all of them in working memory or retrieve them when required due to the cognitive load involved in solving the problem; or (b) to reduce the load on working memory, participants break the problem into two sections, the first allowing them to reach the given location and the second to then proceed to the target location corresponding to the solution.

Peebles and Cheng constructed two ACT-R models of the experiment (one for each graph type) that were able to interact with an exact replica of the software used to run the experiment. The models consisted of a set of production rules to carry out the six basic sub-goals in the task; (1) read the question, (2) identify the start location determined by the given variable, (3) identify the given location on the graph representing the given value of given variable, (4) from the given location, identify the target location representing the required variable, (5) identify the target value at the target location, (6) enter the answer. Many of the production rules were shared by the two models, the main difference between them being the control structure that sequences the execution of the production rules. Figure 4.4 shows that the mean RTs from the parametric and function graph models are a good fit to the observed data ($R^2 = 0.868$, RMSE $= 0.123$, and $R^2 = 0.664$, RMSE $= 0.199$ respectively). Perhaps more important, however, were the insights into the observed eye movement data that came from the modelling process itself. When ACT-R focuses attention on an object on the screen, representations of the object and its location are created in the system's visual buffers which can be accessed by productions. Eventually these representations go into declarative memory with initial activation values and, as long as these values are above a certain threshold, they can be retrieved by the cognitive system and replaced in a buffer. However, as we mentioned earlier, ACT-R includes a mechanism by which the activation of representations in declarative memory decreases over time, which allows it to simulate processes involved in forgetting. These mechanisms played a crucial role in the ACT-R models' ability to capture the eye movement data observed in the experiment. At the start of each trial the models read the three question elements, but during the processing of the trial these elements do not stay in the visual buffers but are placed in declarative memory. As a consequence, at least one question element must be retrieved from memory at each stage of the problem in order to continue. However, as soon as a question element is placed in declarative memory its activation starts to decay and, as a consequence, the probability that it cannot be retrieved increases. Typically, if a retrieval failure occurs, an ACT-R model will halt as it does not have the appropriate information to solve the problem. During the process of model development it was found that on a significant proportion of trials the model was not able to retrieve question elements at the later stages of the trial because their activation had fallen below the retrieval threshold. As a consequence new productions had to be added to allow the model to redirect attention to the question in order to re-encode the element and then return to solving the problem. This was precisely the behaviour observed in the eye movement study. This is illustrated in Figure 4.5, which compares screenshots of the model scanpath and eye movements recorded from one participant for the same question using the 1980s parametric graph. The numbered circles on the model screenshot indicate the sequence of fixations produced by the model. The pattern of fixations in both screenshots is remarkably similar.

4.4.2 Salvucci, 2001

Most HCI research concentrates on understanding users interacting with one desktop interface. However, this research looks at non-desktop interfaces and in fact includes interaction with more than one interface. The starting point for the research was an existing ACT-R model of driving (steering and speed control) which was further developed so that it included user performance of dialling a telephone number while driving. In building the model, Salvucci decided to

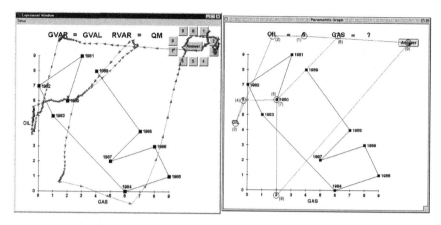

Fig 4.5 *Screenshots showing an experimental participant's eye movement data (left) and the ACT-R model's visual attention scanpath (right) for the QV-QV question 'oil = 6, gas = ?' using the 1980s parametric graph. In the model screenshot, numbered circles on the scanpath indicate the location and sequence of fixations*

compare the effects of dialling a phone number in different modes (full manual dialling, full voice, speed manual, speed voice) on the model's ability to control the car. In order to do this, he took a GOMS description of dialling a telephone number with each method of interaction and expanded it to include cognitive processes. Each of the GOMS operators and cognitive processes included in the task descriptions was taken to represent a production in the model.

This multi-tasking model was used to provide a priori predictions about task performance which were then compared to human data from an experiment. The model made a number of predictions and provided explanations as to why these predictions were sensible. For example, perhaps unsurprisingly, the model predicted that the full manual telephone interface has a large effect on driver behaviour, but, importantly, using the speed manual interface (i.e. using a single digit speed dial number) also has a small but significant effect. The model also showed that use of the voice interfaces has no effect on driving performance. This was because both manual interfaces occupy more visual attention than the voice interfaces as the model needs to look at the keypad while dialling. The voice interfaces require aural rather than visual attention which only detracts a small amount from the model's attention to the driving task. As suggested in the cognitive psychology literature, the model can more easily switch between the different types of attention (visual for driving, aural for dialling) than switch visual attention between the two tasks when using the manual telephone interfaces.

The main benefit of the model is its predictive power. The model closely predicts the baseline dialling times for the four different interfaces when not driving. Coupled with the driving task, the models have the ability to predict interactions between task behaviours which provides us with a real understanding of not just which multi-tasking combinations are easier to use but also why this is the case. In addition, if we created a new form of interaction for this task, we could just build another user model and plug it in to the driving model, enabling us to look at that multi-tasking situation. It would also be possible to change driving conditions to look at whether there are some situations where interacting with the telephone interfaces might be more or less dangerous. Would it be safer to use the manual interface on a single-lane road with no other traffic (as in Salvucci's experiment), on a single-lane road with other traffic or on a motorway, which is likely to be straighter with no oncoming traffic to contend with?

4.5   Critique

The Peebles and Cheng (2003) case above provides a good example of some of the benefits of cognitive modelling. First, engagement in the activity of modelling an aspect of human behaviour helps to clarify the theory about the cognitive processes involved in completing the task of interest. Peebles and Cheng were forced to be explicit about the cognitive strategies they thought humans employed when trying to understand the data presented in the graphs. Second, the behaviour of the resulting model can be compared to that of human participants to ensure that the account of the processes involved is accurate. It was in doing this that Peebles and Cheng realised that they needed to extend their models in order to capture the redirection of attention to the task description before the model could complete the task.

Cognitive models can also be used to make predictions about human behaviour in other situations (such as interacting with other types of graphs), and they can be used to compare systems and/or competing designs as part of the usability evaluation process. Computational cognitive modelling is of particular value to HCI researchers, as models built within a computational environment can be hooked up directly to the software applications that human users use. More recent architectures provide the researcher with the ability to re-use all or parts of previous models, and even to combine two or more existing models in order to investigate how multi-tasking might impact performance (see summary of Salvucci, 2001 above).

4.5.1 What to consider when choosing a method for your own research

Having provided the reader with a description of the benefits of cognitive modelling in HCI, in order for us to give a balanced view it is necessary to consider some of the limitations of the approach because building cognitive models of HCI is not an easy or trivial matter.

First, it is important to spend some time deciding which model or architecture is most appropriate for the task or data set that you are trying to model. For a detailed discussion of how to choose and get started with a cognitive architecture, the reader is directed to Ritter (2004). In practice, unless you are a programmer who is already proficient in the language that underpins the cognitive architecture, the learning curve required to build a computational model is too steep for someone who is undertaking a three-month MSc project. So in this circumstance you are probably better off limiting yourself to GOMS style models. For many system evaluation type projects, using a member of the GOMS family of models is likely to be sufficient. Those involved in a larger project, or at least one that will run over a longer time period, such as a PhD thesis, are more likely to have the time required to learn both the underlying language and how to build a model and will be able to take advantage of resources such as the ACT-R summer school. Tools are already being developed to aid the modeller to automatically generate GOMS (e.g. Vera *et al.*, 2005) and ACT-R models (e.g. CogTool by Salvucci and Lee (2003), ACT-stitch by Matessa (2004)). These will facilitate the move from models of expert behaviour with an interface (in GOMS) to models of novice behaviour (in ACT-R).

Once you have built your model it is necessary to test it against some human data. Many papers report the results of such efforts claiming that because their model behaves in some way similar to their participants this in fact validates their model. However, it is much easier to build a model that behaves in a particular way if we already know how it should behave, i.e. if we have already collected and analysed the human data. Once the modeller has tweaked some of the input parameters, it is perhaps of little surprise that he is able to get the model to match the human data. The cleaner approach is therefore to build the model before examining the human data. If the behaviour of the model does not match the human data then, like Peebles and Cheng, it is important to consider where the model might need to be changed, rather than trying to retrofit the model to the data via parameter fitting.

A final point to remember is that a cognitive model is a model of HCI in an ideal environment where there are no other factors, such as interruptions or emotional issues, which might affect thought processes. As such, predictions made by the model cannot always be taken as absolute truth. This thought may go some way to lessening the blow when, despite your best efforts, you find it difficult if not impossible to accurately model your data.

4.6   Further reading

ACT-R website includes publications, tutorial material, etc. act-r.psy.cmu.edu/

Cooper, R.P. 2002. *Modelling High-Level Cognitive Processes.* Mahwah, NJ: Lawrence Erlbaum Associates.

Gluck, K.A. and Pew, R.W. (eds) 2005. *Modeling Human Behavior with Integrated Cognitive Architectures.* Mahwah, NJ: Lawrence Erlbaum Associates.

Gray, W.D., Young, R.M. and Kirschenbaum, S.S. 1997. Introduction to Special Issue on Cognitive Architectures and Human–Computer Interaction. *Human–Computer Interaction* 12(4): 301–9.

Kieras, D.E. 2004. *EPIC Architecture Principles of Operation.* ftp://www.eecs.umich.edu/people/kieras/EPICtutorial/EPICPrinOp.pdf

Polk, T. and Seifert, C. 2002. *Cognitive Modeling.* Cambridge, MA: MIT Press

Ritter, F. E. 2004. 'Choosing and getting started with a cognitive architecture to test and use human–machine interfaces.' *MMI-Interaktiv-Journal* 7: 17–37.

LIVERPOOL JOHN MOORES UNIVERSITY
LEARNING SERVICES

5 Formal analysis of interactive systems: opportunities and weaknesses

MICHAEL HARRISON, JOSÉ CREISSAC CAMPOS AND KARSTEN LOER

5.1 Overview

Although formal techniques are not widely used in the analysis of interactive systems there are reasons why an appropriate set of tools, suitably designed to be usable by system engineers, could be of value in the portfolio of techniques used to assess interactive systems. This chapter describes the role of formal techniques in modelling and analysing interactive systems, discusses unfulfilled opportunities and speculates about the removal of barriers to their use. It also presents the opportunities that a clear expression of the problem and systematic analysis techniques may afford.

5.2 Introduction

Formal approaches bring rigour and automation to usability engineering. Models capture key features of the interactive behaviour of the design and are then subjected to systematic analysis using verification techniques such as model checking (Clarke, Grumberg and Peled, 1999). The appropriate selection of models and verification techniques is critical to the value of the analysis. Otherwise models can bias the analysis and verification techniques can take the focus away from important safety or business-critical features of the designed interactive system.

Formal techniques have been used to analyse a variety of properties of interactive behaviours in a number of systems including menu structures in mobile phones, flight management systems and other control systems on aircraft, air traffic control systems, interaction techniques for virtual environments and many others. Two categories of (semi-)automated verification techniques can be identified. Algorithmic techniques, such as model checking, are fully automated and, given a suitable model and property, are capable of determining if the property is valid of the model (assuming adequate computational resources are available). Deductive techniques (i.e. theorem proving) are semi-automated approaches where a more traditional mathematical proof is performed by a tool under some degree of user guidance.

An important challenge if these techniques are to be used effectively and efficiently is that there be generic models of interactive behaviour that can be taken off the shelf by the engineer and instantiated to the particular requirements of the system under design. This step has not yet been achieved but forms the basis for speculation in Section 5.7. Model checking as contrasted with other techniques – for example, theorem proving – is a usable, algorithmic approach to analysis, but if verification is required between different levels of system refinement, say between display and state (as might be required in checking the characteristics of a direct manipulation system), then only rudimentary checking can be done using a model checker and theorem proving is required. In the same way theorem proving techniques have been used to analyse consistency between the user's mental model and the display or state (Doherty, Campos and Harrison, 2000). Campos and Harrison (1998) describe a range of techniques that can be recruited together to analyse interactive systems.

Two example 'ubiquitous systems' are used to illustrate two styles of model adopted in this chapter. The first is concerned with the mobile device in context and the mode effects that context will generate – so it is concerned with unexpected consequences of the device. The second example analyses the whole system: the rooms, the public displays, the mobile devices and the timeliness of information in that system. The first model describes properties of the interactive device and its interaction with context (Section 5.5). The second model describes the information flows in the system (Section 5.6). In Section 5.7 the scope for generic modelling and property templating is considered in a little more detail.

5.3   Formal models in interactive systems

The value of formal (mathematically based) models of interactive behaviour of systems (devices or whole systems) is in providing precise descriptions of features of the interactive behaviour of the design early in the process. The features focus on user action, whether explicit or implicit (an implicit action might occur as a result of the user moving into a room for example), and the observable effects that action has in the context. This makes it possible to analyse characteristics of the behaviour of the system before expensive commitments have been made to implementation.

In this chapter, two modelling approaches are taken that share a number of features in common. They are both diagrammatic approaches based on finite state models which capture properties of the system in terms of states (circles or 'blobs' in the diagram) and transitions between states (arcs). The models are based on concurrently executing automata that can synchronise by using labels on the state transitions: a transition can occur in two parallel automata if complementary labels occur on arcs in the two automata and both arcs are enabled at the same stage in the execution of the system. The first approach described uses statecharts (Horrocks, 1999), which has the additional feature that hierarchies of automata may be described. The second approach uses uppaal, which additionally focuses on continuous time (Behrmann, David and Larsen, 2004). Models based on these techniques are good for describing behaviours of actions in the interactive system in terms of the actions to which they will lead. Models can be used to analyse the mode characteristics of an interactive device (see as examples Campos and Harrison, 2001; Gow, Thimbleby and Cairns, 2006).

There are also textual approaches to modelling labelled transition systems such as these. For example, SPIN (Holzmann, 2003) captures the model using a process algebra called Promela. Here the transitions are described using a language that has similarities with a programming language that captures how the processes respond to events. Other approaches, for example Alloy (Jackson, 2006) and Modal Action Logic (MAL, Campos and Harrison, 2001), capture relations between states described textually in terms of typed attributes of the states. A further approach describes interactive systems using matrices (Thimbleby, 2004b).

The advantage of these simple models is that they can be explored using model checking. These approaches explore paths exhaustively to check whether the model satisfies the property. The model therefore is described in one of the languages above. The model checker converts it into an appropriate form for analysis. The analyst provides properties, often expressed in a temporal logic, to analyse the model. The model checker then attempts to find a counter-example to the property, or an instance where the property is true (in the case of some properties), and provides the analyst with a sequence of states (a trace) that describes the counter-example or true instance. SPIN and Alloy have their own model checkers. MAL uses the SMV checker (McMillan, 1993). Model checking has the advantage that it is a decidable algorithmic approach that is therefore relatively easy to use. The disadvantage of the technique is that there are a number of properties of interactive systems that cannot be adequately analysed using these approaches, for example representation properties. To prove that a display representation of some underlying structure faithfully represented the underlying structure (as would be required in a direct manipulation interface such as a text editor for example) it would be necessary to represent the data structures and use theorem proving techniques such as PVS (Owre, Rushby and Shankar, 1992) or Isabelle (Nipkow, Paulson and Wenzel, 2002).

5.4   Verification in development

As briefly summarised, analysis explores behaviours of a device. An important feature of the behaviours of interest is that they correspond to envisaged uses of the device. The analysis is designed to relate to a number of concerns including, for example, whether these behaviours lead to confusing mode shifts

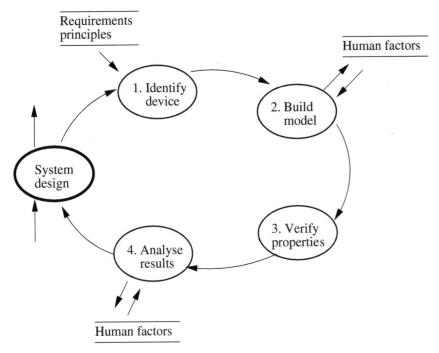

Fig 5.1 *Integration of verification in development*

or whether there are situations in typical sequences where it is impossible to recover. As discussed in Campos (1999), the process of establishing usability requirements, modelling systems and checking the models against requirements can be thought of as a cycle consisting of four steps, as represented in Figure 5.1. These steps may involve discussion between software or system developers on the one hand and human factors specialists on the other. The cycle is as follows:

1 **Identifying usability requirements:** Based on usability guidelines or heuristics or specific concerns derived from a requirements elicitation. They are used to assist the development of a model to be used for the analysis. They involve device descriptions or whole system descriptions – a device might be a mobile phone, the system is the whole system in which the mobile phone is embedded. These requirements are expressed as formal properties.

2 **Building model and formulating properties:** Once the initial requirements have been expressed, a model of the interactive device or system and a set of properties are formulated. This step benefits from the participation of someone with specific user or domain expertise. Models capture assumptions about the user's view of the device or how users are embedded along with devices inside the system. Properties capture constraints that if broken represent potential failures in the use of device or system. This stage could be achieved by re-using an old model or instantiating a generic model.

3 **Verifying properties:** The next stage is to verify whether the properties hold of the device under the constraints imposed by the environment – for example, a property requiring the visibility of actions but only over the paths that relate to expected tasks. Constraints are either expressed in the properties themselves or through additional models capturing relevant characteristics of the environment in which the device is to be considered. The properties could be examples of general property patterns.

4 **Analysing the results:** Finally the consequences of the results are analysed. The technique used in this chapter is model checking. The method of analysis involves checking a property. If the answer is positive then, under the assumptions captured by the model, the usability property is true of the system described by the model. If the answer is negative then the reasons why are investigated. A rationale explaining why the property does not hold is provided by the reasoning tool, in this case a trace representing the confluence of conditions in which the property fails. A negative result might indicate that the device model is incomplete. It may therefore be necessary to determine whether all relevant aspects of the device have been considered. Alternatively it might point to a situation where the assumptions made about the user (or the context of usage) must be refined. For example, it may be necessary to eliminate specific courses of action from the expected user behaviour. Finally, it might be a genuine usability problem.

This exploration of results leads to refinements of the model and/or of the property being proved before a new proof attempt is made. This is a valuable outcome of the process. Usability is not a concept that can be completely defined in a formal context. By enriching the model/property the conditions under which the usability property will hold are being clarified.

5.5   Steps 1 and 2: Modelling the device in its context

The first example (discussed more fully in Loer and Harrison, 2005) illustrates how relevant characteristics of a device model are captured, part of step 1 (Figure 5.1). Hence ways in which a formal approach can help to articulate key properties of a mobile device are illustrated. A mobile device is analysed as an alternative to a centralised control room, using the analysis to make a comparison between behaviours of the two interfaces. The context is a biochemical process. The mobility of the designed hand-held device may have consequences for interaction that were neither envisaged nor intended. A particular set of these possible consequences are the *modal* effects introduced by a device's position within its spatial context. These modal effects occur because action makes use of information about the context that may not be clear to the user.

Context and context awareness in mobile systems can either contribute to the seamlessness of an interaction by making action more natural or implicit, or make the interface more confusing and opaque to the user. Whether it is one or the other is a matter of design. The device model for this example is designed to explore two types of property. The first is concerned with internal modes. These modes arise because (in this case) the display is more limited than that available in the control room and therefore the device displays or hides different information. The second is concerned with external mode that arises because of the position of the device. Different controls are accessible at different positions in the plant. These controls are either accessed directly or saved in locations within the display for future reference. Hence the device may be in the hands of a plant worker who receives an alert that there is a leak in a pipe. She may walk to the upstream pump using the device to turn it off and save an icon representing the capability to control the pump in the device. She may then walk to the site of the leak out of range of the pump and once the leak is fixed use the saved icon to turn the pump back on. In the process of retrieving the saved icon the worker may have to use commands to navigate the displays. The purpose of the hand-held technology is that it will enable staff in the plant to monitor and control the plant while being on site.

Both the control room and the mobile device are designed to control a process. To capture the constraints that govern the behaviour of these two systems, a model of the process is produced. The mobile device must also be associated with a model that captures position constraints within the plant itself. The mobile device is analysed by comparing it with the control room by exploring a reachability property – can the system achieve the goal of producing a defined product? Differences that arise through location and display constraints both provide possible sources of error, and this needs exploring in detail. Differences that are detected may be further explored using usability criteria.

Models are specified using statecharts (Harel, 1987; Horrocks, 1999). A variety of notations could be used to describe the models. Statecharts are used here because they are relatively easy to read (if not write) and because they provide a graphic representation of mode structures. Degani's OFAN approach (Degani, 1996)[1] is followed, which adds additional structure to the statecharts, decomposing models of interactive systems into orthogonal sub-states representing *control elements*, *control mechanism* (the model of the device functionality), *displays* (a description of the output elements), *environment* (a model of relevant environmental properties) and *user task* (the sequence of user actions that are required to accomplish a certain task). The aim of structural decomposition is to ease thinking about the interactive behaviour of the system as well as its refinement.

5.5.1 The plant model

Two different biochemical processes, X and Y, take place in *tank 2* and *tank 3* and these require input of substrates A and B. Process X generates product C when supplied with substrate A. The bacteria in this process are highly temperature- and substrate-sensitive, so the process must be supplied with substrate A only at a certain range of temperatures.

---

[1] This work only appears to be published as part of Degani's doctoral thesis. This makes the work relatively inaccessible though it can be accessed through NASA: ase.arc.nasa.gov/people/asaf/hai/.

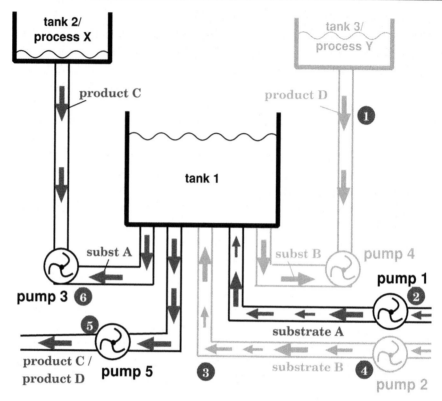

Fig 5.2 *Plant process*

The chemical engineers have decided to share *tank 1* between processes *X* and *Y* by regulating the temperature of the substrates before entering and after leaving the processes. Flows are organised as follows: substrate *A* can be introduced into the system by pump 1 while substrate *B* can be introduced by pump 2. Pumps 3 and 4 are bi-directional which means that substances are transported from *tank 1* in 'forward' mode and from processes to *tank 1* in 'backwards' mode. End products leave the plant using pump 5. For a graphic representation of this process see Figure 5.2. Pumps 1 and 2 are equipped with an optional VOLUME mode that triggers an automatic stop when a selected target volume of the tank is reached. The plant is designed to satisfy a minimal set of safety requirements:

PSR1: Substrates *A* and *B* must never leave the system unprocessed.
PSR2: If its feeding tank is empty a pump must be shut down to prevent damage.
PSR3: If the capacity of *tank 1* is reached, the pump that currently feeds it must be shut down immediately to prevent an overflow.
PSR4: *Tank 1* must never hold more than one substance at any time.

The OFAN model that describes the behaviour of the plant is given in Figure 5.3 and is designed to satisfy requirements PSR1 to PSR4. Pumps 2 and 4 are precisely analogous to the specifications of pumps 1 and 3 and therefore are not

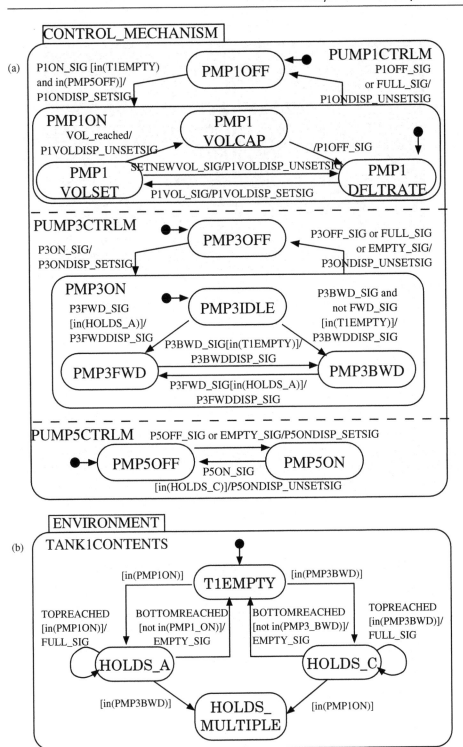

Fig 5.3 *Plant model*

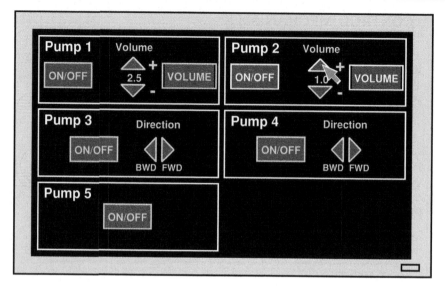

Fig 5.4 *Screenshot of control screen layout (arrow represents cursor/stylus)*

described. Only the *change* of the volume is specified in pumps 1 and 2 because the actual *value* of the volume setting is irrelevant to the contextual assumptions that need to be made. The pump logic is modelled in Figure 5.3a. *Tank 1* modelled in Figure 5.3b is a simple and discrete model of what it means for the tank to hold substances, to be full and to be empty. The tank either holds *A*, *B*, *C* or *D* exclusively, or it can contain multiple substances. The tank can also be in a state where the top is reached in any of these conditions in which case a full signal is sent. When the bottom is reached the state of the tank becomes empty and an empty signal is sent. Hence the model is simple but captures the extreme conditions of the system that are important to the behaviour of the interactive system. No constraints are placed on *tanks 2* and *3* and therefore they are not modelled explicitly.

5.5.2 Modelling the central panel and the hand-held device

The interactive system that controls the process described in Section 5.5.1 is to be designed to satisfy the following requirements: (1) to inform the operator about progress; (2) to allow the operator to intervene appropriately to control the process; (3) to alert the operator to alarming conditions in the plant; and (4) to enable recovery from these conditions. These requirements together form the basis for the overall analysis of the interactive system, and can be considered to be a result of Step 1 (Figure 5.1).

Representing and modelling the central panel

The control room, with its central panel, aims to provide the plant operator with a comprehensive overview of the status of all devices in the plant. The specification (Figure 5.5), designed to analyse properties (1)–(4), describes the behaviour of

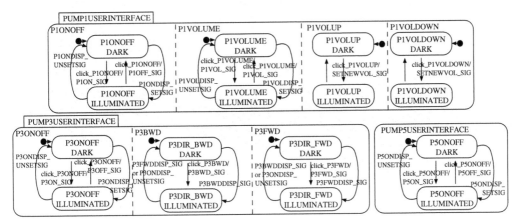

Fig 5.5 *Initial specification of control screen behaviour*

the displays and the associated buttons for pump 1 (and equivalently pump 2). The effects of actions are described in terms of signals used to synchronise with the pump description and the states in which the buttons are illuminated.

The control room display is implemented as a mouse-controlled screen in which icons act as both displays and controls. PUMP1USERINTERFACE supports four simple on/off state transitions defining the effect of pressing the relevant parts of the display.

5.5.3 Modelling the context of the device

The simplified model of the chemical process acts as context for both the control room and the hand-held device. In addition the mobile device requires a model of position. This information constrains device interface behaviour.

Representing the position of the hand-held control device

The hand-held control device (Figure 5.6) is 'aware of' its position within the plant. Hence the ENVIRONMENT model to describe the system containing this device is extended to include both the chemical process and the spatial layout of the plant. In this case a simple model of how an operator can move between device positions in the plant is specified. The user's movements are modelled as transitions between position states, as shown in Figure 5.7.

The hand-held control device enables the capture of information about plant components (i.e. different types of pumps, valves and displays) that are encountered by the operator during their rounds. Both the status information for that component and soft controls can be transferred into the currently selected 'bucket' (a display state where the control icons are displayed for future use). Components can be removed from a bucket by pressing the delete button. With the bucket selector button the user can cycle through buckets thus producing an internally moded display. Control elements for the manipulation of components in a bucket

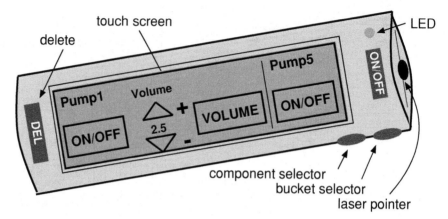

Fig 5.6 *A hand-held control device (modified version of the 'Pucketizer' device in Nilsson et al. (2000))*

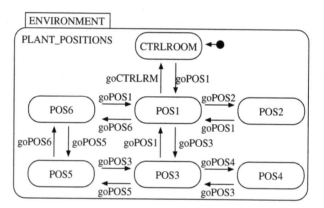

Fig 5.7 *Model of device positions*

are displayed on a touch screen with a display area that is limited to controls for up to two pumps at a time.

The model of the hand-held device describes both the physical buttons that are accessible continuously and other control elements, like pump control icons, that are available temporarily and depend on the position of the device. When the operator approaches a pump, its controls are automatically displayed on the screen. The component may be 'transferred' into a bucket for future remote access by using the component selector button. Controls for plant devices in locations other than the current one can be accessed remotely if they have been previously stored in a bucket. When a plant component is available in a bucket and the bucket is selected, the hand-held device can transmit commands to the processing plant, using the pump control icons.

The model described here presumes that the appliance should always know where it is in the network. This is of course a simplification. Alternative models would allow the interaction analyst to explore the dissonances between the states of the device and the states of the environment, or richer notions of context including the worker's history and intentions, for example.

5.5.4 Steps 3 and 4: analysis

The analysis illustrated here deals with the issue of whether facets of the interaction with the device will be problematic. This is addressed by considering whether there are consequences of the design of the ubiquitous interface that are problematic in comparison with those provided by the central control room. The main mechanism for doing this analysis is to identify how the two different interfaces are used to achieve the same goals. The single goal '*Produce substance C*' is considered. In practice there are many ways in which a given interface can achieve a given goal. The analysis demonstrates how constraints can be used to consider alternative paths. The analysis proceeds by checking that there is a path to a state that satisfies the required property. If the property 'holds', a True answer is obtained. Otherwise, the property is False, and the tool creates a sequence of states leading from the initial state to the violating state. These 'traces' form the most valuable output of the process. They support an understanding of *why* a specification is violated (as opposed to a mere statement *that* a specification does not hold). For more detailed introductions to the technique, see Clarke *et al.* (1999), Huth and Ryan (2000), Bérard *et al.* (2001), Holzmann (2003).

In this case the reachability property concerns a target state representing: '*Produce substance C.*' A trace demonstrating that the property holds provides a possible way of reaching this target state. It can be found by running the model with a negated property – in the case of a reachability property, negation yields a never-claim. Model checkers usually produce only a single trace for each never-claim. To obtain a wider understanding, additional traces may be created by adding assumptions about the behaviour of parts of the model.

In this case the reachability requirement is formulated as an existence property

> **SAN1**: F (PUMP5CTRLM.state=PMP5ON) &
>   (TANK1.state = HOLDS_C),

This states that the plant can eventually (F) deliver substance C from the tank to the outside world (represented by the two properties namely that TANK1 holds C and PUMP5 is taking the finished material out of the system, in other words the pump is switched on). For the model specified, the checker returns True. To obtain a trace that demonstrates one possible way of achieving that goal the negated requirement 'not **SAN1**' is checked. In the case of the model of the control room user interface the resulting trace contains a sequence of user inputs ⟨openPmp1, openPmp3, closePmp1, reverseP3, openP5⟩ which is shown in the first column of Figure 5.8.[2] This sequence of actions represents the following task

---

[2] The traces in Figure 5.8 are filtered and pretty-printed to illustrate the key information of interest with respect to this chapter; the standard outputs of the model checker – ASCII text files or data tables – are not easy to read, see chapter 6 of Loer (2003) for a discussion.

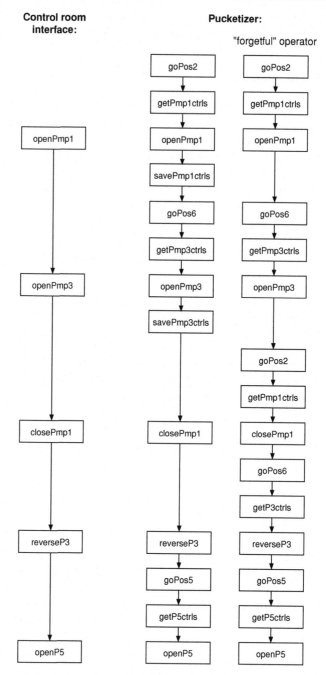

Fig 5.8 *Comparison of behaviours for a goal: 'Produce substance C'*

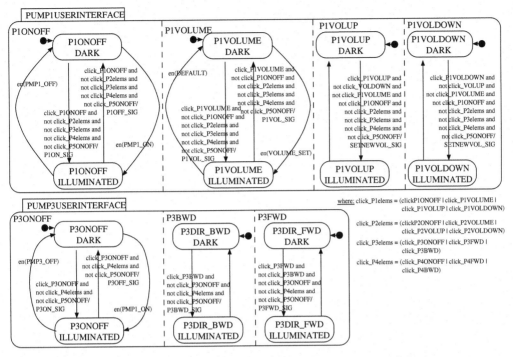

Fig 5.9 *Modified (deterministic) specification of control screen behaviour (cf. Figure 5.5)*

order: (1) insert substance *A* via pump 1, (2) forward substance *A* from the tank to process *X* via pump 3, (3) close pump 1, (4) pump end product *C* into the tank by reversing the flow of pump 3, and (5) deliver substance *C* via pump 5.

Since the aim is to compare the hand-held device with the control room, the same reachability property is checked in the context of the hand-held device specification, which is shown in Figure 5.9. The sequences in Figure 5.8 are visualisations of the traces obtained by checking property 'not **SAN1**' for different models. The first sequence relates to the control room interface. The second and third sequences were generated from the model with the hand-held device. In the case of the third sequence it is recognised that there is a risk that the operator might forget to save the controls into the device. This is introduced as an assumption into the property specification.

Given that the central control panel characterises key actions, the second and third sequences illustrate the additional steps that have to be taken by the hand-held device to achieve the goal. The additional steps represent changes of the physical location and uploading/storing controls of the visited devices. The designer and usability engineer now have information, which in addition to the experience of the existing control room, will enable them to assess whether the new interface will be problematical. For example, action goPOS6 may involve a 100 m walk through the plant, while action savePmp4ctrls may be performed instantaneously

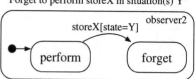

Fig 5.10 *Simple observer automata*

and the performance of action `getPmp3ctrls` might depend on additional contextual factors like the network quality. This approach leaves the judgement of the severity of such differences to the designer, the usability engineer or the domain expert (step 4 in Figure 5.1). It enables these experts to draw important considerations to the designer's attention.

Further information about the design, based perhaps on assumptions about what the user might do, can also be included in the analysis. In the case of the SMV model checker (McMillan, 1993; Cimatti *et al.*, 2002) used here, system assumptions can be introduced in three ways: (1) by adding state invariants, (2) by extending the property specification by temporal assertions, and (3) by binding the model execution to the behaviour of observer automata. Traces that represent behaviours that are infeasible, for example, the possibility that the user carried out two actions at the same time, may be excluded. In such a case it may make sense to investigate the behaviour of the model under the assumption that only a single user input occurs at any step. One possibility stemming from a usability analysis would be an assumption that the operator consistently forgets to store control elements on the handheld device (a trace is described in the third sequence of Figure 5.8). This may be specified as an assertion 'alwaysForget' as follows:

```
assert alwaysForget: G !(savePmp1ctrls| [...]
|savePmp5ctrls);
```

This assertion specifies that always (G) the user omits the actions associated with saving controls `savePmp1ctrls`. It then becomes possible to check the original property **SAN1** under the assumption that this assertion holds:

```
assume alwaysForget; using alwaysForget prove
SAN1;
```

For a list of patterns for specifying more sophisticated sequential properties, see Dwyer, Avrunin and Corbett (1999).

The designer may also want to make less restrictive assumptions about operator behaviour such as that 'the operator will forget to store controls after *n* times' or that 'operator will forget to store controls in certain situation(s) *Y*' (where such situations are described by model states). These behaviours may be formulated as observer automata with violation states, see Figure 5.10. The model checking analysis will only concern those system behaviours that are restricted to what the observer will allow.

5.6   Modelling implicit action and context in the whole system

To demonstrate the model of the whole system and the information flows within it a different example is chosen. This example gives an example where user actions are *implicit* (Schmidt, 2000). The models described in the previous section focused on usability issues associated with interaction with a mobile device within a system. Usability issues may also be associated with the characteristics of the whole system, for example the way in which information is presented to users in different locations within a built environment. The issues that are of concern are about whether implicit actions will have desired effects – for example, will a relevant message be sent to a user within a certain time after arrival at a given location? In this case the implicit action occurs when a user moves into a space. The effect of this movement is that a sensor in the space recognises the presence of the user's mobile device and triggers the system to provide information that is relevant.

Many factors affect users of built environments. These include the texture and physical characteristics of the environment and where information displays are situated. They are also affected by whether relevant information is received by them in a timely way. Consider the example of an airport. In each space within the airport there is a public display of messages about flights relevant to passengers that occupy the space at any one time. Each passenger carries a mobile phone and receives messages on this phone that are specifically relevant to their flight and location. Action is implicit, in the sense that when a passenger walks into a space the location sensor notes the fact and as a result information may be distributed to the passenger's mobile device and possibly to the public display if it is the first time someone for a designated flight arrives in the space. The design that is modelled adopts a simple set of techniques for deploying information to users sufficient to provide a basis for the discussion. Many schemes are feasible for combining public displays with private information, see for example Gilroy *et al.* (2006), Kray, Kortuem and Krüger (2005). The scheme used here is illustrative of a range that could equally be addressed by the techniques described.

5.6.1 Step 1: user requirements for the system

In this example the requirements that relate to the broader system are concerned with the acceptability of the smart environment to passengers in relation to the services that the environment provides. The passenger may have expressed the following concern about the existing system:

I would like to be sure that flight information is up-to-date.

This is an issue of usability because it relates to the *experience* that passengers would have of the total system and would be a property that complements device properties of the kind discussed in the previous section. The user concern (as part of step 1 in Figure 5.1) is translated into the following properties of the model:

P1 When the passenger moves into a location then the flight status information is presented to the passenger's hand-held device within some maximum delay time.

P2 Information on public displays should reflect the current state of the system within a maximum delay time.

P3 When the passenger enters a new location, the sensor detects the passenger's presence and the next message received concerns flight information and updates the passenger's hand-held device with information relevant to the passenger's position and stage in the embarkation process.

P4 When the passenger moves into a new location then if the passenger is the first from the flight to enter, public displays in the location are updated to include this flight information.

P5 When the last passenger on a particular flight in the location leaves it then the public display is updated to remove this flight information.

The next step is to provide a model of the system that can be used to check properties such as these.

5.6.2 Step 2: characteristics of the airport model

Since properties P1 and P2 are timing properties, a model that incorporates time is adopted for this system. The model of the airport system therefore uses uppaal (Behrmann *et al.*, 2004). The model is split into a number of processes describing:

sensor: the activity within a room, including the mechanism for sensing the arrival and departure of passengers. This process updates the room-based display to show flight information for those passengers that are in the room.

passenger: the passenger that receives specific messages relating to flight and location in the airport. The passenger moves from room to room.

dispatcher: the centralised dispatcher that sends messages regularly.

The dispatcher (Figure 5.11) is critical to the timing characteristics of the design and is the basis for exploring the system to ensure that timing guarantees are satisfied. It is assumed that the dispatcher is a human machine system. The dispatching of messages involves human intervention at some level and this is the primary source of delay. This exploration is carried out by adjusting the rate and the order of distribution of messages, as well as passenger arrival volumes. The illustration in Figure 5.11 distributes messages in strict order with a delay between broadcasts specified by the constant `workload`. The model makes a simple set of assumptions about messages and the way they are tagged for recognition. Tags are associated with flight number and location. In practice, of course, the airport system would be more elaborate than this. Many of the potential complexities of the model are removed by focusing on the specific requirements with the proviso that checking the properties does not bias the analysis exclusively to a certain

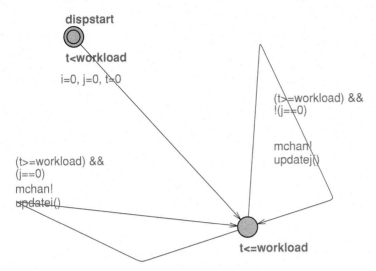

dispstart

t<workload

i=0, j=0, t=0

(t>=workload) &&
!(j==0)

mchan!
updatej()

(t>=workload) &&
(j==0)
mchan!
updatei()

t<=workload

Fig 5.11 *The dispatcher process*

class of properties, thereby providing a model that can be used as a structure for implementation.

Two types of process receive information from the dispatcher. The sensor process (Figure 5.12) combines the behaviour of the public display with the room sensor. Each room or space in the airport contains a sensor (how the sensor is implemented is not the concern of this level of modelling). The generic sensor is instantiated for each space: entry hall, queue 1, queue 2, check-in, main hall, gate. The other type of process is the passenger process (Figure 5.13) that describes the passenger and the relevant behaviour of the passenger's mobile device.

The sensor process (Figure 5.12) describes the key interaction features of:

- the public display located in the room
- the sensor updating its knowledge of whether passengers are present in the space
  – this assumes an interaction between the sensor and the passenger device

The sensor communicates by means of three channels.

- It receives messages that have been distributed to it from the dispatcher by means of the channel mchan.
- It receives requests from the passengers' hand-held devices (via arrive) where they arrive in the room that relates to the sensor.
- It receives requests from the passengers' hand-held devices (via depart) when they leave the sensor's room.

When the sensor receives a message from the dispatcher, the function read() checks the tags on the message and if the location tag coincides with the location of the sensor then the display is updated. Of course, a realistic implementation of this system would update a flight information array for display each time a

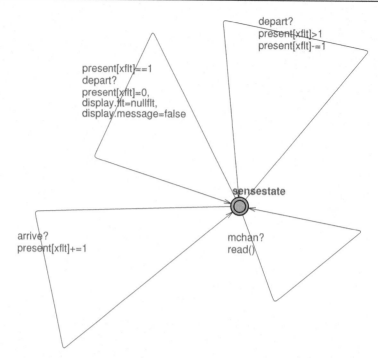

Fig 5.12 *The sensor process*

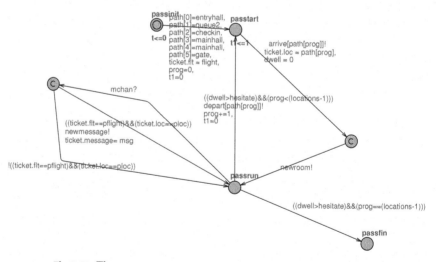

Fig 5.13 *The passenger process*

relevant message is received. The array updating mechanism is not of interest to interaction analysis.

When the sensor receives a message from the arrive channel this signals the entry of a passenger. The array `present[]` keeps a count of the number of passengers present for a particular flight and is incremented with the arriving passenger's flight number. When the sensor receives a message from the depart channel then the array is decremented using the departing passenger's flight number. If the result of this is that there are no passengers for a particular flight left in the room then the flight information is removed from the display.

As a consequence, when the last passenger moves out of the space this information is cleared from the display. When the passenger is newly arrived in the space then the array present is incremented and so next time a message arrives about this flight the information will be displayed for the first time.

The passenger process (Figure 5.13) describes the activity of the passenger and the key features of their mobile phone. This activity has a number of characteristics:

- The passenger is given a specific path to follow. This is defined in the array path, one would anticipate more than one passenger defined associated with different paths.
- The process notifies the room sensor that it has arrived. The passenger ticket is updated to point to the current location.
- The passenger moves to a state where it receives messages from the dispatcher via mchan. If the received message is tagged with the passenger's current location and the passenger's flight number then the mobile phone display is updated.

The next stage is to prove properties of the model.

5.6.3 Step 3: checking the properties

P1 requires that when the passenger moves into a new location in the airport then flight status information is presented to the passenger's hand-held device within a maximum delay time (this is defined by the variable maxdelay). It must be updated within a period of delay after a passenger arrives. P1 can be characterised as proving that from the point that the passenger enters the location (regardless of flight number) the relevant message will be received by the passenger within the time delay. Two transitions are of interest in the passenger process (Figure 5.13). The first occurs as the passenger moves into the new location and the second occurs when the passenger receives a message from the dispatcher that matches the flight number and location of the passenger. P1 is checked by introducing an observer process (Figure 5.14) and adding a communication (newroom) in the passenger process (Figure 5.13) to signal arrival in the new location and similarly a communication (newmessage) to signal receiving a relevant message. If the message does not arrive while the passenger is in a location (this time is determined in the model by the variable dwell) then the observer will deadlock. The deadlock occurs because the observer is waiting to receive notification that a message has been received but instead receives a message from the passenger that it has entered another room. When appropriate diagnostics are switched on, deadlock generates a trace that can then be further analysed to work out why the system does not satisfy the properties.

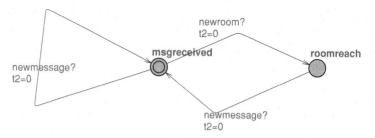

Fig 5.14 *The observer process*

In practice the generalised deadlock property is very computer intensive and on a no-frills specification PC the Uppaal system (Uppaal 4.0.6) ran out of memory after three hours execution. The specific properties relevant to P1 and P2 relate to checking that fresh messages arrive within the maxdelay interval. For example, in the case of P1 A[](o1.roomreach imply (o1.t2<maxdelay)) was checked for different values of maxdelay. This property holds true as long as passenger 1 (this passenger's observer is o1) receives a message within maxdelay after entering any new room. The airport system that was used for analysis contained two instantiations of the passenger process. As a further elaboration, to check that the passenger received regular updates while occupying a particular room, A[](o1.msgreceived imply (o1.t2<maxdelay)), was checked. This property checks whether subsequent messages that are received, while passenger 1 is in a particular space, arrive at intervals of more than maxdelay. This property failed for an appropriate value of maxdelay though it was successful because the passenger had completed its path through the airport and terminated in passfin. While the observer o1 continued to wait expecting a further signal from the passenger to say it had received another message, the observer's local clock t2 exceeded the maxdelay limit.

The second property P2 that relates to the information on the public displays is proved in the same way. The observer is modified to receive messages from both the passenger and the sensor. Hence the passenger sends a message to the observer when it enters a new room and the sensor for that room sends a message to the observer when the dispatcher sends it a message that relates to the flight.

In both cases the properties were checked experimentally for different values of maxdelay. When the property failed, and the passenger did not receive the message in time, the diagnostic trace was investigated to check which assumptions caused this failure to occur thereby allowing the designer to explore alternative strategies for distributing messages so that passengers would receive timely updates.

5.7   Generic models and properties

The analysis of this chapter describes two models that were built specifically in response to the requirements of the two designs. Many of the

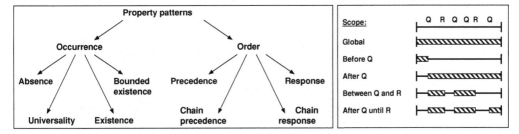

Fig 5.15 *Property specification patterns (Dwyer* et al.*, 1999)*

characteristics of these applications are shared between applications. The generic moding characteristics of the mobile device are shared between a range of similar devices and the fact that a system consists of rooms, displays and people tracked as they move between rooms is likewise a characteristic of many systems. It therefore makes sense to consider generic characteristics: models that can be adopted off the shelf and instantiated for the particular requirements of the system.

The same is true of the properties that can be proven. The *ifadis* tool (Loer and Harrison, 2006) has been developed to support property patterns that correspond to a set of usability requirements. These property patterns are inspired by the work of Dwyer and his co-authors who have extracted 555 property specifications from a range of sources and observed that most properties are instantiations of a limited set of patterns under a particular scope (Dwyer *et al.*, 1999, see Figure 5.15). Scopes describe sub-ranges of the possible state sequences over which the properties can hold. Chapter 5 of Loer (2003) demonstrates that usability guidelines, such as those in chapter 4 of Dix *et al.* (1998) or Nielsen (1992), can be viewed similarly as patterns and may be considered in terms of a concept hierarchy. This can be seen in the screen dump of Figure 5.16. The property editor helps the designer to construct temporal logic specifications by making the patterns available and aiding the process of instantiation. It is envisaged that further generic properties would have general applicability to information flows within built environments.

5.8   Conclusions

A number of studies indicate that human factors account for a very large proportion of failures in systems (Hollnagel, 1993; MacKenzie, 1994). In the past, software development methods have attached relatively little significance to human factors issues. Unless that is changed the proportion of failures attributed to human factors will keep increasing as other aspects of software development improve. Clearly there is the need for a better integration of human factors concerns into the software engineering lifecycle.

One specific facet of such integration is the need to reason about the usability of systems' designs from early in the development process. Usability analysis

LIVERPOOL JOHN MOORES UNIVERSITY
LEARNING SERVICES

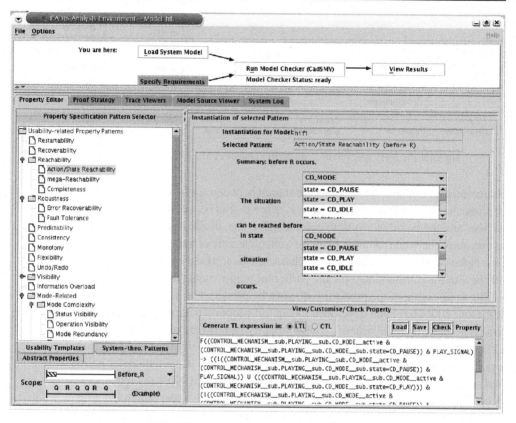

Fig 5.16 *Usability perspective of property editor (*`req2tl`*)*

must not be left to the latter stages of software development when changes will be more difficult and expensive to make. Instead, a number of lightweight methods are needed that enable reasoning about the usability of systems from the early stages of design, thus enabling the design to be shaped by the usability criteria and concerns.

A number of low-cost methods for the analysis of usability have been proposed and studies have shown that they can be useful in detecting potential usability problems (Jeffries *et al.*, 1991; Desurvire, Kondziela and Atwood, 1992; Karat, Campbell and Fiegle, 1992). Low-cost techniques have distinct advantages over empirical methods. They are cheap to use, they do not require extended advanced planning and they can be used in the early stages before a design is implemented.

There are, however, problems when these techniques form part of a process where it is intended that they be applied by software engineers because they require human factors expertise. Questionnaire-based techniques such as cognitive walkthrough can be useful in this respect. Since the analysis is guided by a questionnaire it can, to some degree, be applied by non-human-factors specialists, although there is a danger of bias when applied by people directly involved in the design process.

Another problem is the sheer size and complexity of the models that must be considered when it comes to complex systems. Usually the methods tend to focus on what could be called surface issues in the interaction, with little consideration of more complex behavioural issues of the interaction between user and device that will arise in real usage conditions. In this respect it can be argued that not even empirical evaluation can guarantee absence of such errors, since for complex systems it is usually not viable to test all possible usage conditions/situations.

This chapter presents proposals of more formal and systematic usability analysis methods that attempt to provide answers to these problems. The claim is that these techniques, although narrower in scope, provide a more thorough analysis in which human factors claims are more clearly identified and substantiated using complementary expertise from other parties to the design process. Hence software engineers carry out part of the process, but there are well-defined stages where human factors input is required. In an initial phase human factors expertise is brought in to help select and model relevant system features; the analysis can then progress in a more typical software engineering setting, but finally the analysis of the results must go back to human factors expertise.

The problems with using formal techniques relate to how well the techniques scale, how easy it is to use the methods and whether the methods bias the analysis so that key issues may be ignored. It is not contended that this type of approach is the answer to all of the usability engineering problems. However, if usability engineering is to be a true engineering discipline, it does need rigour and formality. Formal methods of software engineering have a role to play during interactive systems design and analysis. They enable a type of reasoning that is more thorough and repetitive, without precluding the use of other more traditional approaches to usability analysis. How to best integrate the two worlds is a challenging and interesting research area. No single current technique has the expressive power to capture, and enable the analysis of, all interesting facets of an interactive system. Instead, different techniques should be applied as needed.

One final word regarding the practical feasibility of using formal techniques during interactive systems design and analysis. In the context of design problems where there is no obvious pay-off using formal techniques, for example where more exploratory techniques are currently used, it might be argued that the costs of applying these techniques are too high. However, the situations where early analysis can reduce substantial downstream costs, either because the system is safety critical or because the cost of shipping volumes of less than usable systems cannot be countenanced, are increasing.

6 Using statistics in usability research

PAUL CAIRNS AND ANNA L. COX

6.1 Overview

As discussed in the earlier chapters, controlled experiments and questionnaires offer HCI researchers the opportunity to deal with numbers and the hope is that in doing so we can reach solid, secure results like other sciences. Of course, as discussed in Chapter 1, there are a lot of pitfalls in ensuring that these numbers are meaningful. Even if they are avoided there is still the problem that people vary – we all take different amounts of time to do routine tasks such as finding a link on a web page or copying a paragraph from one page in a document to another. Thus, we need to be sure that what we see in our numerical data is not just natural variation between people but variation due to the real differences between interfaces and their effects on people. Statistical methods allow us to do this.

The purpose of this chapter is to look at the two sorts of data that occur frequently in HCI: data from controlled experiments and data from questionnaire studies. We will discuss how statistics can be used to distinguish natural variation from systematic difference, or in other words, how to see the wood for the trees. It is also worth saying that the purpose of this chapter is not to help you choose and execute different statistical tests. There are a lot of excellent textbooks out there, some of which will be recommended later, where you can find out the nuts and bolts of statistics. Instead we will worry more about how statistics helps you make sense of your data and thus draw sound conclusions about the nature of the interactions between people and computers.

The topics covered in this chapter are therefore:

1 Using descriptive statistics and diagrams to help you understand your data
2 How to prove your point with inferential statistics
3 Using inferential statistics in a more exploratory way.

6.2 Exploratory data analysis

Having devised a successful experiment or compiled a valid questionnaire, the researcher goes out and collects their data. After even a modest number of participants, the researcher suddenly finds that they have a whole spreadsheet full of numbers. The question now is what to do with it.

Table 6.1 *Example task completion
times and numbers of wrong clicks*

Participant	Task time	Wrong clicks
1	32	1
2	15	3
3	26	2
4	18	8
5	24	2
6	45	0
7	26	1
8	31	1
9	29	2
10	18	3
11	42	1
12	37	1
13	34	1
14	27	2
15	25	3

6.2.1 Averages and spread

A good starting point for any statistical analysis is to turn the large set of numbers into a small set of numbers to make it easier to grasp what is going on. Specifically, averages are very useful as they indicate roughly where the middle of the data is. So for example, the researcher has collected a whole set of times of how long it took people to find important information on a website together with how many wrong clicks they made along the way. The data collected are given in Table 6.1.

The average task completion time is usually understood to be the *mean* of the times, that is, add up all the times and divide by the number of participants. This is a good indicator of how the 'average person' performs and this comes out as 29.27 s, which does seem to be in the middle of all of the task times. A similar thing can be done with the number of wrong clicks. However, there the mean comes out at 2.06 clicks whereas the researcher can see that generally people were making at most one or two wrong clicks. So the mean seems a bit unrepresentative, a bit too high. Instead, the *mode* can be useful here. This is simply the number of wrong clicks that occurred most frequently of all the possible number of wrong clicks. In this case the mode is 1, which means the most common number of wrong clicks is just one wrong click. In this sense, the mode is not the 'average person' but rather the 'typical person'.

The *median* is the third sort of average and is precisely the value that divides the data into two equally sized groups. So the median time would be the time for which half the participants took longer than that time to complete the task and half the participants took less than that time to complete the task. For the task times, the median is 29. As there were 15 participants, you should check that somebody did actually get 29 s as their time and that 7 people were slower than that and 7 people were quicker. In this sense, the median is literally the middle of the data.

Whilst averages are useful to suggest what is a good single value to represent all of the data, they don't really say how representative it is. For example, only knowing the mean of the task times to be 29.27 s doesn't tell you whether everybody took around half a minute to do the task or whether some people took three or four minutes and some people took just a few seconds. What is needed here is some way of understanding the spread of the data.

The simplest measure of spread is the range and is simply the smallest and largest values of the data. So the range of task times is from 15 s to 45 s. This tells us then that nobody is taking an incredible amount of time on the task and so the mean task time is quite representative of the task times of all of the participants. With the clicks, the mode is 1 and range is 0 to 8. This does not indicate how many people were making eight wrong clicks but simply that somebody did. Fortunately, in a small data set like this example, it is easy to scan down and check out exactly how many people are making eight mistakes, but in general this is not so easy.

A better measure of spread is the standard deviation. Basically the standard deviation is a measure of the average distance that each item of data is from the mean of all the items. Or, in terms of task times, it measures the average number of seconds any particular task time is away from the mean of 29.27 s. This is slightly more complicated than it sounds, as the average used here is not the mean but uses squaring and square-rooting of numbers. It is one sort of average, it is just not the usual sort of average. In the case of task times, the standard deviation is 8.73 s which means that, approximately, the task times for most participants are within 10 s of the mean value.

Similarly, the standard deviation of the number of wrong clicks is 1.87 clicks. Roughly this means that mostly people make two wrong clicks more or less than the mean, so between none and four wrong clicks. From this, the maximum value of eight wrong clicks does stand out: it is a lot more than two clicks away from the mean. We might start to wonder if it was an unusual value in some way. However, as we said earlier, the mean is not a good representative of the number of wrong clicks and the standard deviation is intimately connected to the mean. Thus, the standard deviation is not really the best number here to represent spread. Probably just the range or a graph, as described next, would be the best way to understand the shape of this data.

Thus averages and spread can greatly simplify our data. Starting from 30 numbers in Table 6.1, the mean task time and modal number of wrong clicks give us two averages that usefully represent the two types of data. The standard deviation of the task times gives a good sense of variation in task times and the range of wrong clicks is helpful too. What is more, these numbers would have been useful whether there were 15 participants or 150.

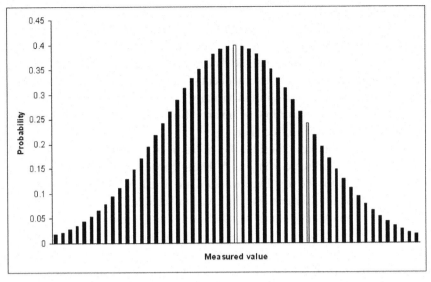

Fig 6.1 *A normal distribution with mean (in white) and one standard deviation from the mean (in grey)*

In practice, many people will simply report means and standard deviations and move on to doing some inferential statistical tests. This seems reasonable – everybody else seems to do that when you read their papers. However, if that is all that is done there is a real risk that you have gone to all of the trouble to collect this data only to ignore most of it! Drawing graphs of data can be very useful as a way of properly seeing data and getting more out of it.

6.2.2 Seeing data

Means and standard deviations are ways of describing a normal distribution: the bell-shaped curve that underlies much of statistics. The mean is where the peak of the bell is and standard deviation indicates the width of the curve, as shown in Figure 6.1. The normal distribution is important in statistics for lots of reasons. The main one is that it occurs as a result of processes where lots of factors come together to determine a particular property of a population such as height. This means it crops up a lot in usability because how people interact with systems tends to depend on lots of factors. It has the added advantage that its mathematical form is entirely determined by just two parameters, namely the mean and standard deviation. This makes it very convenient as well: when data are normal, all the researcher needs to describe it are those two values. Once the data are known to be parametric (another term for normal), it opens up a particular set of statistical tests that can be used to see differences between groups of people. These tests, not surprisingly, are called parametric tests and the two most commonly encountered are the analysis of variance (ANOVA) and *t*-test. But more on those later.

Before using these tests, how can researchers be sure that their data fit this nice shape? Or, in statistical language, how do you know whether your data are parametric? The answer is to look at the data. By inspecting data visually, it is possible to be more confident that the data are parametric. And if they are not, then that can guide the choice of subsequent statistics in the analysis of the data. Moreover, once the data are laid out visually, sometimes it is possible to spot patterns that may be worth following up and also anomalies in the data, such as skew and outliers, as we will see later.

To give some examples, consider the situation of a questionnaire where all answers are on a Likert scale from 1 to 5. Thirty people completed the questionnaires and the data for the first five questions are listed in Table 6.2. The means and standard deviations for this data are given in Table 6.3.

From this summary table alone, it would seem that Q1 gives the highest score overall and Q5 the lowest. But all the means are around 3 and the standard deviations are around 1 with the exception of Q1. But on a Likert scale from 1 to 5, 3 is just the centre of the scale so basically the mean score is the average of the scale and the standard deviation of about 1 is probably about right if the scores are not all the same! This summary data is telling us very little.

The exceptional standard deviation in Q1 should be looked at but, unless you are familiar with working with data, it would be very easy to gloss over this value as 'round about right'. However, looking at the data for question 1 in Table 1, Q1 very obviously stands out as unusual – all the values are either 1 or 5! Thus, whilst the mean is about average, actually people are behaving far from average, they always land at one of the extreme ends of the scale. It is only by looking at the data that this becomes clear.

But what about the other questions, are they really as simple to understand as Table 6.3 suggests? The way to see this is to look at the bar chart. This chart graphically represents the number of people who answered with a given Likert score. The bar charts for questions 2–5 are in Figure 6.2.

From the bar charts, it is possible to get a much clearer picture of the data. Q2 does roughly fit the bell-shaped curve of a normal distribution. It is not perfect, for instance it is not symmetrical, but given there are only five possible answers to Q2, this is not too bad.

Questions 3 and 5 seem to have main peaks like a normal distribution but they are off to one side. This is called skew. Q3 has negative skew because the long asymmetric tail is to the left of the peak and Q5 has positive skew because the tail is to the right of the peak. This need not be a problem for using statistics that rely on normal distributions, but it is nice to know in case some tests are sensitive to skew.

Question 4 presents a curious case. It doesn't really have a peak, nor does it have any extreme values of 1 and 5. The mean in fact is the least frequently occurring value! This is certainly not a normal distribution. At this point, a researcher might wonder if the question is a good one. Perhaps when the question is re-examined it may turn out to be rather hard to answer and this picture is really representing

Table 6.2 *Example questionnaire data*

Participant	Q1	Q2	Q3	Q4	Q5
1	5	2	5	2	3
2	5	3	4	4	4
3	1	3	5	2	3
4	1	3	4	3	2
5	5	2	5	3	4
6	5	3	2	4	2
7	5	3	3	4	2
8	1	2	5	2	2
9	1	2	4	2	2
10	1	3	5	4	3
11	5	3	2	4	4
12	5	4	3	2	2
13	5	4	2	4	4
14	5	5	3	4	4
15	5	3	2	3	3
16	1	2	3	3	1
17	1	4	4	2	5
18	5	5	4	2	4
19	5	3	4	4	3
20	1	4	3	3	2
21	5	3	3	2	5
22	5	3	3	2	3
23	1	2	2	2	3
24	1	3	4	3	2
25	5	4	4	4	2
26	5	2	4	4	2
27	5	3	1	3	5
28	5	3	4	4	1
29	5	4	1	4	4
30	5	3	2	3	3

Table 6.3 *Summary statistics of questionnaire data*

Question	Mean score	Standard deviaton
Q1	3.67	1.92
Q2	3.10	0.84
Q3	3.33	1.18
Q4	3.07	0.86
Q5	2.97	1.13

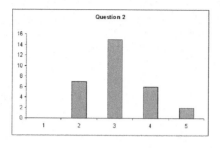

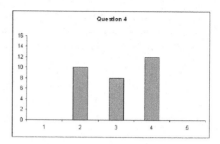

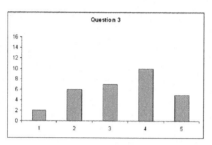

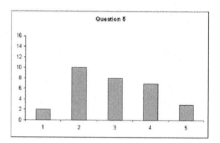

Fig 6.2 *Bar charts of example questions 2–5*

that people do not know what to say, so are giving somewhat neutral, random answers. Or perhaps it is fine and this is how people think! But without looking at the data, the researcher would not even have thought that there could be anything wrong with the question.

And of course, had we been given the bar chart for Q1, it would have been clear that the distribution was unusual because there would have been no bars in the middle of the graph.

Bar charts, or similar diagrams, are therefore a useful way to look at the shape of the distribution. Knowing the shape, we can then assess how useful the usual summary statistics of average and spread really are. This is not to say that summary statistics like means and standard deviations are valueless. They are just not the whole story.

Another very useful way of picturing data is scatterplots. This is when two different measures gathered about people are plotted as the x and y co-ordinates of a graph. The result is a scatter of points where each point represents two items of data for a particular participant. Scatterplots are useful because they can help identify relationships, or lack of relationships, between the different measures collected.

For example, the scatterplot of the task times and number of wrong clicks data from Table 6.1 is given in Figure 6.3. The scattering of points does not seem as random as looking at the table of data might suggest. The longer the task time seems to be, the fewer wrong clicks people make. This is of course not a perfect relationship, but the data do seem to suggest that something like that is going on. Thus, from the scatterplot, a researcher could begin to speculate what the cause of the relationship might be, if it is a real relationship. For instance, it may be

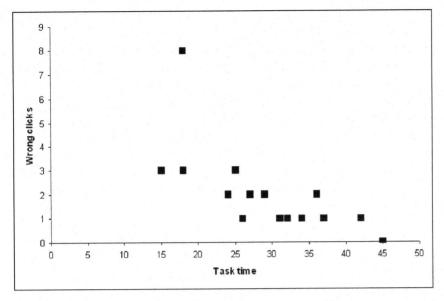

Fig 6.3 *A scatterplot of the data in Table 6.1*

that to do the task accurately requires a lot of thought and so people who spend longer thinking about it make fewer mistakes. Or alternatively, the more errors made, the quicker the time and so it was not worth people trying to be precise and accurate – they might as well just try something and they would be able to do the task. Neither of these explanations is proven by the scatterplot. The scatterplot is just representing the data, but having spotted a possible relationship, it can be further investigated with perhaps some more experiments that specifically look at whether this relationship is really there or just a random variation in the current data.

The scatterplot also makes it clear that the person who made eight wrong clicks is very unusual. That participant did not have a particularly quick time but did make lots of mistakes. An unusual point in the data like this is called an outlier – it lies outside the normal range of the rest of the data. There are lots of reasons for outliers: some people may have unusual abilities (either better or worse) that mean they perform unusually in an experiment; or something went wrong with that participant's session; or the participant was wrongly instructed; or possibly only that the data was mis-typed as it was entered.

Whatever the reason, having identified an outlier, it is useful to go and check why that person may be producing an outlying result. Sometimes they are just unusual and their data can be excluded from the analysis. Other times, the very fact that they are unusual is indicating something deeper about the experiment that needs to be investigated. But without looking at the data in the first place, such outliers are not easily spotted.

It should be noted that even had we just plotted the bar chart for the number of wrong clicks, the eight wrong clicks would have stood out as an outlier. However, if, for the sake of argument, that person had also completed the task in under ten seconds, the outlier would suddenly look less odd. It would fit into the general scheme of the rest of the data, the participant being a person who took a very short time as a result of making many mistakes. Thus, in the scatterplot picture, they would be an outlier but not a peculiar, inexplicable one.

Thus, simple bar charts and scatterplots can be enormously valuable when it comes to understanding the data collected in an experiment. They complement an understanding of the data suggested by descriptive statistics like averages and measures of spread. At the same time, they offer opportunities to see the shape of the data and any unusual features in it. Also, as will be seen in the full example, it is often possible to take steps to account for these problems in our statistical analysis.

It is perhaps because these methods are so simple that they are so easily overlooked. Nonetheless, rather as a gardener needs a good understanding of the soil and drainage in different parts of a garden and can only do this by getting their hands into the soil, so a good researcher needs a good view of the relationships and oddities in the data from experiments. Exploratory data analysis is the way that a researcher begins to get their hands dirty.

6.3   Inferential statistics

Having found out a lot through exploring data, it is time to consider more carefully what features of the data are real and what are merely chance variations. This is what inferential statistics is all about. We recognise that in any experiment involving people we expect to see variation. The problem is identifying what aspects of the variation are the interesting systematic differences that we are looking for and what are just chance variations that happen to look like patterns in the data.

The best way to see the value of inferential statistics is with an example. Suppose a designer is trying to work out a new way of doing a search on a website. The designer comes up with three search tool designs that seem to have some merit and being a good user-centred designer puts them to a user trial to see which one users prefer. Thirty users are given each of the three designs A, B and C to perform some searches (experimentally speaking, this is a within-subject design). Afterwards, the users have to say which of the three designs they prefer. The results are summarised in Table 6.4.

At this point, the designer can come away from the user trial happy. Design A was preferred by half the users and, given there were three alternatives, this is a good sign that it is the best design. But is this conclusion correct? Thinking a bit harder, if people really had no preference, you would expect people's preferences to split evenly between the three designs, so ideally each design would have 10 people identify it as their preference. Of course, in reality, even if there were no preferences between the designs, it would be unlikely to get this split. It would be more likely to get a split not exactly like this but something similar to it. Is the actual data so far from an even split that it does show a preference for design A?

Table 6.4 *Number of users
preferring given designs*

Design A	Design B	Design C
15	7	8

There is a statistical test, the χ^2 test or chi-squared test (χ being a Greek letter and usually pronounced in English the same as 'ky' in 'sky'), that is able to say what the probability is of getting this particular result. Performing the tests and finding out the probabilities gives a result that this particular data would occur more than 1 in 7 times each time this trial was run *if the users have no particular preference*.

Suddenly, the designer's conclusions do not look so convincing. The data is still a bit unusual as it is only likely to happen 1 in 7 times by chance, but, at the same time, the designer might just have obtained an unusual sample. It seems a real possibility that none of the designs is preferred more over the others.

There is also a deeper problem. Even if the data had come out as really unlikely, say less than 1 in 100, the designer does not necessarily know that even this unlikely data is not just a chance variation. An unlucky variation, admittedly, but chance nonetheless. In which case, how can anyone come away from a user test with any certainty that what they are seeing is real, systematic variation rather than just natural variation between people?

The strict answer is that no one can. However, inferential statistics provide an approach to answering questions in the face of this sort of natural variation between people. The remainder of this section will not discuss any particular statistical test in detail, but will discuss how to conduct statistics so that you can be confident that what you find in your user trials really is something interesting.

6.3.1 The gold standard statistical argument

There is no way round the uncertainty that natural variation between people brings to an experiment with users. Instead, statistical tests act as evidence towards a viewpoint and the key to ameliorating the effect of random variations is to make predictions. Again, an example of how this works is useful.

Suppose a person has two normal dice. They roll the dice in front of you and score a double six. This is an unusual outcome (it occurs 1 in 36 times on average), but there is nothing really interesting about the outcome – it happened by chance. If, however, the person first told you 'I am going to throw a double six' and then promptly rolled a double six, then the situation becomes much more interesting. The prediction has no effect on the chances of the outcome, but the fact that it did come out the way it was predicted suggests that the person knew something you did not. In fact, you would either suspect that the dice were not as fair as you originally thought, or you would ask the person to repeat this remarkable feat just to check it was not a fluke.

Similarly, for a statistical test to have any relevance, there needs to be some sort of prediction of an unlikely outcome. Moreover, there needs to be some expectation that the outcome will come out in some other, more normal way. Ordinarily, the expectation should be that nothing interesting will happen and this is the null hypothesis in an experiment (see Chapter 1). The prediction of something interesting for the statistical test is called the alternative hypothesis. This should state clearly how the experimental data should turn out if things are working the way you believe. It is still not possible to prove the alternative hypothesis, but you are able to show that the null hypothesis is unlikely to be holding. For instance, if the search tool designer mentioned earlier had first suggested that design A was likely to be best, this would have added weight to the outcome of the experiment. In the case of the search tool designer, the null hypothesis is that there is no preference between the three designs.

The next step in the statistical argument is to collect the data and to collect it fairly. For instance, the experiment should be fair, allowing the possibility of people preferring any of the three designs, but some theory or insight into design A suggests that it is the one that should be preferred.

Having collected the data, a statistical test is used to analyse the data. In almost all cases, the test takes the null hypothesis as a predictor of the expected outcome. Moreover, usually, the null hypothesis says that there will be no particular pattern or difference between different parts of the data. In our example, the null was that there was no difference between the levels of preference of the three designs. Given this assumption, it is possible to calculate the probabilities that the data gathered really are just natural variation and this is the p value that comes out of statistical tests. One way to understand the p value is as the probability of getting this result if the null hypothesis holds. That is, if nothing is really going on and you are just seeing chance variation, the p value is the proportion of times that you would get a difference like the one you have obtained or a more extreme difference. So for instance, if the null hypothesis really does hold and your p value is 0.04, then for every hundred times you run the experiment, four of the runs would be at least as extreme as your result. Or one in twenty-five of the runs would appear like your actual results.

In an actual study, if this p value is small, usually less than 0.05 (or 0.01), then the data is said to be significant (or highly significant). This level of significance is a convention. There is nothing to say that it really is the level at which the data become interesting. It is, however, a level which is sufficiently unlikely to have occurred by chance, particularly if it was what was predicted to happen beforehand by the experimenter. Having gained a significant p value, it is now possible to put the whole argument together:

1 A prediction, the alternative hypothesis, was made about the outcome of an experiment.
2 The null hypothesis is what would ordinarily be expected and contradicts the alternative hypothesis.

3 Data was gathered fairly.
4 A statistical test is used to show that under the null hypothesis the data should only occur rarely.
5 Thus we conclude that not only have the data occurred as predicted but that they were unlikely to have occurred by chance.
6 This means the data are very interesting and provide evidence in support of the prediction and the theory or viewpoint that informed the prediction.

This is what we have called the gold standard of statistical analysis because, if done like this, the conclusion of an experiment is on the firmest foundation.

It should be clear though that this is not a proof of the alternative hypothesis. There never can be a proof when there is natural variation. Moreover, just like the person rolling two dice, you would be reasonable in asking the experimenter to do it again just to prove it was not a fluke. This is why isolated experiments, whilst they are interesting and may initiate some good research, are not as valuable to research as a good sequence of experiments all in the same area. The more experiments that work out in favour of a particular theory, the more that theory looks like it is correct. One experiment is useful but it could just be a fluke.

This argument form also addresses a common complaint that students have about statistics which is 'Why can't I do more than one test on my data?' This is usually said by students frustrated that an experiment, and all the work that entails, has resulted in no significant outcome. So to try to rescue their work, they consider other tests to do in the hope that something comes out significant. However, if those tests are done without a prediction, what do they prove? With significance levels at 0.05, 1 in 20 tests (on average) will come out significant by pure chance. If a researcher does enough tests, they will be unlucky not to get a significant result at some point! But this argument form requires a prediction and that prediction cannot be made once the data has been collected since then it is no longer a prediction.

This seems harsh. To do really good statistics using this gold standard gives the experimenter only one chance to get a good result. But it is precisely this harsh standard that makes the experiment valuable. Unfortunately, in reporting work, no one can tell whether or not this is what the experimenter really did. The consequence is that people, even those trying to do good work, do publish work that does not meet this standard. The result is the gold standard is diluted and the value of the research accordingly debased.

6.3.2 The silver standard of statistical argument

In some experiments, having managed to get users through the door, experimenters do not just settle for asking one question with an experiment. They therefore try to collect lots of data from the users in the hope of finding out more about them. This data may be independent of what is needed for the gold standard. Or it may help shed light on why the main predicted outcome works. In either case, the experimenter does not have a clear prediction to make but does feel that there may be interesting things to be found from some carefully collected data. For example, the designer may be wondering if one of the search tool designs really is preferable to the others and if so which one.

This is quite reasonable, but the conclusions from this sort of exploration should not be given the same weight as those from the gold standard. For this reason, we call this sort of statistical analysis the silver standard. It is still valuable, just less valuable. The argument therefore works as follows:

1 There is a null hypothesis of what would ordinarily be expected.
2 Data are gathered fairly.
3 A statistical test is used to show that under the null hypothesis, the data should only occur rarely.
4 This means that the data are unlikely to have occurred by chance so may be an indicator of some interesting underlying phenomenon.

Clearly, without a prediction, the unlikely finding in the data could still be a chance finding. Nonetheless, the very fact that it is unlikely makes it interesting. As usual, 0.05 is taken as the threshold at which probabilities become interesting. It is best still to stick to this even in exploratory studies because it is what a lot of researchers understand and are comfortable with. It would only be reasonable to start adjusting this threshold if there were good theoretical reasons to do so.

This silver standard also provides a fallback for the unsuccessful experimenter. The failed gold standard experiment may still yield some interesting data. The silver standard argument allows the experimenter to exploit the data, but at the cost of drawing much less firm conclusions.

Regardless of why the silver standard is applied, the conclusions from this sort of argument cannot be given anything like the same status as conclusions from the gold standard. At best, these conclusions suggest interesting ideas for future experiments. Ideally they should be framed in some sort of theory that can make predictions about experiments not identical to the one where they were found. In this way, the data provide some valuable inspiration but nothing more.

Sadly, when it comes to publishing statistics, referees and readers are more likely to be happier with gold standard rather than silver standard statistics. And as mentioned earlier, without some way of managing predictions, it can be impossible to tell from a write-up of an experiment what was really done. However, this does not mean that you as a researcher in HCI should not strive to maintain the strength and vigour of research through appropriate, careful statistical argument.

6.3.3 Choosing a test

No matter how carefully you explore your data and think about the evidence you need to prove your point, there comes a point in the analysis where you must choose a statistical test and carry it out. This is where things get technical very quickly and before you know it you are swamped with t-tests, ANOVAs, correlations and so on. Even an elementary text on statistics like Rowntree (2000) covers a range of tests. To really help you to do statistics, you would not need a chapter like this but a textbook. However, what it is possible to do here is to give a couple of pointers to help you get started.

Possibly the best thing to do is to remember that a statistical test does not provide proof, it provides evidence. You as the researcher will have to interpret the evidence so it is best to do statistics that you feel you can interpret. There is always the temptation when devising an experiment to collect lots of data. This is actually quite efficient and you can be confident that out of the hundreds of statistical tests available there is one somewhere that can analyse your data. However, if you do end up performing a multivariate analysis of covariance with two covariates, would you really be able to interpret what the test is telling you? Actually, more importantly, even if you could, could your readers? If your readers are the jury weighing up your evidence, you had better make sure that they are actually capable of understanding the evidence you provide them.

Statistical analysis complements the experiments that you do. Thus, you can always design your experiment carefully to collect the data that you know you can analyse. Sometimes, this may seem like making an experiment too simple. But actually, if the experiment still provides evidence that you need, then it is valuable. Also, if your experiment is simple, you may find you can run it several different ways in a relatively short period of time. Evidence from several simple experiments can make a much more convincing case than evidence from one complex experiment that is hard to interpret.

The lesson then is that you should always try to keep things simple. This makes interpreting statistics clearer and therefore more convincing, though it is always worth bearing in mind Einstein's wise saying that your work should be as simple as possible but no simpler.

Even keeping things simple, there is still a huge range of tests to choose from. The reason for such a range is not only for analysing different sorts of data but also so that you can use everything you know about the data to produce more accurate probabilities. One way to think about this is that a statistical test is a machine for turning lots of numbers (the data you collect) into a single probability. As far as the gold standard argument is concerned, that is all a test is for. However, the more you know about your data, the better the machine you can choose so that it can produce more accurate probabilities from even a small amount of data.

To make things concrete, one of the simplest experiments is to compare how two groups of people perform. For example, you have two different ways of selecting songs on an MP3 player and you want to know which one is quicker for people to use. You devise your experiment where each person uses each interface and you time how long it takes them to select a song. This is a within-subject design, in the terminology of Chapter 1. Thus, for each person you have two times, one for each interface.

The most basic way to see if people are quicker would be to see how many people are quicker with one interface rather than the other. There is a test that does exactly this by ignoring everything about the actual times and looking just at whether the changes in timings were faster or slower. This is called the Sign Test. However, as you do know the precise timings, you could look at the actual differences in times for each person and use not only the direction of the change in timing but also the size of the change. The test that uses this information is called the Wilcoxon test.

If also, from other studies, you knew that timings on this sort of task tend to be normally distributed, then you could use this knowledge as well by using a t-test. This test assumes that the data you are analysing are normally distributed. Of course, you had better check this out when you actually collect your data.

What is the advantage of these tests? Well, if your data really were normally distributed but you only used a Wilcoxon, you would need 10 per cent more participants to get the same probabilities as the t-test would produce. You could need up to 50 per cent more participants if you used the Sign Test when you could have used a t-test. So using the right test really can save you effort. However, if you don't know whether the data should be parametric, then using the t-test could be a disaster – the machine would churn out a probability that is just a meaningless number. In this case, you would be better off being more cautious and using the Wilcoxon or the Sign Test.

Out of all the basic tests that it is worth you getting to grips with, there are probably five or six key ones. These are:

1 t-test for comparing two groups when the data are parametric
2 analysis of variance (ANOVA) for comparing more than two groups when the data are parametric
3 χ^2 test for comparing the actual number of people in different categories to an even splitting between the categories (as in the example earlier)
4 Wilcoxon and Mann-Whitney tests which are like a t-test but when the data are not parametric; Wilcoxon is for within-subject designs and Mann-Whitney for between-subject designs
5 Pearson correlation which shows the degree of association between two different things you have measured provided they are both parametric

If you can learn these and be confident in employing them in your analyses then you will be in a very strong position to do a wide range of experiments and to provide a lot of good evidence to support your research. These tests are covered by most basic statistical textbooks such as Pagano (2006) and Greene and D'Oliveira (2006).

6.4   Applying the method

To demonstrate how inferential statistics works, we will use as an example the study used in Chapter 1 into investigating alternative modalities for entering text (SMS) messages into a mobile phone (Cox *et al.*, in press). Thus, you can use the two chapters together to see how the experimental design and statistical analysis support each other in ensuring a good quality result.

Briefly, the experiment was intended to explore the viability of speech recognition as an alternative method of text entry. The intention was not to replace the traditional keypress mode of interaction altogether, but instead to add functionality to the existing user interface, thus addressing the limitations of keypress input. Speech (S) could be used at two different points in entering text messages: it could be used to actually enter the words of the message and it could be used to allow the user to navigate through the mobile phone menus both to start entering the message and to send it off. To see the effect of speech on the interface, it was compared to other methods of entering messages. For entering the message itself, the two most common ways of entering the message are predictive text (P) and multi-tap entry (M). Navigating round the phone menu is usually done via the keys on the phone (K). Thus, there were three ways of entering the message, S, P and M, and two ways of doing the navigation, S and K, giving six combinations of entry methods overall: SSS, SPS, SMS, KSK, KPK and KMK. Another way of putting this is to say that there were two factors in the design: one for message entry with three levels and one for navigation with two levels. This helps to guide us in the choice of statistics that we want to do.

The study itself considered several different aspects of all of these interface types including how long people took to enter messages, number of errors they made, the workload on their mental resources and so on. For this discussion, though, we will focus only on how long it took people to enter messages using the different interfaces. Each user was given six messages to enter, one message for each version of the interface. The times to navigate through the menus, enter the message and send off the message were recorded. Thirty-six participants took part in the experiment.

Whilst it was hoped that speech would indeed prove to be a better user interface in terms of time to enter messages, this is not a firm foundation for making predictions. However, in human–computer interaction, there is a system of modelling user interactions called GOMS. This allows us to break down the task of entering a message into its individual components and from those components derive an estimate of how long it should take people to complete the tasks. More details are given in Chapter 4 on cognitive modelling. This analysis gave the time estimates shown in Table 6.5.

Breaking the predictions down in terms of the two factors, speech should be quicker than predictive text, which should be quicker than multi-tap for message entry. Also, speech navigation should be slightly slower overall than keypress navigation.

We are now in a position to start looking at the data to see whether our predictions are satisfied. In fact, the type of data and the prediction we have made suggest that we should be doing a specific test called an Analysis of Variance, or ANOVA. This is usually how statistical tests are chosen – once the type of data is known and the predictions about it made, the test is simply the one that can analyse that sort of data the way that is needed.

Table 6.5 *Predicted time (in seconds) for each task condition based on the GOMS model*

	Text entry		
	Multi-tap	Predictive	Speech
Keypress navigation	25.14	16.01	9.21
Speech navigation	26.02	16.89	10.09

Table 6.6 *Mean time taken (and standard deviations) to complete each task for all combinations of input modes. Time is shown in seconds*

	Text entry			
	Multi-tap	Predictive	Speech	Overall mean
Keypress navigation	36.67 (8.53)	25.63 (7.97)	9.51 (1.85)	23.94 (13.09)
Speech navigation	45.77 (11.56)	32.23 (8.48)	16.20 (2.52)	31.40 (14.72)
Overall mean	41.22 (11.08)	28.93 (8.82)	12.85 (4.02)	

Just because we know what test to do, this does not mean we should ignore looking at the data and making sure we know what they are like. For our analysis we will be using the statistical package SPSS. This is able to do lots of different tests and analyses including everything that we would like to do with this data. Better yet, it can do all these things with just a few mouse clicks, once the data have been entered. This makes it very tempting simply to enter the data and let SPSS do the work without getting too close to the numbers. However, as we shall see, the basic exploratory analysis is essential if we are to understand what systems like SPSS end up telling us.

6.4.1 Exploring the data

As we have a prediction of how the task performance times should come out, we first look at the data to find out if, on average, the actual task times fit this pattern. As we have many participants and times that can be essentially any value, the mean and standard deviation are the usual ways to analyse this data. These are given in Table 6.6.

We should also look at the data to see what shape it is. In particular, because we are planning on using an ANOVA test, we need the data to be approximately normally distributed (parametric) for each interface. We therefore plot the bar charts for the task times. In the earlier examples with Likert scales, the bar charts had natural bars – one bar for each value on the Likert scale. However, this won't

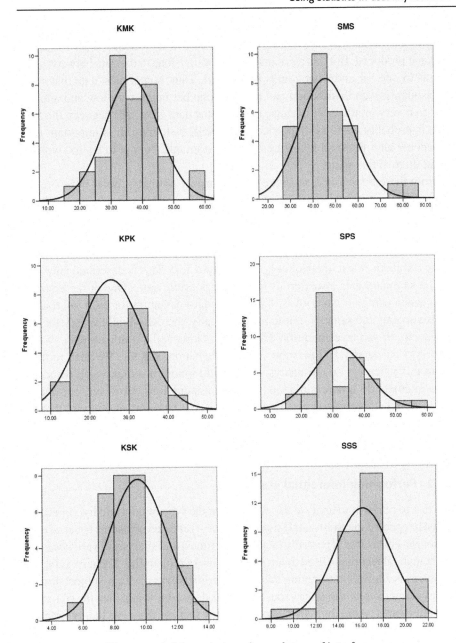

Fig 6.4 *Histograms of the task times for each type of interface*

work for times because each time will be different from all the others. Instead, we plot a particular type of bar chart, called a histogram, where we choose the intervals into which to group the task times. These are shown for each interface in Figure 6.4. Normal curves are also shown on the bar charts to help us assess whether these data really are normal.

Using your eye to examine these graphs, it is clear that none of the histograms perfectly fit the normal curves drawn over them. This is to be expected. Another issue is how histograms are made. The number of bars in a histogram is not pre-determined, so in this case we have simply used whatever the SPSS statistical package produced. But this can cause arbitrary divisions in the data between what counts in one bar and what counts in the next. Thus, sometimes, data that show a reasonably even distribution can result in one bar being very low and another next to it very high simply because of where the data were split between the two. This is probably what has happened in the KSK histogram. It is important then to become alert to possible features in the histograms, but not to get too worried about them at this stage.

From these histograms, most are approximately normal – this is not a precise measure, it is just judged by eye. Two that give cause for concern are KPK and SPS. The shape of the KPK histogram looks too flat to be normal and the SPS shape is rather more like a sharp peak than a normal curve. Neither of these might be problematic, but knowing that they might be, we did some further analysis using a statistical test, the Kolmogorov Smirnov test. This is described later.

The summary data also alert us to another possible issue. One of the assumptions when using an ANOVA is that the standard deviation for each interface is approximately the same or, put more technically, the data should satisfy the homogeneity of variance condition. However, looking at the summary data, we see that SMS has nearly 10 times the standard deviation of KSK. We need to think about this when we do our analysis. We could ignore it – many well respected experimenters do ignore violations of these assumptions. However, our goal is not to do what everybody else does but to do the best sort of analysis that we can. We may end up ignoring this problem, but we will do so from an informed position rather than just because we could get away with it!

6.4.2 Performing inferential statistics

The test to perform to analyse this data, given the type of data and hypothesis, is called a repeated measures analysis of variance – repeated measures because each person was measured repeatedly (actually six times) and analysis of variance is the mathematical technique used to turn the data into a probability. The term repeated measures is equivalent to saying that the experiment was a within-subject design. It may seem from this that the experiment was devised first and then the statistical test afterwards. Actually, what happened was that, in devising the experiment to test the ideas, it was first ascertained that there was a suitable statistical test available to analyse the data. Many new researchers often make the mistake of assuming that having gathered the data they can then choose the test later. Sometimes this works. Sometimes it does not, in which case the researcher has gone to an awful lot of effort to produce data which then cannot be analysed.

Even having designed the experiment with the test in mind, each test has its own set of assumptions and it is only when the data have been collected that these assumptions can be checked. The assumptions on a repeated measures ANOVA are that the data are normally distributed and the standard deviation in each condition is the same. If the test's assumptions are not met, the calculated probability can bear very little relationship to the actual probability of getting these particular data and this undermines the whole argument form for both gold standard and silver standard statistics.

Of course, in practice these assumptions are never going to be met perfectly so they require some sort of interpretation. Also, some tests still work reasonably well even when the assumptions are not satisfied. These tests are said to be robust. Sadly, a repeated measures ANOVA is not robust to violations of its assumptions, meaning that if our data do not satisfy the assumptions then the probabilities it produces may have little relation to real probabilities of getting such data. For the gold standard argument to work, we need to have reasonable confidence that our probabilities are accurate.

The initial exploratory analysis by eye has alerted us to possible issues with both of the assumptions. We therefore examine statistically how far each of the distributions deviates from normal. There is another statistical test called the Kolmogorov-Smirnov test (or KS test) to see how far the data stray from a normal distribution.

The KS test, like other tests, produces a probability that a null hypothesis holds – for this test the null hypothesis is that the data are normally distributed. For five of the six conditions, the probability that the data in those conditions are normal is quite high – that is, quite likely – so we are safe to assume the data are actually normal in those conditions. However, condition SPS still gives cause for concern because the KS test gives a very low probability suggesting that this condition's data deviate significantly from a normal distribution. Is this a problem? Well, it is only one of six conditions and also its shape is not radically different from a normal distribution, just a bit too 'pointy'. So the best thing for now is to bear it in mind and see what else might be wrong.

When we come to do the repeated measures ANOVA in SPSS, we cannot test for homogeneity of variance (similar standard deviations in all of the groups), but this is not a problem if another property of the data, sphericity, is satisfactory. (Sphericity is a technical condition meaning that the data in the different conditions relate to each other in similar ways.) SPSS automatically tests for deviations from sphericity and fortunately our data do not cause any problems in that regard.

Given that none of these problems seems too serious, it is worth doing the ANOVA. The ANOVA will test three things all in one go. First, it will give a probability that the three message entry types, M, P and S, are not really different regardless of navigation type. Second, it will give a probability that the navigation type, S or K, is not really different regardless of message entry type. These two probabilities are looking at the *main effects*, that is, the differences between the two factors in the experimental design. The final probability produced by the ANOVA is that there is no particular difference between the cells other than what the first two probabilities already account for. This is called the interaction between the two factors of entry type and navigation type because this probability is only significant if there is some interaction between the different combinations that mean, for example, M is only different from P in the S condition and not the K condition.

The result of the ANOVA is the statistic for each of these tests and it is usually given the symbol F. Associated with each F value is the probability of getting such an F value if the null hypothesis is true. Here the null hypothesis is that there are no differences (on average) between how long it takes to send a text message regardless of the method for entering the message and the method for navigating the phone menu.

Under this hypothesis, the F value for entry method is 246.35 and $p < 0.001$, that is, the probability of getting this F value is so small that it is less than one chance in a thousand. In fact it appears in SPSS as 0.000 but as we can't be sure of the exact value we report it as shown. For navigation method, $F = 120.09$, $p < 0.001$ and for the interaction, $F = 2.77$, $p = 0.070$. Another important factor in helping other people to assess the statistics that have been done is the degrees of freedom. This is a very important but quite complex idea that is key to many statistical tests. It is not worth trying to explain now how it works, but it should always be reported with the results of any test. For an ANOVA, there are two degrees of freedom and they are usually put in brackets after the F.

Thus, the outcome of the ANOVA is formally reported as: there is a significant main effect for entry method ($F(2, 70) = 246.35$, $p < 0.001$), a significant main effect for navigation ($F(1, 35) = 120.09$, $p < 0.001$) and no significant interaction effect ($F(2, 70) = 2.77$, $p = 0.070$).

What does this mean? It means that there are real differences between our data both in terms of which entry method is used and which navigation method is used. We need to refer back to the actual means in Table 6.6 though to understand this fully. First, consider the main effect for navigation. The two means for keypress and speech navigation (overall, not for each type of message entry) are different – speech is slower than keypress. The main effect here tells us that this difference is unlikely to be by chance. Moreover, we predicted that this would be how it would turn out from our GOMS analysis. The gold standard argument now gives us confidence to say that the theoretical advantage of keypress over speech for navigation is actually seen with real people. This supports our analysis as being appropriate to analyse this sort of navigation method.

The main effect for entry type is a bit harder to analyse as there are three conditions. The three means at the bottom of Table 6.6 look as though they are decreasing as you read from left to right. The ANOVA tells us that the means really are different but it does not tell us whether it is because all three means are different from each other or whether two means are actually about the same probabilistically and only one mean is truly different. This can be analysed further with *post hoc* tests, special tests to be done after an ANOVA, but they are not worth going into here. It is enough to say that the pattern of the means is coming out as predicted by the GOMS. Moreover, the GOMS method is a well-understood and well-verified theory. Thus, we can be reasonably confident that the entry type is having a real effect on task performance, with speech being the fastest, then predictive text, then multi-tap.

There is no significant interaction effect. This means that any differences between individual combinations of navigation type and message entry type are accounted for entirely by the two main effects. Some people might say that the calculated interaction probability $p = 0.070$ is tending to significance even though it falls short of the threshold of 0.05. This is rather like a silver standard argument saying that something is beginning to be interesting there. If it were really important to our understanding, we might devise further studies to see if there really is something going on there. However, our primary focus is on the two main effects and hence we can simply accept the absence of interaction effect and move on.

This discussion has covered a lot of ground and there have been some tricky considerations along the way. Thus, it is worth restating the whole analysis in terms of the gold standard argument. The basic set-up is that we are looking at different methods for navigating and entering text messages on a mobile phone.

1 From the GOMS analysis, we made two predictions. First, speech navigation would be slower than keypress navigation. Second, multi-tap would be slower than predictive text, which would be slower than speech for entering the messages.

2 The null hypothesis is therefore that there is no real difference between these methods, that is, on average people enter messages and navigate at about the same speed regardless of the methods that they use.

3 We gathered timing data from different interfaces where the only difference between interfaces was the method of navigating and entering messages. Thus, as far as possible, the data we gathered were fair and unbiased.

4 We used an ANOVA that is able to compare the timing data across both factors at the same time to produce probabilities. These probabilities mean that if nothing is happening (the null hypothesis holds) then they are the probabilities of getting our data by chance alone. For both of our predictions, the chances of getting the differences we saw were very low, well below 0.01, which makes our results highly significant.

5 Thus we conclude that the data are unlikely to have occurred by chance and indeed have come out as we predicted.

6 This experiment has therefore provided evidence that speech for entering text messages is likely to improve the speed with which people enter messages but may slow them down if used for navigation.

Of course, the experiment is just one study and so provides some evidence but not proof. We would need to do a lot more experiments to see if different age groups perform similarly and if they perform similarly in real contexts where people text each other, not just in the lab. Nonetheless, our study does suggest that this is an interesting new type of interface that is worth investigating and developing further.

There is also the problem of the fact that the assumptions for a repeated measures ANOVA were violated. Actually, it is possible to address these concerns, and we have done so in our full analysis of the data, but it is not worth going into the full details of how we did that here. The details do not illustrate the main points of this chapter any more clearly and indeed may give a level of mathematical and statistical detail that could be off-putting. The final story, though, is that when we did account for the violation of assumptions, the probabilities told the same story. Thus, our gold standard argument is still sound.

6.5   Critique

In usability studies for which clear, quantitative results are required, there is little choice but to do some sort of statistical reasoning. Without statistical methods, any variations that you see between users or groups of users can merely be attributed to chance variation. The gold standard argument of combining prediction with careful analysis, however, provides a way to combat this unavoidable uncertainty. The gold standard does not provide 'proof' in the sense of irrefutable conclusions, but a sound basis for any insight that studies may give. Through combining several studies, possibly including studies in the appropriate academic literature or from previous projects, and a theory to explain your understanding, it is possible though to bring very convincing evidence to support your understanding.

This strength of a rigorous statistical approach, however, is also its greatest weakness. Statistics are not easy to master and involve becoming well-versed in statistical language, a range of statistical tests and software packages to help you perform the tests. All of these together present a steep learning curve to a newcomer. The example above used a repeated measures ANOVA which is one of the more standard tests in the statistical arsenal. Even so, as was seen, when things are not quite right in the data it can suddenly get much more complicated. Navigating the complexity requires extensive expertise and experience to be sure that the analysis retains the appropriate level of rigour.

Good statistics also rely on good experiments. To borrow a term from computing, statistics operate on a GIGO basis – garbage in, garbage out. That is, the assumption in statistics is that the numbers being analysed are meaningful. This meaning is founded on the experiment that provided the numbers having been done well. If the experiment was not done well, no amount of statistics will rescue it.

This adds an extra layer of complexity to doing statistical analysis. For the gold standard argument to apply, and we really do want it to apply as often as possible, it is only reasonable to devise an experiment that can answer one question and moreover that question generally needs to be very focused. Thus, there is a huge expenditure in learning how to devise good experiments and to do the statistics to analyse them. Moreover, the outcome is only evidence to support an answer to a very narrowly defined question. Is it really worth it?

Of course, once you are adept at statistics and experimental design, this is when you can reap the rewards. It can become routine to devise and analyse experiments to answer the sorts of questions that you are researching or to analyse the usability of the systems that you regularly consider.

There is also an external drive to use a statistical approach and this comes from the perceived value of numerical results. Indeed this is reflected in the term 'hard data' which is usually referring to actual numbers. This is opposed to 'soft data' that might be obtained from more qualitative approaches. The very fact that statistics is difficult, and even regarded by some as arcane knowledge, lends weight to your case if you can demonstrate mastery of the area. Whether this view is accurate is another matter! Nonetheless, academics do accord higher respect to more statistical approaches. And in business, the need for hard data to support a business case, particularly when talking about a return on investment, makes statistics a useful tool in any usability expert's portfolio of research methods.

6.6   Related studies and reading

There is no doubt that a good place to start learning statistics is from a textbook and there are many and varied examples to choose from. Which to choose depends very much on your confidence and previous experience with statistics. If you really are utterly new to this area, a classic (justly so) is Rowntree (2000). It provides a good introduction to the basic concepts of statistics with almost no mathematical formulae. Once you need to start actually performing calculations, there are innumerable textbooks that would guide you through the mathematics to help you understand and perform the core basic statistical tests such as t-tests, ANOVA, chi-squared and so on. To some extent, this is a matter of personal tastes and a browse through a good library or bookshop would help you decide. Two texts stand out in quite different ways. Pagano (2006) is an extensive and careful discussion of most of the standard basic statistical tests. It has lots of examples and works hard to motivate the concepts. In contrast, Greene and d'Oliveira (2006) covers the same ground as Pagano but does so in a much more concise form. It is no less useful but is very different in style.

When it comes to more advanced statistics, there are innumerable texts, some leading up to research level statistics. Choosing a good one from amongst these can be a very hit and miss affair. Whilst learning advanced statistics has its advantages, particularly when data are more complicated than you expected, there is still the problem of how much statistics your audience knows. For example, you may become adept at multivariate analysis of covariance (MANCOVA), but if your audience is not so adept, it can be hard for them to judge the value of your research.

Simpler statistics have the benefit of being easier to understand. Simpler statistics usually reflect a simpler experimental design as well. Statistics, as described here, is an argument form and if your argument is difficult and involved either through using difficult statistics or having a complex experimental design then you have to question how effective an argument you can make.

If you do feel, though, that you are asking truly multivariate questions, then a good starting place is Foster, Barkus and Yavorsky (2005). It covers a wide range of multivariate techniques in a very readable and maths-free way.

The only advanced technique that we would single out as particularly useful to a usability researcher is factor analysis. This is a method that is mostly used for analysing questionnaire data. With it, you can find out which questions are related to each other and therefore which factors underlie what the questionnaire is about. Sometimes these factors are ones that you built in. For example, you may ask multiple questions about how satisfied users are with a particular interface. If the questions are good ones, this should result in a factor that you can identify as 'satisfaction'. Alternatively, you may be looking to relate questions on satisfaction to those on willingness to re-use a particular system. Thus, your factor analysis could help identify if there is a clear relationship between 'satisfaction' and 'intention to re-use', though both factors will only be asked about indirectly through a sequence of non-leading questions, as discussed in Chapter 2. Foster *et al.* (2005) does provide a good introduction to factor analysis but it is brief. A better and more extensive introduction is Kline (1993).

When it comes to the conceptual understanding of statistics in terms of the gold and silver standards, most major texts make no reference to statistics as an argument form. The only example that we know of is Abelson (1995) and, fortunately, it is a very good example. It covers the wide variety of ways in which statistics can be used to support an argument. Not only is it useful if you want to do statistics, but also if you simply want to read studies that use statistics but not be blinded by the figures.

There is a whole distinct approach to writing up the results of statistical analysis. The best way to learn this approach should be from examples in the HCI literature. Unfortunately, not all statistical analysis in HCI is of the high standard that other disciplines, such as psychology, would expect. This is true even of well-respected authors in well-respected conferences and journals (Cairns, 2007). This makes it particularly challenging for a new researcher to understand what constitutes a good statistical analysis and what is poor – both are commonly found. It is also worth making it clear that the fault for this does not just lie with the researchers: any paper in a good outlet is usually seen by three or four referees and an editor. They must all take some responsibility for the poor standard of statistics in HCI research literature.

There are, however, some very good examples of the use of statistics in HCI. The work of Andy Cockburn has looked at navigation in all sorts of devices and interfaces. He does not rely on one particular experiment, but rather over a series of experiments, and even projects, develops a sound body of evidence to support the usability of the different systems he considers. A good example is Savage and Cockburn (2005) but you should also look at others of his publications available from www.cosc.canterbury.ac.nz/andrew.cockburn. Also, Prof. Stephen Payne's work is more in the psychological tradition of HCI and Payne, Duggan and Neth (in press) is a good example of statistical work as done in psychology but for HCI purposes.

It is also worth reading papers in psychology journals related to your chosen area of study. The standard of writing up statistics and the editorial standards are much higher in psychology than in HCI. Thus, you can get a good idea of what you should be expected to do. At the same time, it is a good way to broaden your perspective on your work.

Despite HCI's current poor regard for statistical reporting, you should be striving to do statistics to the highest standards. You may be able to get away with a lower standard, but then what really is your research saying? As the Nobel laureate, Richard Feynman (1992), pointed out, doing research requires a sort of radical honesty on the part of the researcher. It is hard to tell from a paper whether the statistics was done to the gold standard, to the silver standard or even just made up. Thus researchers must be as honest as possible to make sure the research is making a sound contribution. Sound research relies on sound analysis and you should be aiming to do the soundest possible research, even if your audience cannot tell the difference.

7 A qualitative approach to HCI research

ANNE ADAMS, PETER LUNT AND PAUL CAIRNS

7.1 Overview

Whilst science has a strong reliance on quantitative and experimental methods, there are many complex, socially based phenomena in HCI that cannot be easily quantified or experimentally manipulated or, for that matter, ethically researched with experiments. For example, the role of privacy in HCI is not obviously reduced to numbers and it would not be appropriate to limit a person's privacy in the name of research. In addition, technology is rapidly changing – just think of developments in mobile devices, tangible interfaces and so on – making it harder to abstract technology from the context of use if we are to study it effectively. Developments, such as mediated social networking and the dispersal of technologies in ubiquitous computing, also loosen the connection between technologies and work tasks that were the traditional cornerstone of HCI. Instead, complex interactions between technologies and ways of life are coming to the fore. Consequently, we frequently find that we do not know what the real HCI issues are before we start our research. This makes it hard, if not actually impossible, to define the variables necessary to do quantitative research (see Chapter 2).

Within HCI, there is also the recognition that the focus on tasks is not enough to design and implement an effective system. There is also a growing need to understand how usability issues are subjectively and collectively experienced and perceived by different user groups (Pace, 2004; Razavim and Iverson, 2006). This means identifying the users' emotional and social drives and perspectives; their motivations, expectations, trust, identity, social norms and so on. It also means relating these concepts to work practices, communities and organisational social structures as well as organisational, economic and political drivers. These issues are increasingly needed in the design, development and implementation of systems to be understood both in isolation and as a part of the whole.

HCI researchers are therefore turning to more qualitative methods in order to deliver the research results that HCI needs. With qualitative research, the emphasis is not on measuring and producing numbers but instead on understanding the qualities of a particular technology and how people use it in their lives, how they think about it and how they feel about it. There are many varied approaches to qualitative research within the social sciences depending on what is being studied, how it can be studied and what the goals of the research are. Within HCI, though, grounded theory has been found to provide good insights that address well the issues raised above (Pace, 2004; Adams, Blandford and Lunt, 2005; Razavim and Iverson, 2006).

The purpose of this chapter is to give an overview of how grounded theory works as a method. Quantitative research methods adopt measuring instruments and experimental manipulations that can be repeated by any researcher (at least in principle) and every effort is made to reduce the influence of the researcher on the researched, which is regarded as a source of bias or error. In contrast, in qualitative research, where the goal is understanding rather than measuring and manipulating, the subjectivity of the researcher is an essential part of the production of an interpretation. The chapter therefore discusses how the influence of the researcher can be ameliorated through the grounded theory methodology whilst also acknowledging the subjective input of the researcher through reflexivity. The chapter also presents a case study of how grounded theory was used in practice to study people's use and understanding of computer passwords and related security.

7.2   The method

Despite the name, grounded theory is not a theory of qualitative research. Instead, it is a method of qualitative research that aims to produce new theories that are grounded in the qualitative data gathered during the research. Grounded theory was originally identified within social science as the product of close inspection and analysis of qualitative data (Glaser and Strauss, 1967). Later Strauss and Corbin (1990) used the term to refer to a data collection and analysis technique that they formulated which was no longer restricted to qualitative data. Grounded theory is, therefore, an approach to theory building that can incorporate both qualitative data sets (e.g. interviews, focus groups, observations, ethnographic studies) and quantitative data sets (e.g. questionnaires, logs, experimental). The methodology combines systematic levels of abstraction into a framework of interpretation of a phenomenon, which is iteratively verified and expanded throughout the study. 'The research findings constitute a theoretical formulation of the reality under investigation, rather than consisting of a set of numbers, or a group of loosely related themes' (Strauss and Corbin, 1990, p. 24).

A key feature of grounded theory is that it does not require a prior hypothesis for focusing the research (Strauss et al., 1964). That is, the researcher may go into the research knowing that they want to find out about a particular area, such as people's perceptions of passwords (Adams, Sasse and Lunt, 1997) or how people perceive immersion in games (Brown and Cairns, 2004), but without knowing exactly what it is that they expect to find. The process of doing the research formulates the theory and therefore produces potential hypotheses for further study. A side-effect of this is that research data previously collected on the same phenomena can be used for further research.

Moreover, the theory is not developed once the data collection is complete. Instead, the theory is developed as soon as there are data to analyse, say, after the first interview. The researcher, of course, acknowledges that one interview is not likely to produce a good theory, but the initial formulation of a theory means that the researcher can gather more data with a view to validating and expanding the theory. So in an interview study, the first interview leads to a tentative theory. In the next interview, the researcher can ask questions that may specifically probe the theory so far. In particular, the researcher should explicitly probe the limits of the theory to see when it no longer holds and within what parameters it does hold. The second interview would then be analysed to modify or even reject the theory and produce a new theory. Thus, the method proceeds through cycles of data gathering, analysis and theorising. Note, in particular, that interview questions are actually adapted to investigate the developing theory and thus the initial interview may be very different from interviews later in the study. This is an important contrast to the focus on reliability through systematic repetition of observations in quantitative research.

Another particular feature of this approach is that the researcher is explicitly trying to test the limits of the theory at all times. This leads to theoretical sampling, where the researcher deliberately chooses where to collect the data next in order to test the theory to date. So as a very straightforward example, the researcher may decide that having learned something about how men experience immersion in computer games, the next interviewee should be a woman to see if her experience is in accord with the theory or whether she provides data that do not fit with the theory so far and require the emerging theory of immersion to be expanded in new ways.

The question then becomes one of when to stop. This is when the theory reaches saturation, that is, each new item of data can be fitted into the existing theory without requiring the theory to be modified. The theory at this point is considered to be complete because there are no new ideas to be accounted for. Moreover, the theory is grounded in the existing data and should fully account for them. Successful application of the methodology is, thus, assessed both in terms of the validity of the engagement with the diversity of concepts in use in the interaction with the technology and the fit between the data and the thematic interpretation that emerges in the analysis.

Strauss and Corbin (1990) suggest that grounded theory is especially useful for complex subjects or phenomena where little is yet known. The methodology's flexibility can cope with complex data and its continual cross-referencing allows for grounding of theory in the data, thus uncovering previously unknown issues. Although there is flexibility in the type of information used for grounded theory analysis, a greater emphasis is placed on theoretical sampling and contextual considerations so that later transferability of findings can be increased.

As the data are collected, they are analysed in a standard grounded theory format. Data, in whatever form, are broken down, conceptualised and put back together in new ways. To enable this to occur in a structured manner, Strauss

Table 7.1 *Example of a category broken down into properties and dimensions*

Category class	Properties (attributes)	Dimensional range (domains)
surveillance	frequency	often ... never
	scope	more ... less
	intensity	high ... low
	duration	long ... short

and Corbin (1990) have devised three major coding stages – open, axial and selective – in the analysis procedure. It must be acknowledged, however, that the lines between these forms of coding are artificial, as is the divide between data collection and analysis. This is an analytic distinction, but in practice all of these elements of grounded theory analysis intersect as the interpretation proceeds.

7.2.1 Open coding

The open coding stage involves identifying concepts in the empirical material and, as the interpretation proceeds, joining similar concepts together into categories. The coding is open because there is no pre-determined set of codes but the researcher is open to learn what these codes are as the analysis proceeds. Concepts pertaining to similar phenomena (categories) along with identifying the properties and dimensions of the said category are central to this part of the analysis.

1 Concepts are identified.
   - *Concepts* are conceptual labels placed on discrete happenings, events, and other instances of phenomena to name those aspects of the phenomena.
2 Concepts are compared to see if they pertain to a similar phenomenon (category).
   - *Categories* are where concepts are classified and grouped together under a higher order – a more abstract concept is called a category.
3 The properties and dimensions of the category are identified (see Table 7.1).
   - *Properties (attributes)* are characteristics pertaining to a category.
   - *dimensions (domains)* are locations (values) of a particular property along its range.

7.2.2 Axial coding

This coding stage identifies the high-level phenomena, that is, the central ideas and events, along with the conditions and participants' strategies pertaining to those phenomena, for instance causal conditions or intervening conditions.

1 Key high-level phenomena are identified.
   • *Phenomena* are central ideas and/or events.
2 Conditions pertaining to those phenomena are identified, namely the causal condition, context of the phenomenon and any intervening conditions.
   • *Causal conditions* are events that lead to occurrence or development of a phenomenon.
   • *Context* is the specific set of properties that pertain to a phenomenon; specifically, locations pertaining to a phenomenon along a dimensional range.
   • *Intervening conditions* are the broader structural context.
3 Any action/interaction strategies produced in response to the phenomena are identified.
   • *Action/interactional strategies* are behaviours devised to manage, handle, carry out or respond to a phenomenon under a specific set of perceived conditions.
4 Any consequences from these action/interactional strategies are identified.
   • *Consequences* are outcomes or results of actions or interaction.

For example:

> When I want to have (context) a personal conversation (phenomenon), I encrypt the message (strategy). I think that makes the email private (consequence).

7.2.3 Selective coding

Finally, the analysis is elaborated upon and interpreted in the selective coding stage. The core category (the central phenomenon around which all the other categories are integrated) is defined here and a conceptualisation of the descriptive narrative, set around the core category, is exposed. This whole process is iterative so that it is validated by continual comparisons with the raw data to confirm or refute conclusions. This continual validation can identify gaps in the framework that can only be filled in by further research using theoretical sampling.

1 The core category and a high-level storyline are defined. The storyline is set around the core category which defines the whole.
   • *Core category* is the central phenomenon around which all the other categories are integrated.
   • *Story* is a descriptive narrative about the central phenomenon of the HCI study.
   • *Storyline* is the conceptualisation of the story – the core category.
2 The subsidiary categories around the core category are related by means of its properties.
   • This is best done with graphical representations of the core category and subsidiary categories. The core category properties are high-level definitions.
3 Categories are related at the dimensional level.

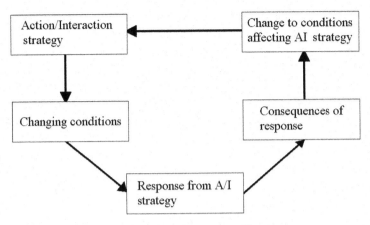

Fig 7.1 *Graphical representation of a process effect chain*

- This then ties up in detail, finally, all the categories into a whole HCI model/framework which is defined by the storyline and the core-category.
4 Relationships are validated against data.
  - The process of building the core-category and storyline is an iterative process which is validated by continual comparisons with the raw data to confirm or refute your conclusions.
5 Categories which need further refinement are filled in.
  - Often, after defining some categories, gaps appear in the high-level storyline which can only be filled in by further research.

The last stage in the analysis is the integration of *process effects*, that is, factors changing over time, so that changing factors within the framework can be identified.

1 Define any process effects that may be occurring.
  - *Process* is the linking of action/interaction sequences over time (see Figure 7.1)

7.2.4 Performing coding

As a new grounded theorist, it is important to realise that the lines between the different levels of coding are artificial. Unfortunately end-users often jump between different levels of abstraction when they are talking. This means that data can frequently be presented at a dimensional and selective level with elements of action/interaction strategies thrown in. For example, in the humorous statement:

> I find computers always break down for me when I have a lot of things to do. So I try not to use them when I have a lot to do. Which slows everything down a bit!

the user is talking about dimensional concepts (e.g. always – sometimes, a lot – a little, slow – fast) at the same time as they are using strategies (e.g. 'try not to use them when . . . ') and consequences (e.g. 'slows everything down a bit'). It is useful to be able to code different levels at the same time (e.g. open and axial together) while keeping an eye on the different levels of abstraction being employed. Some researchers have found that computer-based analysis tools (e.g. ATLAS.ti, Nvivo) can help them in this codification process. Ultimately it is important to understand the complexities that are inherent in human behaviour and to ease up on yourself and your ability to codify it all. Keeping the data collection and analysis tightly interwoven, for instance conducting an interview and analysing it before the next interview, can help to support a richer, flexible and more explorative understanding of the data and the research process.

Even so, these analysis stages initially seem quite daunting and the biggest question facing a researcher new to grounded theory is: where to start? *Microcoding* is a very useful strategy suggested by Strauss and Corbin (1990). The researcher simply starts with some part of the data, possibly the first interesting part of the interview (once the 'hello's and 'how are you's are completed), and then looks at each word and tries to work out what it means. And this really does mean each word. The barrier in understanding is that of course we already naturally understand the words that people use, but are we really understanding the words as the interviewee means them? To overcome this, *asking questions* is the primary way to sensitise the researcher to the data. Consider as an example the simple quote from earlier:

> When I want to have a personal conversation, I encrypt the message. I think that makes the email private.

The first word is 'when' and naturally we would understand this word in the context of the sentence to mean 'on occasions or in situations where'. But now start asking questions: Which occasions? Which situations? Literally at what times of day/week/year do these occasions occur? Are these common or rare occasions? Does something prompt the occasion? The next word is 'I'. Well that really is just the person and to ask questions on this may be too far down the road of philosophy, but the word after is 'want'. The questions suggesting themselves here are: What would make you want a personal conversation? Is it want in the sense of deep need? Or want in a more whimsical sense? Is the wanting ever-pressing or urgent? Is the wanting provoked by other people? Or the person with whom you'll converse? Now 'personal': does that mean intimate? Or just friendly? Or just not work-related? Is a conversation with a spouse personal? With a parent? A child? A friend? Would all such conversations always be personal? Could you have personal conversations with a colleague? Could they be about work? Already we have more than a dozen questions and we have only really thought briefly about three words! Some of these questions may seem trivial or overblown – surely the interviewee didn't mean that much by these words – however, if you go in thinking that you know what their words mean then you will struggle to go beyond your own understanding. By questioning what words mean, you open the opportunity for them to mean something else and hence for you to see something in the data that was previously closed off from you.

The data do not contain the answers (at least not in the quote here), but you are now sensitive to look for the answers and seek them in the rest of the data even if you did not explicitly ask for them. Or you could probe subsequent interviewees to find out the answers. Also, this might suggest a first concept 'conversation'; one attribute of that is how personal it is, another being when such conversations occur and a third being the motivation. Now it may be that conversation is not a dominant feature of other interviews and so this concept is replaced or superseded. Or it may be that motivation for a conversation is a separate concept in itself and this leads to links between the motivation for a conversation, the conversation itself and the use of security techniques to preserve privacy. But already, even with these three words, you could begin to formulate a (very tentative) theory based on conversations and how people determine the need for privacy and when that privacy is enough to warrant using encryption. This theory can be tested with the rest of the interview.

Of course, no one could do grounded theory by simply doing microcoding, otherwise no grounded theory study would ever have been finished! Once you are feeling sensitive to the data and alert to their potential interpretations, you can begin to read the data in large portions in an attempt to gain a bigger picture, but all the while asking questions about what you think you understand. However, if the data become challenging and hard to interpret, reverting to microcoding can be enormously helpful in refreshing your sensitivity and helping you to continue making progress.

This sort of work clearly very rapidly generates a lot of ideas that are hard to maintain in the head. This is partly why grounded theory places emphasis on documented forms of the data so that the documents can be annotated either physically with scribbles or post-its, or electronically in Word or using a specialised software package for grounded theory such as ATLAS.ti. All interviews or focus groups should be recorded and transcribed for this reason.

Annotations though may not capture the richness of some of your ideas. Thus, grounded theory also recommends *making memos*, or 'memoing'. Memos are longer than annotations and are intended to capture the thoughts of the researcher as the analysis proceeds. They do not need to be polished or well written but sufficient to help remind the researcher of their thoughts and ideas as they developed. They do not even need to relate closely to the data but may be ideas that the researcher feels could be valuable at some point. The memos then become an important tool for theorising as they allow the researcher to track the growth and development of the theory as the data accumulate and the cycles of theorising progress. They can allow the researcher to resurrect previously abandoned ideas or to avoid re-inventing old ideas in a slightly different guise.

As the analysis progresses, some of the memos will inevitably formulate the theory in terms of concepts (open coding), the links between them (axial coding) and the overall narrative of the theory (selective coding). This perhaps also indicates that though there are three types of coding, they should not occur in isolation but are strongly interwoven and may even occur at the very earliest stages of microcoding.

Even with the grounded theorist's tools of microcoding, asking questions and memoing, you may not feel sure about how to do grounded theory. This is normal. Indeed, there is a strong degree of craft skill in doing grounded theory. Do not be put off by this and do not succumb to the criticism of the more quantitative researchers who point out the inevitable bias that craft skill suggests. Doing experiments is also a craft skill! At the end of the day, to do this or any other of the methods in this book, the only way to learn how to do them properly is to try. The nice thing about grounded theory is that this learning process is an acknowledged aspect of the theorising, whereas it is entirely ignored in more positivistic approaches. This will be discussed in more detail in the critique of the method towards the end of the chapter.

7.3 Applying the method

In this section a series of study examples (Adams *et al.*, 1997; Adams and Sasse, 1999) are given for the different approaches to qualitative analysis to help clarify a series of application issues in relation to passwords and computer security. The same studies are being used in the chapter on questionnaire, interview and focus groups (Chapter 2) and so both chapters can be used to cross-reference for the whole research process.

7.3.1 Questionnaire and interview study

Authentication, and in particular passwords, plays an important role in organisational security. Security breaches and adapting security procedures (e.g. password changing regimes) have been a major organisational system issue for the past decade (Hitchings, 1995). The ever-growing costs from security breaches and re-instating forgotten passwords is a major problem within modern organisations. Chapter 2 introduced a series of password studies (Adams *et al.*, 1997; Adams and Sasse, 1999) that identified the need for a balance in password construction and implementation procedures between secure yet effective passwords. The usability, yet effectiveness of system security, is a field growing in importance. The study described in Chapter 2 and here initially sought to identify relationships between memorability and security to support users in designing memorable yet secure passwords. Later studies built on initial findings that inappropriate password procedures and organisational security practices were the major problem in modern-day security systems.

7.3.2 Method

It is interesting to highlight that the following sequence of studies concisely details some interesting differences and applicability of varying levels of analysis. Initially, a questionnaire was designed and implemented, the findings of which are presented in Chapter 2; 139 questionnaire responses were received with questions ranging from factual to open-ended questions. The findings verified some initial hypothesis that the researchers were proposing. The open-ended questions, however, identified a range of issues not previously conceptualised (e.g. password procedures such as change regimes inhibiting the memorability of passwords). These issues were noted by the respondents to be of greater importance to them than the ones previously conceptualised for the questionnaire. Because of these findings it was decided that further in-depth investigations were required.

Study 1 and thematic analysis

Initially a set of 15 in-depth interviews were conducted within a technically based organisation (Organisation A). The interviews lasted approximately 30 minutes and were used to complement the qualitative data from the questionnaires. Respondents had varying levels of password expertise, both over period and frequency of use. Participants were asked a series of semi-structured questions that covered issues of password generation and recall along with more general system and organisational factors. The interview format allowed participants to introduce new issues to the discussion that they regarded as important.

The initial analysis of the interviews and questionnaire open-ended answers took a thematic approach guided by the frequency and fundamentality of the issues raised by the users (that is, putting emphasis on those issues that occurred frequently or that were deemed of fundamental importance). This produced four factors influencing effective password usage. Problem areas for password usability were password content, multiple passwords, users' perceptions of security in the organisation and the novel concept of 'information sensitivity'.

Password content is defined here as the character content of the password reviewed in terms of its memorability and security. Initial results found that users' knowledge of secure password design was very inadequate. This leads users to create rules and judgements on password design strategies which are anything but secure. Words contained in the dictionary and names are the most vulnerable form of password. These results showed that many users do not realise this:

> I mean I would have thought that if you picked something like your wife's Christian name or something then the chances of a complete stranger guessing ********* in my case were pretty remote.

It must be noted, however, that further analysis (see grounded theory analysis below) revealed that these behaviours were related to perceptions of the physical security and information sensitivity.

Many users have to remember multiple passwords, that is, they have to use different passwords for different applications and/or change password frequently because of password expiry mechanisms. A high number of passwords was found to reduce memorability and to increase insecure work practices (e.g. writing passwords down) and poor password design (e.g. using 'password' as their password):

> Constantly changing passwords results in very simple choices which are easy to guess or break within seconds of using 'Cracker'.[1] Hence there is no security.

> But basically because I was forced into changing it every month I had to write it down.

Many users devise their own method for beating memorability problems. One approach was to devise 'linked passwords' where passwords are linked via some common element (e.g. tom1, tom2, tom3). Such methods are devised in response to password expiry mechanisms, and by users who have a multitude of different passwords for different applications. The initial analysis identified that linked passwords were both memorable and yet had memorability problems. This inconsistency in the findings was not resolved until a full grounded theory analysis was conducted.

Initial analysis of the results revealed that users' perceptions of security levels and potential threats was a key element in motivating their work practices. Without clear feedback from the organisation, users construct their own model of security threats and importance of security. The two extracts below illustrate users' misconceptions in their perceptions of both organisational security and possible breaches:

> I don't think that hacking is a problem I've had no visibility of hacking that may go on. None at all.

> I think that security problems are more by word of mouth than computer problems.

The study identified that users' security behaviours often depended on their perceptions of the information sensitivity. Users identified certain systems as worthy of secure password practices, whilst others were perceived as 'not important enough'. In the absence of guidance, users concluded that confidential information about individuals (personnel files, email) was sensitive; but commercially sensitive information, such as customer records and financial data, were often not regarded as sensitive. Some users stated that they liked the classification of printed documents (e.g. Confidential, Not for Circulation) as this gave them clear feedback on what the organisation perceived as sensitive information. Although the first pass analysis identified this concept, it did not reveal complex contradictions related to differences in organisational procedures.

---

[1] A password dictionary checker.

Study 2 and grounded theory analysis

As detailed above, the initial findings were analysed at a thematic level. Although this approach was reasonably simplistic (for example, identifying relevant themes from the data), it helped to identify concepts and potential issues not previously identified. This analysis led the researchers to realise that there was a need for further in-depth qualitative research and analysis to explore these issues. The second stage of research sought to verify and expand on issues identified within the first set of interviews. The second study was conducted with 15 users, within a comparable organisation (a company in the construction sector). Participants from Organisation B were less experienced with technology and used it sporadically. Again, interview questions covered general security, systems and organisational issues as well as questions about password generation and recall strategies. Subsequently some of the data were analysed twice at different levels. The different types of issues uncovered reveal the strengths and weaknesses of each approach.

The analysis provided a step-by-step account of user authentication usage problems and possible intervention points. Key issues identified through research at Organisation A were substantiated and expanded upon by the research in Organisation B. This study identified two major benefits in using grounded theory as an HCI methodology:

1 Because of grounded theory's conceptual depth (a hierarchical analysis with cross-links) and the absence of a pre-defined theory to restrict research, the data could be tested and re-tested to identify the source of initial contradictions in the data. This means that whole data sources are not disregarded because of confounding contradictions.
2 Because grounded theory relies on iterative development of interview questions this allowed different perceptions to be sampled and analysed with regard to issues which did not emerge until the data was analysed. This means that valid and complex relationships can be identified in shorter time frames.

Several of the interviews show users identifying one perception of their behaviour and then later stating the opposite. Such contradictions make it hard to establish relationships between factors which influence user behaviour. In the initial thematic analysis the processes that led to these contradictions were not identified. The contradictory statements could have been caused by users being unsure of their own descriptions, or discussing complex issues which involve several factors. The application of grounded theory techniques for analysing the free-format statements on the questionnaires and the interview data identified the latter as the case. For example, the initial analysis revealed that for multiple passwords users often use a strategy of 'linked passwords' (e.g. tom1, tom2, tom3). The linked password strategy was identified by users as both improving and decreasing password memorability. Further grounded theory analysis of the data meant that this apparent contradiction was re-visited. The researchers proposed a

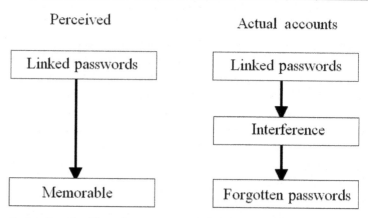

Fig 7.2 *Perceived/actual memory contradictions*

hypothesis of why the contradiction existed. It was proposed that these two sets of perceptions might be the result of individual differences. This in turn would mean that some people were better at remembering linked passwords than others. The data was re-investigated to identify to whom these perceptions were related and if there were any other traits persistent with these users. Further analysis identified that these two concepts were often related to the same person, thus discrediting the notion of individual differences. Further hypotheses were proposed and reviewed through re-analysing the data until it was noted that a key difference between these perceptions was the notion of the respondents recounting perceptions (for example, 'I think that ***** makes it more memorable') and accounts of what actually occurred (for example, 'I kept forgetting which of the passwords it was'). Frequently the perceived/actual distinctions were made by the same person without them realising that they were contradicting themselves (see Figure 7.2).

The actual poor memorability of linked passwords was identified as due to the previously identified cognitive limitation of within-list interference (Wickens, 1992). The common password element was easy to remember, but the changing element produced interference between the versions. It has been noted as similar to the problem of not being able to remember where you parked your car today but remembering where you parked it yesterday. The poor memorability of linked passwords caused users to write passwords down which in turn reduced password security levels.

Initially, analysis identified isolated concepts and user strategies, but did not identify how these could be mapped into a sequence of events with potential intervention points for changing practices and negative perceptions. Analysis of grounded theory process effects, the sequence of events leading to a concept, meant that the concepts of 'information sensitivity' and 'threats' were re-visited. User perceptions of their environment, such as the physical security around them, were found to relay assumptions and in turn incur related user strategies. For example, within organisation A, the technically biased organisation, users were

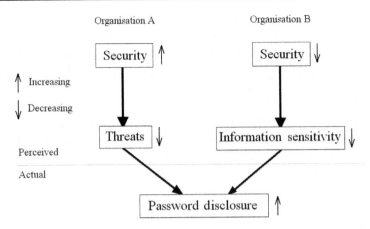

Fig 7.3 *User behaviours produced by perceptions of physical security levels*

identified as perceiving the organisation's general security level as high (increased). Further process effect analysis identified this as related to decreased overall perceptions of threats to the information. This was in turn found to relate to increased insecure work procedures such as password disclosure ('Well, security for getting into the site is so tight, there's no harm in writing down my password and leaving it on my desk.'). In comparison in organisation B, the company in the construction sector, users were found to perceive the organisation's general security level as low (decreased). Reviewing processes effects for these perceptions it was found that this related to decreased perceptions of how sensitive the information is. Ironically, this was also found to relate to increased insecure work procedures such as password disclosure. ('Well, if the information isn't important, why make a big fuss about keeping your password secret?') The two situations are illustrated in Figure 7.3.

The conceptual depth of these grounded theory relationships was noted when relating them to previously identified concepts. The initial thematic analysis identified a simple relationship between poor password construction and security awareness. However, further grounded theory analysis identified relationships between password construction behaviours and assumptions around physical security levels and threats.

Once a sequence of relationships has been identified it is easier to identify positive relationships and potential intervention points to counteract negative relationships. For example, in Figure 7.3 we can see that for organisation A negative behaviours were the results of perceived low threats. Increasing awareness of potential contextually relevant threats could counteract these perceptions. In comparison, within organisation B poor awareness of information sensitivity for the organisation could be increased by effective feedback from the organisation of how sensitive specific information is. This type of HCI feedback to users can provide them with guidance in adapting their security behaviours according to organisational needs. The concept of identifying behaviour–perception sequences and potential intervention points is one of the major benefits of this approach for HCI designers.

Ultimately, these studies uncovered a complex web of variables interacting to produce users' password behaviours. Grounded theory was able to relate descriptively these variables in a way that enabled possible intervention points to be identified. In a field where there has been little previous research, the direction of the initial study could be biased by the researcher. Grounded theory enabled the research to be grounded in the data obtained so that the validity of the theories produced was increased. The structured format of grounded theory encouraged the building of a framework and theories that were grounded in the data thus improving the external validity of the research conducted.

7.4   Qualitative methods and grounded theory in HCI

HCI often needs to review complex phenomena and develop applicable frameworks for action, yet due to its short history it has not yet established an extensive knowledge base on which to base its research. Ultimately HCI research requires the in-depth nature of qualitative research to review these complex phenomena with the structure of quantitative research. It is worth briefly discussing other qualitative methods that may be useful in HCI research and what it is about grounded theory that makes it stand out.

A variety of methods of data collection under the broad rubric of qualitative methods have been applied in HCI research, including a range of observational and ethnographic methods and various forms of qualitative interviewing. In addition, a variety of approaches to analysis have been developed to complement these including thematic analysis, grounded theory, discourse analysis and conversation analysis. Such methods and approaches to analysis are not without controversy. In the past, the debate between the quantitative and qualitative paradigms has become very heated (Morgan, 1996; Sherrard, 1997; Stevenson and Cooper, 1997). Henwood and Pidgeon (1992) argue that the debate should move away from a destructive epistemological battlefield and concentrate on identifying criteria for good research in all its formats.

In the worst scenario, qualitative analysis is reduced to poorly applied 'eyeballing' of the data with 'general impressions' identified. It is hard to know what are true features of the data and what are simply things that have stood out for the particular researcher. Moreover, it is very hard to know what has been missed. This is sadly quite common in HCI research, where it seems there is a poor understanding of how to approach this type of data. Perhaps to ameliorate this, HCI qualitative data is increasingly being turned into quantitative data by means of counting terms (e.g. content analysis). Although these approaches give some useful initial descriptive data, they lack the rigour of quantitative approaches and lose the depth and richness of some qualitative analysis techniques (e.g. words out of context can be incorrectly interpreted).

More constructively, various social science methodologies have been used for some years in HCI, particularly in the field of computer-supported collaborative work (Suchman, 1987; Fafchamps, 1991). However, these studies tend to be restricted to observational, ethnographic style research, limiting their applicability as the ethnographic approach shies away from making value judgments in preference to revealing people's behaviour in a descriptive way. This makes it hard to move away from the particulars of one ethnographic study to the general situations that may be experienced by many users.

Some research has taken a more empirical approach, with methodologies such as conversational analysis (Bowers, Pycock and O'Brian, 1996; Hindus *et al.*, 1996). Discourse and conversational analysis methods sequentially break down a broader set of discourses or more specifically speech. Both seek to finely break down communication sequences, such as turn-taking. As these methods relate more to the actions of discourse and speech, they would be useful for a detailed HCI analysis of technology-mediated communications. They would struggle to be of more general use in studying technology where usually there is very little by way of a rich dialogue.

Thematic analysis, in comparison, seeks to identify patterns of experiences both of processes and attitudes to those processes. Attitudes are abstracted, catalogued and related to themes and sub-themes. This approach is often related to patterns of experience which would nicely support an analysis of many HCI interactions. However, this approach lacks a depth of analysis across different levels of abstraction and thus can be insufficient for detailed theory-building.

Henwood and Pidgeon (1992) argue that the goal of both qualitative and quantitative research paradigms is to build relevant, applicable theories. Normally, in science, theory is based on previous research, but at some point a researcher has generated this theory in an unstructured manner and, in the reporting of scientific work, this theory development stage is largely absent. In contrast, HCI can be (though it is not always) very explicit about developing the theory underlying a new design, though it is noted as being something of a craft. In a new field of exploration like HCI, there must be an increase in this unstructured approach to the discovery stage as there are fewer relevant papers to look to for assistance. Henwood and Pidgeon (1992) argue that the discovery stage is a fundamental role in the scientific process. It could be argued that it is even more fundamental within the design procedures of HCI. This suggests that the particular value of grounded theory in HCI is its structured approach to theory generation. Developing theoretically informed explanations is the most powerful way to highlight reality. Building theory implies interpreting data, for the data must be conceptualised and the concepts related to form a hypothetical rendition of reality. The rendition that results, the theory, cannot only be used to explain that reality but also to provide a framework for action within that context.

Thus, grounded theory has the potential to provide a more focused and structured approach to HCI qualitative research and to provide theories and applied models based on both qualitative and quantitative data. Indeed, its particular approach is closer in some ways to quantitative methods and that is why it is sometimes referred to as a post-positivistic method (Stevenson and Cooper, 1997). Within HCI, grounded theory has been growing as an appropriate qualitative analysis methodology, particularly as a way of analysing usability in complex social, international settings (Adams *et al.*, 2005; Pace, 2004; Razavim and Iverson, 2006). The nature of many HCI phenomena, such as user satisfaction, engagement, privacy and trust, advocates a qualitative approach, although the requirements of the HCI knowledge base imply that a systematic quantitative approach is required. The post-positivistic grounded theory methodology potentially fulfils both of these requirements because it combines a rich, detailed analysis of qualitative material with an attempt to provide a systematic portrayal of the main concepts and themes in public discourse. Grounded theory as an HCI approach is an appropriate method for:

- building HCI theory (in research fields that are conceptually immature) which is empirically based and systematically developed
- integrating current interdisciplinary knowledge into the theory
- dealing with the complex nature of the phenomena (e.g. user perceptions, privacy, trust, technology engagement)
- providing designers with accessible and applicable guidance.

It should be noted that the use of grounded theory methodology has diversified into two approaches: the classic version supported by Glaser (1978) and the Strauss and Corbin (1998) version. It is primarily the Strauss and Corbin approach that is described here. These variations are argued by McCann and Clark (2003) as a sign that the method is maturing and developing as the domains of application widen. Nowhere is this more evident than in the field of HCI where the need for valid yet flexible research is essential.

7.5   Critique

Most qualitative approaches, not just grounded theory, are frequently criticised for being subjective. An important defence against this criticism is to point out that all methods, not just qualitative methods are open to being done poorly and that all experimenters may bias the outcomes of their research. Poorly constructed experiments and applied statistical analysis can lead to bias and subjectivity in the research process just as surely as grounded theory. It is, therefore, advisable that HCI researchers and designers applying any of the methods in this book consider the concepts of reflexivity and quality.

As mentioned in other chapters (see Chapters 2, 6 and 10) it is invaluable to reflect on your research design decisions and how they match with your analysis methods. This concept is known as reflexivity and it deals with the researchers' reflection upon the inevitable impact they have on the research they are conducting. It is through reflexivity that, as HCI researchers, we are able to interpret, understand and improve our own research. Reflexivity compels us to investigate how we as HCI researchers interact with, influence and inform the subject of our research (Nightingale and Cromby, 1999).

Reflexivity can support us in identifying appropriate HCI methods to use and any potential research biases that may occur. This is particularly useful when designers are conducting HCI research on their own developments. The ability to reflect effectively on the limitations of a design we have developed is a difficult one to master. The desire to turn an empirical evaluation into a training session can be overwhelming when the researcher is both the developer and researcher. Carla Willig (2001) describes two different aspects of reflexivity which can help to support effective reflection on these issues: personal reflexivity and epistemological reflexivity. Personal reflexivity can help designers identify their own interests, experiences and beliefs that are helping to shape and potentially bias the research. This approach also supports a reflection of how much this research has affected and changed us both as designers and researchers. Epistemological reflexivity helps HCI researchers reflect on the research question and methodology. For example, what are the different HCI issues that could be identified through a heuristic evaluation compared to an experiment or an in-depth interview? Epistemological reflexivity supports an analysis of our assumptions upon which the research is based and the implications of those assumptions for the research and its findings.

All research methods must be defensible in order to ensure the quality of the research they produce. There are several arguments put forward to disclaim the usefulness of a grounded theory approach. It has been argued that this type of research lacks repeatability (Morgan, 1996). Repeatability is used to verify that findings can be generalised to other participants in similar situations and are not just specific to the particular study. Strauss and Corbin (1990) argue that as long as the data used are comprehensive and the interpretations made are conceptually broad, the theory developed should be abstract enough and include sufficient variation to enable its application to a variety of differing phenomena-related contexts. Thus, HCI research of technology within one context may reveal something of relevance about the technology in another related context.

The subjective elements of grounded theory have also been criticised. However, Sherrard (1997) argues that the apparent lack of opinion within science is merely the product of avoiding socially controversial issues. Many of the research projects in HCI would be difficult to approach purely experimentally either because it would be unethical or because of the complexity of the issues involved. It is also argued (Henwood and Pidgeon, 1992; Sherrard, 1997; Stevenson and Cooper, 1997) that subjectivity and bias are apparent, in varying degrees, in all research. The move, it is suggested, should therefore be to acknowledge these biases for scrutiny by professional counterparts, rather than denying that they exist. Henwood and Pidgeon (1992) suggest that all good quality research should provide documentation of the analytic process and a reflexive account of researchers' research backgrounds and perspectives. They also detail seven rules that should be followed to increase the quality of grounded theory research. To ensure a high standard of analysis Henwood and Pidgeon's (1992) rules can provide guidance to ensure quality within qualitative analysis procedures:

1 A constant comparison method should be used as an internal check on validity ensuring that the framework developed retains the importance of fit to the raw data.
2 Multiple testing of hypotheses will result in identification of relationships that are integrated at all levels of abstraction.
3 Increased validity of the research can be obtained by endeavouring to increase its theoretical sensitivity using previous research comparisons.
4 Theoretical Sampling allows for elaboration of the model and increases the conceptual depth of the analysis.
5 An account of the contexts in which the studies were completed should be provided. This increases the transferability of the findings to other contexts.
6 Detailed documentation of the research process should be made and a sample of the process provided.
7 To obtain reflexivity an account of the author's attitudes and approaches to research in general should be provided.

Another criticism is that, because of the complexity in applying grounded theory appropriately, researchers' experience levels will alter the level of quality in the analysis and also the degree of subjectivity. However, the same could be said for quantitative research in which an experienced researcher would be able to identify potential confounding variables in an experimental design sooner than a less experienced researcher. Strauss and Corbin (1990) argue that a study's reliability (and some aspects of its validity) are still down to the researcher's own theoretical sensitivity, which should be encouraged to reduce bias (Glaser, 1978).

Thus, all of these criticisms, which seem initially most relevant to qualitative approaches in general and grounded theory in particular, only seem so relevant because of the explicit role of the researcher and because qualitative researchers actively acknowledge that role. In fact, though, these criticisms are true of all research methods, and all research methods would benefit from such critical scrutiny.

What cannot be disputed is the time-consuming nature of these approaches. Consider an apparently straightforward interview study. An hour-long interview can easily end up as 10 pages of type. Fifteen interviews make 150 pages that need to be coded, cross-referenced and related. In addition, the researcher will be continuously producing memos that are frequently reviewed and updated. In total, then, developing a grounded theory from even a modest study is a substantial effort. What an HCI researcher must consider, however, is the depth of knowledge they require to increase the effective design of their systems. To get an effective answer may simply require more research input.

Ultimately, through reflexivity, you should decide which alternative methods are suitable and the appropriate way to apply these methods. Latour (1987) argues that there is basically little difference between the two paradigms, quantitative and qualitative methods, as both endeavour to arrange and rearrange the intricacies of raw data. Bryman (1988) additionally suggests that the distinction between these two approaches is purely technical, so that the choice between them relies on their suitability in answering particular research questions. It is suggested that a valuable approach towards strengthening the quality of research is to use a principled combination of methods (Strauss *et al.*, 1964; Henwood and Pidgeon, 1992). It should be acknowledged by advocates of qualitative approaches that there is a lot to be learned from the quantitative paradigm just as there are lots of critical issues addressed by the qualitative approach. This therefore highlights the value of a methodology, such as grounded theory, that seeks to and can encompass both paradigms.

8 Methodological development

ANN BLANDFORD AND THOMAS GREEN

8.1 Overview

One feature of HCI research is that a broad range of methods have been developed to support the design and evaluation of interactive systems. In this chapter, we focus on evaluation methods – not because they are more important than design methods, but because we have more experience of them. In particular we consider the excitements and challenges of research on developing and testing new methods for evaluating interactive systems.

Evaluation methods can be broadly classed on three dimensions:

- with or without the active involvement of users
- with or without a running system
- with or without a realistic context of use.

Most methods fit into one position in this three-dimensional space. For example, controlled experiments typically involve the active participation of users with a running system in a laboratory setting (a non-realistic context of use), while contextual inquiry (Beyer and Holtzblatt, 1998) involves users with a running system in a realistic context. Conversely, interviews involve users but typically not a running system (though they may sometimes take place within the intended context of use). Most of the techniques that involve the active participation of users have drawn on and adapted methods initially developed within the social sciences, and methodological development has been relatively minor and definitely incremental.

In this chapter we focus on the other set of methods – those which do not require the active involvement of users, being applied, rather, by HCI experts. These experts are not necessarily members of the original design team: they may be second-generation designers looking for a way forward; alternatively, they may be informing purchasers choosing between competing offerings.

These methods are usually referred to as either 'analytical' or 'inspection'. The earliest analytical methods, such as GOMS (Card, Moran and Newell, 1983) and Task Action Grammar (TAG: Payne and Green, 1986), can trace their roots back to research in cognitive science. Although widely regarded as methods, the early emphasis in these approaches was on the notation and on describing a system in terms of that notation, then reasoning about it using the underlying theory on which the notation was based. Let us take these two examples a little further.

GOMS is based on a theory of human problem solving, focusing on how experts structure their goals and make choices between alternative courses of action. Average timings for basic actions, both physical and mental, have been established from empirical data; these can be used to calculate typical times for expert users to achieve specified goals. These calculations can, in turn, be used to compare alternative interface designs (e.g. Gray, John and Atwood, 1993), or to identify points where a system's efficiency is low. John and Kieras (1996b) outline methods for performing GOMS analyses and discuss in detail the range of insights a GOMS analysis can yield about a system. Kieras (1997) goes further in terms of articulating a clear method for applying one particular variant of GOMS (NGOMSL).

TAG also considers users' tasks, but is based on a theory of how learners generalise from what they have already learnt to make reasonable guesses at what they don't know. In a highly systematic or 'consistent' interface language, guessing is easy, because tasks with similar semantics have similar commands (e.g. 'move pointer 1 place forward' $\Rightarrow$ CMD-F, 'move pointer 1 word forward' $\Rightarrow$ CMD-SHIFT-F); in a very unsystematic, arbitrary one, guessing is impossible. TAG used a phrase-structure grammar to describe the interface language, then a simple semantic description of tasks and a two-level attribute grammar to summarise the first grammar: a consistent interface language could be summarised by a very short two-level grammar. Evaluating a design therefore required the users' tasks to be summarised in a semantic dictionary and the interface language to be restated as a two-level grammar entered via that dictionary, a hefty process resulting in a very detailed description but not easily compared to any other such evaluation, nor yielding much insight as to how the target design could be improved. Schiele and Green (1990) achieved a fairly thorough analysis of a real-life system, but the approach has been little used subsequently.

Cognitive science has been the theoretical foundation for many of the analytical methods developed to support reasoning about HCI. As well as GOMS and TAG, as outlined above, cognitively oriented techniques include Task Knowledge Structures (TKS: Johnson, 1992), cognitive walkthrough (Wharton et al., 1994) and CASSM (Blandford, Green and Connell, 2005). Other approaches, such as Thimbleby's (2004b) work on matrix algebra and methods based on formal notations of computer systems (see Chapter 5), draw more directly on theories of computing rather than cognition.

Another body of methods that do not require the direct involvement of users is checklist-based approaches (e.g. heuristic evaluation, Nielsen, 1994a). These typically draw less directly on any theory, being based largely on the craft skill and experience of practitioners. Such methods involve inspection but minimal analysis.

In this chapter, we consider the issues involved in developing new analytical methods for evaluation in HCI. This is surprisingly poorly articulated in the literature on methods. Sometimes, such methods and notations appear not to have been designed or developed systematically, but to have happened more by accident. Maybe this is natural: method development is itself a form of design. Cross (2004) presents a compelling argument that design is nothing so simplistic as 'top-down' or 'bottom-up', as in the textbook descriptions of authors such as Pahl and Beitz (1984), but instead is a much more complex process of choosing where to invest effort, moment by moment – a process that may seem haphazard to the onlooker but is in fact quite rational. Top-down design can be viewed as goal-driven: systematically working from the current situation to the goal state; conversely, bottom-up design is driven by the resources and ideas that are currently available.

The paucity of accounts of how methods have been developed in the past represents a challenge in terms of presenting a method for developing methodologies. Unlike most other chapters of this book, there is minimal literature to base the method description on. There are, however, three sources of evidence on which we can draw to develop our account of method development:

1 The snapshots of methods as they are presented in the literature over time – for example, the different descriptions of cognitive walkthrough as it evolved from 1990 (e.g. Lewis *et al.*, 1990) to the present (e.g. Blackmon, Kitajima and Polson, 2003; Allendoerfer *et al.*, 2005).

2 The literature on design. Method development is, as noted above, a form of design.

3 Our most compelling source of evidence is personal reflection. We have been directly involved in the development of at least ten methods and notations between us, and have therefore built up substantial experience of method development and testing:

- TAG (Payne and Green, 1986), as described above
- Cognitive Dimensions of Notations (CDs: Green, 1989; Green and Petre, 1996; Green *et al.*, 2006), a language for discussing properties of notations (particularly programming languages)
- Programmable User Modelling (PUM: Young, Green and Simon, 1989; Blandford and Young, 1996), an approach based on describing the knowledge a user would need to use a device, based on a model of human problem solving
- Entity-Relationship Modelling of Information Artefacts (ERMIA: Green and Benyon, 1996), a more formal approach to describing information artefacts
- Interacting Cognitive Subsystems (ICS: May, Barnard and Blandford, 1993; Barnard and May, 1999), a more abstract approach to reasoning about a user's cognition while working with a system
- Interaction Framework (IF: Blandford, Harrison and Barnard, 1995), an approach that aims to abstract away from details of the individual actors (people and computer systems) and focus on the patterns of interaction between those actors

- Evaluating Multi-modal Usability (EMU: Hyde, 2002), a method that focuses particularly on the ways multiple modalities are recruited in an interaction
- Distributed Cognition for Teamworking (DiCoT: Furniss, 2004; Furniss and Blandford, 2006), a methodology based on the ideas of distributed cognition (Hutchins, 1995; Hollan, Hutchins and Kirsh, 2000)
- CASSM (Blandford et al., 2005; Connell, Blandford and Green, 2004), as described below in the case study
- Claims Analysis for information systems (Blandford, Keith and Fields, 2006), an adaptation of claims analysis (Carroll and Rosson, 1992) that tailored it towards the design of digital libraries and similar information systems

As this list makes apparent, our experience is entirely in developing evaluation methods rather than (for example) design methods, and this bias permeates the rest of this chapter.

In presenting the method below, we draw on these different sources of evidence to construct what we hope is a coherent account of the principles underpinning methodology development. You should note that we tend to use the terms 'method' and 'methodology' interchangeably. We tried sticking with one of these terms rigorously, and found we could not – for example, some authors refer to cognitive walkthrough as a method and others as a methodology, and when we adopted their terminology we inherited inconsistencies. Broadly, we view a methodology as a collection of methods used in a systematic way, but of course at a higher level of abstraction that collection of methods can be regarded as a 'bigger' method.

8.2   The method

Developing and testing a method is not quick. Neither is it for the faint-hearted. As is indicated by the spread of dates on the citations for some of the methods outlined above (notably GOMS, cognitive walkthrough, cognitive dimensions), method development has often taken place over many years. Nevertheless, substantial work can be done within the limits of a Masters or Doctoral project. For example, DiCoT (Furniss, 2004) was developed as a Masters project, using ambulance control as a case study, though it has subsequently undergone further testing in a different domain – namely agile software development (Sharp et al., 2006). Similarly, EMU (Hyde, 2002) was developed and tested as a doctoral research project. It is also possible to test a methodology developed elsewhere, as John and Packer (1995) did with cognitive walkthrough, and refine or extend it, as we did with claims analysis (Blandford et al., 2006), so that any one project does not necessarily have to cover all phases of the development lifecycle.

In simple terms, the development of a method involves some key phases of activity. While we present them here in a linear fashion, the actual development of a methodology will typically be iterative (with testing leading to the identification of further requirements), and phases may sometimes be interleaved in apparently arbitrary and chaotic ways. The core phases of development are:

- identification of an opportunity or need
- development of more detailed requirements (optionally)
- matching opportunities, needs and requirements
- development of the method
- testing of the method

We consider each of these phases of activity in more detail here, and present a single example of the development of a methodology (CASSM) in Section 8.3.

8.2.1 Identification of an opportunity or need

As with any design, the development of a methodology starts with either an opportunity or a need. For example, a cognitive or computational theory (e.g. the matrix algebra underpinning the work of Thimbleby (2004b) or the distributed cognition theory that formed the basis of DiCoT (Furniss and Blandford, 2006)) might suggest a new way of analysing a system to yield new and valuable insights. Conversely, there might be a need to evaluate a system that is not supported by current methods: our development of claims analysis (Blandford et al., 2006) fits into this category. In that development, we were seeking an approach that: (1) would support digital libraries developers in thinking about their design from a user's perspective; (2) fitted within their ongoing development practice; and (3) allowed us to codify an understanding of cognition and information seeking.

In an ideal world, opportunity and need will come together. This was the case for CASSM (as described below), in that we drew on existing resources (our earlier work on CDs, ERMIA and PUM), but also had reasonably clear goals for what we wanted to achieve with our new approach.

8.2.2 Development of more detailed requirements

Developing a new methodology is expensive, in time and resources. It is important to consider what future benefits will accrue from that investment. That sounds a mercenary way to think about research, but a method has to have some benefits. Those may be direct benefits, in terms of a method being taken up and used in practice and hence influencing the designs of future systems, or they may be indirect, for example helping researchers to better understand the challenges inherent in developing methodologies, or being a vehicle for encapsulating a theory of cognition. Whatever the goals of a methodology development project, it is a good idea to be reasonably clear about what they are. If you are really, sincerely trying to develop an approach that is to be taken up and used in practice, then it is important to understand the requirements of practice. If, on the other hand, your interests are more theoretical (e.g. to explore the feasibility of applying entity–relationship modelling to the design or evaluation of information artefacts

(Green and Benyon, 1996)) then it may be less important to identify more detailed requirements on the method.

There is still no clear set of requirements for HCI methodologies to be taken up in practice. Some of the requirements that have been discussed are as follows. Some of these apply equally to both design and evaluation methods; others apply particularly to evaluation methods.

Validity: For analytical evaluation methods, it is important that the method should, as far as possible, support the analyst in correctly predicting user behaviour or identifying problems that users will have with the system, minimising the number of false positives (issues that are identified as problems when actually they are not) and misses (failures to identify actual problems). Of course, some issues will be outside the scope of a particular evaluation method (e.g. a matrix algebra approach is unlikely to have much to say about the effectiveness of team working), so another requirement concerns scope.

Scope: The scope of a method, in terms of the kinds of issues it does and does not address, should be clear to users of the method. This is important so that analysts can both select an appropriate method for addressing their current concerns and also appreciate the limitations as well as the value of their analysis.

Reliability: The extent to which different analysts applying the same method will achieve the same results (the same design or evaluation insights) is considered by some to be an important consideration (e.g. Hertzum and Jacobsen, 2001).

Productivity: In the past, simple problem count (the number and/or severity of problems an evaluation method helped identify) was considered an important criterion. Since the work of Gray and Salzman (1998), this criterion has been relatively de-emphasised. Nevertheless, any method should somehow either spur developers, or else assist users trying to choose whether to adopt a particular device.

Usability: Surprisingly little discussion has focused on the idea that HCI methods must themselves be usable. This means that they must fit within design practice (one might want to be more specific about what particular kinds of design practice are to be addressed; for example, the practices of safety critical systems development are normally different from those of website development).

Learnability: How easy it is for a practitioner to pick up and work with a method will be a strong determinant of take-up and use in practice. We are not aware of many studies of the learnability of methods in HCI, although Blandford *et al.* (1998) studied the practicalities of teaching (and learning) PUM, and John and Packer (1995) investigated the learnability of cognitive walkthrough.

Insights derived: Wixon (2003) argues strongly that the most important criterion for any HCI method (he focuses on evaluation methods, but the same argument surely applies to design methods) is whether or not it gives the designer insights that will help to improve design. Never mind how valid, reliable or productive a method is: does applying it result in a better system?

Wixon's (2003) work, in particular, highlights the fact that there is still little agreement on what features an HCI method should possess. The list of possible requirements presented here is by no means complete; some of them may, indeed, be regarded as unimportant or irrelevant to future HCI practice. Also, as noted above, for many methodology development projects, practitioner-oriented requirements may be of secondary concern to scientific requirements such as the feasibility of encapsulating a particular theory in a method at all.

8.2.3 Matching opportunities, needs and requirements

Whatever the starting point (need or opportunity) and requirements, it is then necessary to consider what theories, tools or resources are available for addressing the need (or, conversely, to identify what unrecognised needs a new opportunity addresses). This is typically an exploratory step.

   If you start with a need, then the question is: how might that need be addressed? If we dismiss as unrealistic the possibility that the answer will emerge as if by magic, this phase typically involves searching through work that has been done before to find likely candidate approaches, then testing them to establish how well they address the need. For example, when we were looking for suitable methods for supporting digital library development, we started by testing some widely used methods, namely cognitive walkthrough and heuristic evaluation. This involved applying these methods ourselves to selected digital libraries and also running some user studies to find out what difficulties the users of those libraries were actually experiencing, to establish how well the methods were supporting reasoning about real user difficulties. We found that the methods were delivering useful insights about surface difficulties (e.g. poor labelling, or unhelpful help messages), but not giving leverage on why real users were having such difficulty working effectively with the digital libraries (Blandford *et al.*, 2004). We therefore scoured the literature to find less familiar methods that might fit our needs better. Claims analysis (Carroll and Rosson, 1992) seemed to fit the bill in that it was intended to be used within an ongoing design process (good!) and focused on the positive and negative effects of design decisions on the user, which looked like a promising approach. Blandford *et al.* (2006) report on our experience of learning, applying and adapting claims analysis; the key points to emerge from that study were that: those learning a new technique are highly dependent on published descriptions of the approach, unless they have direct access to the method developers; and that there were substantial cultural gulfs between ourselves (as human factors specialists) and the digital library developers with whom we worked, in terms of prior knowledge, expectations and values. These differences had to be accommodated in the way that we developed and communicated the approach with them. In summary, then, the identification of possible approaches for addressing a need is typically highly exploratory, finding and testing work (often by others) on which to build.

   If you start with an opportunity, or resource, the exploration is typically less concerned with finding appropriate theory and more with finding ways to develop theory into a method. This may involve minimal exploration, moving swiftly on to the next step of developing the method. However, it is often helpful to have identified existing methods that can be adapted to encapsulate the new theory. For example, having synthesised the elements of distributed cognition from multiple sources, Furniss (2004) searched for data-gathering and representation methods to support the approach of reasoning about a work context in terms of the constructs of distributed cognition. After extensive reading, he adapted the method and representations of contextual design (Beyer and Holtzblatt, 1998) to develop DiCoT; these were chosen because they matched his requirements well.

This phase of matching needs, requirements and opportunities can be regarded as a process of gathering together suitable ingredients for developing the method. Whether particular ingredients fit well together is often a matter of trial and error, explored within this phase or within development or testing of the method.

8.2.4 Development of the method

The development of a method is the creative step that is the hallmark of all design. As such, there is relatively little that can be written about it in terms of structured processes (though drawing on examples of existing methods that share similar features is often a good place to start). Development is itself often iterative: for example, investigating the strengths and weaknesses of particular data gathering techniques (about users or computer systems or work contexts or some combination of these elements), or the effects of changing the representations used or the detailed analysis techniques, or the tutorial or other description of how to apply the method. In the account of how we developed CASSM (below) we recount some of the main design decisions we made, and changes we subsequently made, but we are unable to clearly articulate where each of the ideas that have gone into the method came from – only how we implemented and tested those ideas. We describe some of the insights we had in terms of 'eureka!' moments: we can't tell you what made those moments happen.

8.2.5 Testing of the method

As outlined above, there may be many kinds of requirements on the method that has been developed. What kinds of testing are needed will depend on what the requirements are. For some of the cognitively oriented techniques, such as GOMS, the primary concern, particularly in the earlier stages of development, was cognitive validity: that the findings from a GOMS analysis should match as closely as possible the findings from empirical studies of experts working with the same systems. Through the 1980s and early 1990s, the emphasis for testing was on productivity (e.g. Desurvire *et al.*, 1992; Sears, 1997; Cuomo and Bowen, 1994) – an emphasis that was criticised on scientific (though not on practical) grounds by Gray and Salzman (1998). As outlined above, other criteria for testing have become more widely recognised (though not yet universally agreed) in recent years.

One way to think about testing a method is to consider the following six questions (which we will refer to as the 'PRET A Rapporter' framework):

1 Purpose of evaluation: what are the goals of the testing, or the detailed questions to be answered in the study? These will reflect the needs and requirements that the method was developed to address.
2 Resources and constraints: what resources are available for conducting the study and, conversely, what constraints must the study work within? For testing methods this question usually presents the most challenges, so we consider it in more detail below.
3 Ethics: what ethical considerations need to be addressed? In method testing, the main ethical concerns are likely to relate to privacy of participant information. We do not consider this in more detail here.
4 Techniques for gathering data must be identified, such as those described in Chapters 1, 2 and 3.
5 Analysis techniques must be selected, such as those described in Chapters 4, 5, 6 and 7.
6 Reporting of findings is (usually) the final step, though not necessarily, see Chapter 10.

Testing a method is important because how a method is used depends so heavily on who is using it. The knowledge and expertise of the analysts working with the method simply cannot be ignored. Hertzum and Jacobsen (2001) refer to this as the 'evaluator effect'. In early tests of methods (many years ago), people tended to ignore the evaluator effect – indeed, this was one of the criticisms made by Gray and Salzman (1998) of those early studies. Nielsen and Landauer (1993) turned this issue upside down and asked how many evaluators you needed to be reasonably sure you had identified most of the important usability problems with a system (the widely quoted answer is five, though the origins of that number are disputed and, as Woolrych and Cockton (2001) argue, that answer makes many presumptions about the spread of evaluator expertise; it also assumes the value of productivity as a way of assessing the value of a method).

Many of the tests of methods that have been conducted are comparative: they have pitted methods against each other. This is a fine thing to do (we have done it ourselves), provided that you accept that such a comparison can never be scientifically 'clean': if different analysts use each method then the individual differences of the analysts is a confounding variable; if the same analyst applies the different methods then as they work they will gradually learn about the systems being evaluated, and they may have different levels of skill with the different methods – it is simply not possible to conduct scientifically rigorous comparison of the style discussed in Chapter 1. However, qualitative studies (for example, Connell *et al.*, 2004) that compare the experiences and outcomes of applying different methods can yield valuable insights into their strengths and limitations (see Chapter 7).

You may only want to test an individual method, in which case probably the dominant concern is with ecological validity. How much does it matter that the method should be used by practitioners, or will (for example) HCI students serve as a good surrogate? If the concern is with learnability (e.g. John and Packer, 1995; Blandford *et al.*, 1998) then working with students seems a reasonable approach, and the next question is whether to work with a very small number or with a larger group (studies have been done with a single student, tracking their learning and use of resources in detail). Recruitment and scheduling of training sessions are likely to be the next issues to consider. How you address these will very much depend on circumstances: on the timing of the study and the available resources.

If the testing really needs practitioner involvement then what is possible depends on the duration and level of commitment required of those practitioners. It is important to consider the costs and benefits to the practitioners of involvement in any study. In our experience, few practitioners have much time to commit to learning or applying a new method unless it fits snugly with their existing practices and gives clear benefits. Certainly, longitudinal studies (e.g. Blandford *et al.*, 2006) are demanding, on both investigators and practitioners, though in our experience they are also enjoyable and enlightening.

8.2.6 Summary

It is impossible to be prescriptive about the method for developing a method. There are huge variations in the motivations for developing a method and the contexts within which it happens – and hence the available resources and constraints under which that development and subsequent testing occur. In this section, we have aimed to highlight what are, in our experience (and also based on our readings of other people's work in this area), the important phases of activity and key issues to consider in developing a method. In the next section we present an account of our development and testing of CASSM to date, as an example of method development.

8.3   Applying the method

Concept-based Analysis of Surface and Structural Misfits, or CASSM, is an approach to assessing the 'quality of fit' between the way users think about their activity and the way a system represents it. We have been developing the approach over about 11 years at the time of writing, although most of that time progress has been slow because the development has been in our spare time. CASSM started life as UUUM (Usable, Useful, Used Modelling – an ambitious, but rather non-specific name), then became OSM (Ontological Sketch Modelling – a name that we explain below), before becoming CASSM (pronounced 'chasm') – a name that is intended to evoke the 'gulf' between user and system.

The development of CASSM has been, in Suchman's (1987) terms, 'situated'. Like her canoeist shooting the rapids, we knew where we were aiming, we had some initial ideas of how to proceed, but each particular development manoeuvre was constructed in response to the current situation: to what we had found out so far through empirical studies and personal reflections and to the opportunities that presented themselves. The requirements for CASSM were hatched somewhere unlikely – we now disagree about whether it was in a pub in Sheffield or on a bus in Norway. Either way, we agreed that there was a need for an evaluation method that:

- would be useful: it should reveal important things about usability of tools such as drawing packages that were not well suited to task-based analyses (what makes a drawing package hard to use is typically not the task structures but the appropriateness and obviousness of the concepts – such as drawing objects, layers, 'handles' and fills – with which the user has to work to achieve what they want);
- would be usable, treading an appropriate path between the 'death by detail' that characterises many rigorous evaluation approaches (including the ERMIA and PUM on which we were working at the time) and the vagueness of CDs and checklists;
- would ultimately be used by people other than its developers and their close friends.

'Useful, usable, used': we conclude this section with our current assessment of how well we have met those objectives.

With our backgrounds in modelling (and methods based on the construction of models), it was perhaps inevitable that we would think of our method as involving some modelling work, although we did not want that modelling to be onerous: we had learnt through our experiences of trying to teach ERMIA and PUM that sophisticated modelling activity is not an attractive proposition to many people, and that the initial learning curve for any new method would have to be relatively small. The fact that we wanted to focus on concepts and relationships between them (to provide a complement to the many task-oriented methods that were available at the time) led us to the second name for the approach Ontological Sketch Modelling (OSM). This name reflects that we were interested in the ontology with which users were working; that the modelling was sketchy; and that the approach was model-based.

The first version of OSM focused on concepts and relationships. Examples of concepts and relationships are that layers and drawing-objects are concepts, and they are related by a drawing-object being on a layer. We were interested in reasoning about Green's CDs, many of which are concerned with how easy it is to make changes to systems, and initially we tried to do this just by focusing on concepts and relationships; after weeks of struggling and arguing (the path of research collaboration does not always run smoothly), we eventually accepted that we would need some representation of actions (i.e. what actions need to be performed in order to create or delete entities, or to change attributes or relationships).

Drawing particularly on our experience with PUM, which included a complex representation of actions, our first attempt at representing actions in OSM involved

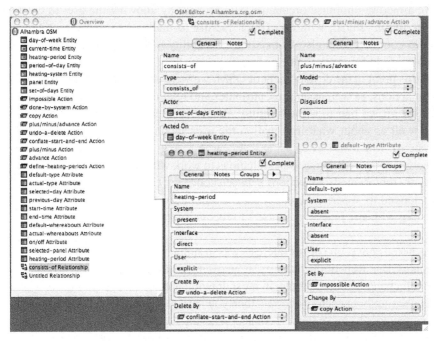

Fig 8.1 *A screenshot of the OSMosis editor, showing example windows for entities, attributes, actions and relationships*

describing them in detail – an approach that we abandoned reasonably quickly as being too time consuming and having limited return on investment.

Early OSM analyses (including the first versions of it we taught to students) were entirely paper-based. This had the advantages of paper, such as being flexible and easy to present in a classroom setting. However, we believed that the ideas would be easier to communicate (e.g. via the internet) and more likely to be taken up by others if we had tool support for the approach. Our first attempt at tool support, OSMosis, is shown in Figure 8.1. The process of designing OSMosis was immensely useful: it forced us to make explicit what we meant by terms (in a way that could be fudged on paper) and it forced us to think about what we really wanted to be able to say about different elements of the model. For example: what did we want to be able to say about an action? At the time of OSMosis, what we chose to say was what the action's name was and whether or not it was moded or disguised: i.e. whether the same physical action would have the same effect on the system state under all conditions, and whether the user could easily discover and predict the effect of the action, because the examples we had been working on up to that point led us to believe that these were the important features of an action for reasoning about usability.

We could go on at length about the design of OSMosis, but will resist. The details really do not matter for the purposes of this chapter. The important points that we should note are that:

- We aimed to minimise premature commitment by allowing the user to create description 'stubs', with an explicit facility to mark when item descriptions were complete, and also to maximise flexibility of expression by creating a 'notes' field for every item.
- At this point in the development of OSM, we were explicitly naming all important actions, as well as entities, attributes and relationships.
- Although we had thought carefully about the interface design for OSMosis (as well as about what information the user should be able to enter into the system), when we started using it 'in earnest' (e.g. for the system description shown in Figure 8.1) we found it tedious to work with: too many windows, and poorly represented connections between concepts (e.g. the idea that an attribute 'belonged to' a particular entity). We did not need to subject OSMosis to user testing with any independent users to recognise its limitations.

As noted above, one of our interests was in supporting reasoning about some of Green's CDs. 'Repetition viscosity' is an example of a CD, describing 'resistance to small changes': for example, in most drawing applications, if you move a box in a boxes-and-connectors diagram then you have to separately move each one of the connectors to make them reconnect with the box. Our hope was to generate formal descriptions of those CDs in terms of the ontology of OSM – i.e. entities, attributes, relationships and actions. Somewhere in this process, we had a 'eureka' moment when we realised that the representation was wrong: that we had to explicitly link attributes with their entities, and that the names of actions were unimportant but that what mattered was how easy or otherwise it was to create or delete entities or change the values of attributes. Actions per se disappeared from the representation, although their properties remained.

Another 'eureka' moment came when we realised that there were two broad classes of misfits that we could reason about with this representation. One was what came to be called 'surface' misfits, which were simple instances of concepts that mattered to the user that were not well represented in the system or, conversely, concepts that were central to the operation of the computer system that were difficult for the user to grasp. The other was 'structural' misfits: ones which related to the internal structure of the computer system representation which made activities that were conceptually simple to the user (like moving a box on a boxes-and-connectors diagram) difficult to achieve in practice (e.g. because of repetition viscosity). The surface misfits could be easily spotted just by 'eyeballing' an appropriately designed system description; the structural misfits required some additional (computable) analysis. With OSMosis, this computable analysis was only achieved by exporting the description to a file which was subsequently analysed as a separate program. The 'eyeballing' was not supported at all.

By this point, another difficulty we were experiencing was with the name of the approach: the word 'ontological' was either unfamiliar to people or was associated with a particular approach to knowledge representation in artificial intelligence; the word 'sketch' made some people think we were only interested in interfaces

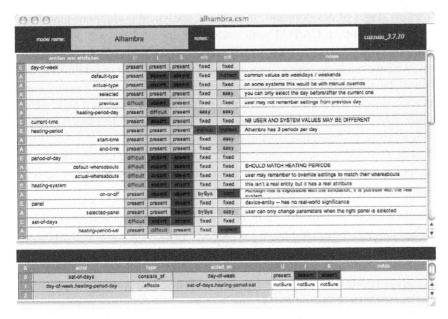

Fig 8.2 *A screenshot of Cassata, showing a complete system description*

to sketching (i.e. drawing) systems; and the word 'modelling' evoked links to the Unified Modelling Language (UML). All wrong! After much head-scratching and playing around with terms and acronyms, we opted to rename the approach as CASSM. We do not think this is the perfect name, but we have not yet conjured up a better one. At least this name is pronounceable ('chasm') and has not been found to evoke inappropriate associations.

These many insights were brought together in a refinement to the method and the implementation of a support tool that we called Cassata (see Figure 8.2). Cassata allows the analyst to describe the properties of actions (e.g. 'fixed', 'easy', 'indirect') but not name them, and includes a facility to automatically analyse a system description for various CDs. It also retains the idea of the analyst writing freeform notes to capture related insights or explanations, explicitly links attributes to the corresponding entities and supports 'eyeballing' of the description to spot surface misfits (they are red (or dark if viewed in greyscale) in Figure 8.2). The complete package of a CASSM tutorial, the Cassata tool and several worked examples of analyses are available via the internet (www.uclic.ucl.ac.uk/annb/CASSM/). This was important to us: for any method to be taken up and used, it has to be accessible to potential users; the tutorial package includes all the materials a novice needs to start working with CASSM.

Throughout the development process, various forms of testing have been conducted. Many of these have been informal, largely concerned with the learnability of the approach – by teaching it to students and presenting it as a conference tutorial and informally establishing what difficulties people have with learning and applying the approach. This kind of informal testing has been conducted since the earliest stages of development. In addition, analytical evaluations have been conducted to compare CASSM with evaluation approaches such as cognitive walkthrough (Connell *et al.*, 2004 and Blandford *et al.* (in press)). In these evaluations, we have not been pitting approaches against each other to establish which is 'better', but to find out more about the scope of each (what kinds of systems and users each approach is suited to, and what kinds of usability issues it highlights). We have also engaged in testing the approach with software developers, and on various kinds of systems; this work is ongoing.

Overall, CASSM has undergone iterative development and testing, and we do not consider that process to be complete yet. In terms of the phases of activity discussed in the previous section:

- Identification of an opportunity or need started from the desire to develop a method that was useful, usable and used, and that gave the kinds of insights we have outlined about misfits, including CDs.
- Development of more detailed requirements has largely refined the initial need.
- Matching opportunities, needs and requirements involved drawing on our earlier work on ERMIA, CDs and PUM.
- Development of the method involved a lot of trial and error and eureka moments, as outlined above.
- Testing of the method has involved using it ourselves on a variety of systems, teaching it to others and comparing the outputs of CASSM analysis with those of other methods.

All the development and testing have been conducted keeping the initial needs and motivations in mind. At the time of writing, we have established that CASSM is useful, we have a reasonable understanding of which elements of it are usable and which are (still) difficult to learn and we have made some limited progress on it being used. The next focus will be on communicating the approach to practitioners and testing it more thoroughly for take-up and use in practice.

8.4   Related studies

To the best of our knowledge (and we have looked in all the obvious places and many non-obvious ones too), there are no accounts of how to develop methods and few case studies of how methods have been developed. The only case study we are aware of is our own (Green *et al.*, 2006) account of the development of CDs. This dearth makes it difficult to present an account of related studies with any confidence. We can tell stories based on snapshots of methods as presented by their developers over the years, but cannot account for the detailed deliberations or serendipitous events that nudged the developments.

Green *et al.* (2006) highlight the serendipity that has characterised the development of Cognitive Dimensions. From an initial aim of developing a way of describing relevant features of designs compactly and with limited ambiguity

(Green, 1989), CDs came to be viewed as 'discourse tools' for information-based artefacts (Green, 1994) in which the dimensions were identified, described and refined largely from the personal experiences of the members of the development team. A publication on the application of CDs to visual programming languages (Green and Petre, 1996) unexpectedly led to them being regarded as only applying to that kind of system. Nevertheless, the vocabulary was sufficiently lightweight, flexible and expressive to be fairly rapidly taken up by others, particularly within the Psychology of Programming community. One of the effects of this – a point that we have not discussed previously in this chapter – has been that CDs have been adopted and adapted in ways that were not intended by their originator, resulting in offspring like CASSM, as described above, CiDa (Roast, Khazaei and Siddiqi, 2000) and CD-oriented personas (Clarke, 2005). In the process, the set of dimensions has been debated and modified; while there remains a 'core' to CDs as originally conceived, there is arguably no longer a single focus or direction to the development as CDs are taken up and used more widely.

Heuristic evaluation (Nielsen and Molich, 1990) is another approach that has been taken up, adopted and adapted. In this case, it appears that the original set of ten heuristics was developed based on craft skill; subsequent sets of heuristics have been published for specific types of systems such as websites and e-commerce sites – again, apparently based on the experience of Nielsen and others (see www.useit.com). In the case of heuristic evaluation, the main evaluative focus has been on costs and benefits of the approach – a question addressed not just by Nielsen himself (e.g. Nielsen, 1995) but also by others (e.g. Woolrych and Cockton, 2000).

The adoption and adaptation that characterise the development of CDs and heuristic evaluation are less obvious in the development of other, arguably more complex, approaches. GOMS (Card et al., 1983) has been developed into four variants, each focusing on a slightly different aspect of user–system interaction, but all based on the same core representation and all assuming expert behaviour (John and Kieras, 1996b). Various tools for supporting GOMS analysis have been developed by different research groups (Baumeister, John and Byrne, 2000) to facilitate take-up and use within industry. Nevertheless, while GOMS has been applied to industrial software systems (e.g. Gong and Kieras, 1994), the published evaluations of GOMS focus on its validity (how well it can be used to predict actual expert behaviour) and not criteria such as learnability or fit with industrial practice, and we are not aware of any case studies of the use of GOMS by (non-academic) practitioners.

This contrasts with the development of cognitive walkthrough, where much less emphasis has been placed on validity and more on usability and utility of the method. The earliest papers on the approach are largely concerned with the theoretical foundations of the method, but through the early 1990s the developers were clearly working to achieve a balance between providing good support, encouraging rigour and avoiding inflicting mind-numbing boredom on analysts. They also focus directly on how to apply the method, rather than on constructing a model as such. Over the early years of development, the number and complexity of questions an analyst was expected to answer for every step of a walkthrough changed from nine relatively sophisticated questions (Lewis *et al.*, 1990) to four more straightforward ones (Wharton *et al.*, 1994), and more recently to three (Blackmon *et al.*, 2002). Recent work has, like heuristic evaluation, focused on adapting the approach to apply particularly to website evaluation. Also, a case study on how the method needed to be simplified and adapted to fit with the constraints of commercial software development has been conducted and reported (Spencer, 2000).

In summary, different methodology development projects have had different focuses in terms of goals (the criteria against which they appear to evaluate their methods) and outcomes to date (e.g. extent and type of take-up and adaptation by others, whether other academics or commercial users). In all cases, it would appear that development has been situated, responding to opportunities that arise and exploiting the strengths and values of the individuals involved in the development projects. Some stages of development are explicit in the publications about various methods; others can only be inferred.

8.5   Critique

As should be obvious, the method for method development is under-defined. All attempts to define systematic design methods have constrained creativity and not proved that helpful for anything other than routine design. The design of new methodologies certainly is not routine. Nevertheless, good design typically contains certain ingredients (including, but not limited to, inspiration and insight). In this chapter, we have aimed to outline important activities, goals and techniques that contribute to methodology development.

Probably the biggest challenge is evaluating evaluation methods. As discussed above, there are many possible evaluation criteria including validity, scope, reliability, productivity, usability, learnability and insights derived from applying a method. In principle, any new method should be assessed against all relevant criteria; in practice, there has been limited work on assessing many methods against any of the criteria, never mind all of them. Indeed, there is scope for conducting informative and rewarding evaluations of methods as separate research projects, and there is a need for innovative methods for evaluating methods.

Stepping back to consider the whole development cycle again, we are not yet in a position to critique the approach we have outlined and exemplified. However, we hope that this chapter is informative and inspirational for others who are up to the challenge of developing or testing methods to address future needs in HCI.

9 Theoretical analysis and theory creation

ALAN DIX

The initial impetus for research is the search for theory.

Fawcett and Downs, 1986

9.1 Overview

A chapter on theory as a research technique is strange as, in a way, what is academic research about if it is not about theory? Without theory we may be engaged in product development, or data gathering, but not research. This said, there is of course also a *spiritus mundi* against theory: in abstracting away from the particular, theory is seen as at best simplistic and at worst reductionist and dangerous. And of course in popular language a theory is an unsubstantiated guess, almost the opposite of the scientific understanding of theory!

A theoretical approach is also not so much a method or technique that is applied to research, but an attitude and a desire to make sense of and to understand, in some ordered way, the phenomena around us. This approach can influence design and research methodology; indeed those most avowedly atheoretical in their methods are often most theoretical in their methodology!

Theories, that is systematic and structured bodies of knowledge, are the raw material for both research and practical design, but are also the outcomes of research and often the results of more informal reflection on experience. As we shall discuss shortly, theory is the language of generalisation, the way we move from one particular to another with confidence.

And theories can be more basic still. A tiny baby watches her moving fingers, hits out at a ball and sees it move, gradually making sense of the relation between feelings and effects; the building, testing and use of theory are as essential a part of our lives as feeding and breathing.

In HCI, developing, understanding and applying theory are particularly important. Technology and its use move so rapidly that today's empirical results are outdated tomorrow. To be proactive rather than merely reactive and to produce research results that are useful beyond the end of the current project or PhD require deeper knowledge and informed analysis.

In this chapter, we will first spend some time examining what theory is about: why it is important, what it is and is not, and what different kinds of theory there are. We will then look at different ways of using theory in HCI practice and research and ways of producing new theories. These techniques will be demonstrated by a number of real examples in research and commercial practice. Finally, we will look at some of the strengths and weaknesses of theoretical approaches and the way they relate to other techniques.

9.2   About theory

9.2.1 Why theory?

As we have noted, theory is the language of generalisation. There are two main ways in which we can generalise from past experience in order to deal with new situations:

- **Analogy:** Here one looks for a past situation that is similar to the current one and then tries to use parallels between features of the past and current situations in order to explain aspects or predict outcomes.
- **Abstraction:** Here one tries to find common features from past experience and use these to create more abstract concepts. When new situations arise, they are expressed in terms of the abstract concepts.

We do both these things in day-to-day life and are usually not aware that we are doing them. In particular, our brains do a lot of analogical 'reasoning' in the form of associative pattern matching at subconscious levels including interpreting raw perceptions. In any analogical reasoning there is already an implicit theoretical model that determines what is considered important in comparing two instances. However, it is when we give names to the attributes and classes that we move from analogical to theoretical thinking.

If we say 'drunk drivers are dangerous because they take risks and have slower responses', then we have taken experience (our own, national statistics, medical facts) and put it into concepts ('drunk driver', 'risk') with relations between them – a theory. This language of generalisation makes it possible to reason more explicitly about the subject of theory, as well as communicate general observations. Theory is not just the language of generalisation; it is the language of technical culture.

The main difference between work-a-day theories (like the above) and academic theories is that in the latter we take an additional step of identifying and naming the collection of concepts and relations that make the theory. When the theory is given a named identity it can then become the subject of more explicit critique and analysis. It is discussable, refutable and sometimes even provable.

Theory and analogy interweave. We often derive our theories after previous more analogical thinking, so analogy helps abstraction. But also theory helps analogy: if we have ideas of abstract concepts and properties, we can use these to explicitly retrieve previous examples ('I recall a case of a drunk driver last year ...')

and then use the retrieved examples to draw conclusions that perhaps the theory does not (yet) support. Furthermore, having seen a past example that is similar to a new one, we need to adapt the past case, and to do that, we need to understand sufficiently the implications of the differences – which is precisely what theoretical understanding helps us to do.

The power of abstraction is not just about communication, but also that it gives us the means to reason about things. As we shall see later this has enormous practical benefits in HCI research and practice.

9.2.2 What is theory?

Theory is a hard word to define. As noted, in common language a 'theory' is a hunch or bright idea. But scientific theories are very different. The *Oxford English Dictionary* has a number of definitions of different uses of the term (including the common use one!), but the one most pertinent to scientific theory is:

> A scheme or system of ideas or statements held as an explanation or account of a group of facts or phenomena; a hypothesis that has been confirmed or established by observations or experiment, and is propounded or accepted as accounting for the known facts; a statement of what are held to be the general laws, principles, or causes of something known or observed.   (*OED*, 1973)

If we were describing a theory in the social sciences rather than the natural sciences, we might use slightly different words, but the essentials are the same:

- **Structure:** A theory is not just an isolated set of statements, laws or facts, but has some level of structure or interrelation.
- **Explanation:** Because of this, theories can be used to give an explanation of how or why things are true, not just what is true.
- **Abstraction:** Theories account for more than single observations, offering more general or abstract accounts.
- **Verity:** However, theory is not divorced from particulars; it is usually based on experience or observation (induction) and can be used to explain or predict future observations.

The last of these is the critical difference from the common use of the word. While theories differ in the extent to which they have been justified or verified, they must all have some relation to reality, not mere hunches. However, theories may be wrong. For example, I might have a theory that gravity is caused by the pressure of air holding you down and that as you go higher up the air pressure reduces and hence so does gravity. This happens to be a false explanation of gravity, but is not without some justification from experience (air pressure is indeed powerful, although caused by gravity rather than the other way round). Critically, the theory has enough explanatory power to make predictions: for example, if we make a vacuum where there is zero air pressure, then things will be weightless in it. Because we can make predictions we can then test this theory, and in this case find it was wrong.

Karl Popper, a philosopher of science, regarded this ability to test scientific theory, falsification, as being a key element that distinguishes true science (Popper, 1959). By this criterion, if it is inconceivable that a theory could be disproved, then it is not a scientific theory. While this captures some aspects of science, in fact science often works by holding on to theories and modifying them rather than discarding them 'just' because the evidence does not fit. This is partly a human tendency towards conservatism and partly a sensible use of the intellectual investment of a community.

Theories may be built upon other theories or laws; for example, the Model Human Processor (MHP; Card *et al.*, 1983) is a theoretical model of human information processing built upon older psychological theories and results. I might then construct a theoretical account of text entry on mobile devices based on MHP and other knowledge of mobile use as described in the example of Chapters 1 and 6.

9.2.3 Things like theories

Theories differ from *laws*, which are also abstractions over observed phenomena, but which do not offer systematic explanations for the phenomena. For example, Boyle's Law says that if you double the pressure on a gas and maintain the temperature it halves in volume, but does not say *why* this is true. Similarly Fitts' Law says that the time to hit a target varies logarithmically with the distance to the target, but again, as a formula, does not say why this is true.

Theories do relate to laws. Theories may explain laws: for example a molecular theory of gases where the gas molecules cause pressure by bouncing off the walls of a container can be used to explain and derive Boyle's Law. Similarly, you can offer theories of Fitts' Law in terms of information theory (as in Fitts' original paper (Fitts, 1954)) or in terms of the feedback loop between perception and action (Keele, 1968; Meyer *et al.*, 1988). Theories may also build on laws: for example, we may use a combination of Boyle's Law and observed data on the calorific value of coal to develop a theory of steam engines. Similarly, we may use Fitts' Law as part of a theory of pen-based mobile interaction.

Theories also differ from paradigms, which are more 'worldviews', ways of looking at things. Theories are framed within a paradigm, as it is the paradigm that gives the theory a way of looking at phenomena, and so for someone outside that paradigm a theory may be hard to comprehend (imagine explaining quantum mechanics in the fourteenth century). There may be many theories operating within a single paradigm, and theories may develop and change while still operating within the same paradigm. We have already noted that real science tends to modify rather than discard theories, but sometimes as an area develops it gets harder and harder to 'fix' the theories until eventually a whole new way of thinking about things is required. Thomas Kuhn, another philosopher of science, identified this phenomenon; he describes these times of critical change as 'scientific revolutions' with associated 'paradigm shifts' in the way people think (Kuhn, 1962/1970).

Perhaps the best-known example of paradigm shift is the change from a Newtonian worldview in the early years of the twentieth century. Until this point, the very small and very large are seen as operating very much like the 'normal' world we experience (a form of reasoning by analogy). However, experiments were increasingly at variance with the associated theoretical models (problems of verity) until the point at which the Newtonian worldview was challenged and superseded by Einstein's general relativity (for the large) and quantum mechanics (for the small).

In HCI, a similar (although less dramatic) shift happened in the late 1980s when the more cognitively based theories of early HCI were challenged by more situated accounts in Winograd and Flores' *Understanding Cognition* (1985) and Suchman's *Plans and Situated Actions* (1987). Because theories in HCI are by their nature partial and approximate, the disparity with the 'facts' of observation is less clear and so, rather than replacing an 'older' view, this is more an additional way of looking at things. Naively, one might imagine that when the 'truth' of theories and paradigms is partial, or not easily verified against the world, academics would tend to use them more pragmatically. However, the opposite tends to be the case and in HCI (as in the social sciences) one tends to get partisan adherents of one viewpoint or other!

Finally, another related idea is that of a model. Minsky (1965) defined a model using the following: 'To an observer B, an object A* is a model of an object A to the extent that B can use A* to answer questions that interest him about A.' This definition is remarkably similar to attempts to define metaphor or analogy, and indeed, writing from a social science perspective, Hawes (1975) defines a model precisely as an analogue. Models are similar to theories and operate at a similar 'level'; however, whilst models, like laws, are mainly about telling you what is true, theories are more about why things are the way they are; or as Hawes puts it, 'the former [theory] is an explanation whereas the latter [model] is a representation'. A model is often an embodiment of a theory. For example, the explanation of Boyle's law in terms of a molecular theory involves a model of molecules hitting the walls. The theory is the combination of the idea of having macroscopic phenomena explicable through microscopic causes, the use of Newton's laws for the individual molecular collisions, and rules about the relationship between temperature and velocity of molecules. This theory is then embodied in a mathematical model, which can be used to derive the laws.

The boundaries between these terms and others such as 'frameworks' is somewhat fluid, and it is not uncommon to find referees of papers arguing that what an author has called a model is actually a framework, or an architecture, or something else. Whilst it is important to be careful in your terminology, it is more important to know whether you have understanding that is sufficiently deep to be able to explain the phenomena you see and perhaps predict what will happen in new, unseen and potentially radically different situations.

9.2.4 Types of theory

There are many types of theory, from the mathematical equations of general relativity to theories of social relationships.

One important distinction is in the generative power of the theory:

- **Descriptive** theory, given a cause and its effect, tells you why it happened. This kind of theory is applied after you have observed a phenomenon and allows you to explain and make sense of what you have observed. The danger of purely descriptive knowledge is that it can often be 'twisted' to explain any results (failing Popper's falsification test), so you have to be very careful in formulating and applying it so as to avoid this.
- **Predictive** theory, given a cause, tells you what effect will follow. This kind of theory can be applied before you have seen the effect of an action. It is the point at which most sciences stop. With a predictive theory of some aspect of user interaction, you are able to look at a design and say 'ah yes, this will/is likely to happen'. Evaluation techniques such as cognitive walkthrough or heuristic evaluation, whilst lacking the structure of a theory, do have this form of predictive power.
- **Synthetic** theory, given a desired effect, tells you what to do to cause it. This last form of theory is most useful in design and engineering ... but least common. Like predictive theories, it can be applied before you have observed a phenomenon. However, in addition it can be used backwards to ask, 'I want this to happen, what should I do to make it happen?' In user interface terms this may be 'I would like users to enjoy/be efficient with this interface, what should I design to achieve this?' It is in this highest form of knowledge that the power and importance of theoretical understanding is most clear.

Where the space of potential causes/actions/designs is small it is often possible to move from description to prediction and from prediction to synthesis through 'what if' thinking. However, once the complexity of the design space becomes large this is impossible.

We can also characterise theories by the kinds of knowledge they provide along a number of dimensions / categories:

- **Qualitative vs. quantitative:** Some theories deal with precise numbers (time, error rate) or clear countable categories (male/female), others with more qualitative concepts such as happiness.
- **Precision:** Actually there are a number of different criteria that lie under this heading. Are the predictions/explanations precise or approximate, deterministic or probabilistic? In a more qualitative theory does the theory say 'sometimes' or 'always'? Theories do not need to be precise to be useful: when buying a car it is useful to know that a Porsche is more likely to win a race than a Lada, even though, occasionally, through breakdowns or better driving, the Lada may win.
- **Aggregate or individual:** We may be able to say things that are true of each user, 'interface A is always faster to use than interface B', but some theories

may only tell us about aggregate or average properties: 'most users will find interface A faster than interface B'. Even for a single user, some things may hold true for every interaction, whilst others only apply to averages. For example, a user may generally prefer one device to another, but under certain (uncommon) lighting conditions the opposite may be the case.
- **Scope:** Is the theory universal, applying to everything, or are there limits?

While scientific theories are often associated with predictive, quantitative, deterministic, universal knowledge, in fact many combinations are possible:

- *The probability of a die falling on 3 is exactly 1 in 6* – universal, predictive, quantitative, probabilistic knowledge
- *There is no smoke without fire* – universal, predictive, qualitative, deterministic
- *Small targets on average take longer to select, so to speed up data entry use larger buttons* – aggregate, synthetic, quantitative data (size and time measurable), but not precise (just longer not how much longer)

These are often linked. In particular, it is common in HCI to have qualitative theoretical explanations of quantitative measurements.

9.3   The method

Theories are so varied it is hard to talk about a single 'method'. We will look at three facets: the relation between theory and empirical methods, methods for deriving theories, and finally the relation between abstracted theoretical understanding and specific situations. This is not exhaustive, but gives a start point for applying and delivering theory.

9.3.1 Theory and empiricism

In the physical sciences measurements are taken so that they are as 'pure' as possible in order to reduce the possible causes of an observation to the single phenomenon being studied. Psychological experimentation emulates this, although the complexity of the human subject makes assigning single causes more difficult, but given this constraint the aim is again to minimise the possible causes. In HCI, we may wish to experiment in near-real settings as we know that the effects seen in the laboratory are often very different from those in the field. Even when we experiment in a laboratory we will still use realistic tasks and user interfaces. This leaves us with multiple causes: the task chosen, the context of the experiment, the fine details of the prototype interface, the chosen user group, etc. and amongst all this the actual effect we wish to study. These problems are discussed in more detail in Chapter 1.

Theoretical understanding can help to unravel this knot of potential effects. Most important is understanding *mechanism* – the details of what goes on, whether in terms of user actions, perception, cognition or social interactions.

Theory can help in the design, analysis and application of experiments and empirical data gathering:

- **Design of empirical studies:** If we understand the details of how we expect a user to interact we can predict what tasks will amplify the desired effects and minimise the 'noise'. For example, as soon as people need to think in a task, the variability between people (and between runs with the same person) increases dramatically, which in turn makes it difficult to run experiments that yield statistically significant results. However, careful choice of tasks and measures can increase the likelihood that effects can be measured. In qualitative experiments also, understanding what is likely to happen enables you to choose appropriate measurement techniques (video, keystroke logging) and tasks that again make it easier to see effects.

- **Analysis of empirical data:** Experiments are often reported in terms of end-to-end measures such as overall error rates, or task completion times. Because there are often interaction effects[1] between the many phenomena affecting the data, these end-to-end measures are often as much about the particular choice of task or system as the target phenomenon. If you understand the details of the mechanism, the steps and phases of the interaction, you can choose finer measurements and use these.

- **Application of empirical data:** From experimental data alone, it is possible to interpolate between measured values. If a user takes 30 seconds to do two tasks and 50 seconds to do four tasks, it is reasonable to expect three tasks to take about 40 seconds. Even here you need to know that there are not likely to be any odd intermediate effects. However, to extrapolate is far more dangerous: no tasks would probably take no time, not 10 seconds! There are often limits to effects where things get much harder or easier. However, with some theoretical understanding of the underlying mechanism, we can know whether to expect such limits, and whether extrapolation beyond the bounds of our empirical data is likely to be sound.

- **Recontextualisation of empirical data:** As well as extrapolation beyond the quantitative limits of our data, we typically want to extrapolate from a study performed on a particular interface with particular tasks, to similar interfaces and similar tasks. Again it is the theoretical understanding of why we see the effects that we see that enables us to make this generalisation.

---

[1] Here this means interaction effects in the statistical sense (see Chapter 6). An interaction effect is where two conditions cannot be treated entirely independently. For example, in a study we might find that women are wiser than men and that people get wiser as they grow older – independent effects. Together these might go some way towards describing the data; however, it may be that even when we take both these effects into account women get wiser more rapidly than men – this would be an interaction effect.

- **Synthesis of empirical data:** In practical design situations we typically know bits of psychological knowledge, data or models of the system behaviour, perhaps previous experimental evidence related to parts or aspects of the system we envisage. If you have some idea of how things work it is easier to bring these together.

To see several of these aspects at play, consider a recent experiment where we varied delays during web page navigation. In addition to end-to-end timing measures, we also measured the average time users took making decisions at intermediate 'menu' pages (time from page presentation to menu selection). This decision time increased markedly when the website was slower, showing that people adjust their behaviour. The end-to-end timings were much less clear, as they were influenced by effects such as the number of pages that the user visited.

The choice of the decision time as a measure was not arbitrary. A previous experiment had observed improved learning of menus when delays were longer. Constructive learning theory suggests that the more you 'work' on information, the more integrated it becomes into your personal knowledge structures and hence you get better learning. We hypothesised (based on cognitive ideas of effort minimisation) that users would think more carefully about decisions for the slower interface. This is because the 'cost' of failure (waiting for the page and then hitting 'back') would be greater when the delay was longer, therefore the menu of the slower interface would be more thoroughly processed and hence more effectively learnt.

So, here we see theoretical understanding being used to synthesise existing theoretical and empirical results in order to analyse the results of the first experiment, and this then being used in the planning of a further experiment and the effective choice and interpretation of measures.

9.3.2 Developing theory

Theory construction is a creative process, so there are no simple handle-turning rules to create a theory. However, there are a number of techniques that can help you.

Abstraction and organising: Those tables and taxonomies that appear in so many papers are not just ways of laying out information to make it more readable. In addition, they create terms, concepts and categories that form the basic vocabulary of many theoretical descriptions. These taxonomies, dimensions, etc., may be drawn from professional experience, existing theoretical knowledge, or different forms of primary data. The concepts on their own usually generalise over many instances, and if the concepts are gathered into some form of classification or taxonomy, then they provide the means for further generalisation. However, while taxonomies are useful for giving an overview, the greatest analytic power comes when there are multiple simultaneous classification schemes (dimensions,

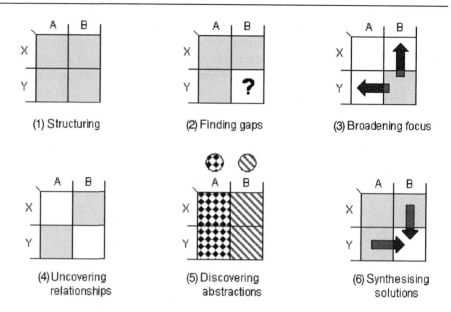

Fig 9.1 *Uses of multiple classification (from Dix, 2002)*

simple categories or taxonomies). With multiple classifications, you can tabulate one against the other and look at how examples (transcript utterances, previous systems, experimental data) fit into the table. Where there are gaps this may signify impossible situations, or potential for novel solutions. Where there are patterns this may suggest systematic relationships (see Figure 9.1).

Exploring definitions and boundaries: Academics also love precise definitions and they are of course important to help make sure we share a common vocabulary. Definitions also enable one to draw precise bounds on concepts, but in a human-centred discipline like HCI, these hard-edged categories often stand at odds with the more nuanced realities of situations. This can be seen as a 'problem': either requiring more rigorous and careful definition, or as an argument for rejecting the process of definition per se. However, it can instead be seen as an opportunity. The boundaries at the edge and between categories are often the most fruitful areas for learning about them. Look at the terms, dimensions and properties you have used to formulate the definition. The definition itself is not the real value – this vocabulary is. By attempting to articulate the criteria that delineate the edges of the category you have learnt about the properties that characterise and explicate its heart! The power lies not in definition (which will be wrong!), but in the activity of definition.

Critical transitions: This is a particular form of boundary exploration that can be used to explore categories that you can recognise when you see them, but find hard to define more precisely, for example, fun. You choose one example that is in the category (e.g. playing party games) and one that is not (sitting an exam) and then produce a series of intermediate examples between the two (sitting an exam

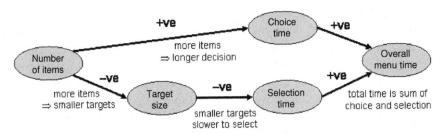

Fig 9.2 *Network of influences of number of items shown on screen*

in a party hat, playing Trivial Pursuit). As you trace the trajectory there comes a point when you start to say that the examples cross the boundary (between fun and non-fun) – the critical transition – and then you can ask yourself 'what happened?', and so uncover critical criteria, dimensions or properties of the core category.

Child-like questions: Listen to a small child and they constantly ask 'why? why? why?'; this is the intellectual equivalent of the baby playing with its hands. Each question probes and builds richer models of the world. And the child is never satisfied with the first answer, always probing deeper. Why is it dark at night? Because the sun goes down. Why does the sun go down? Because the earth turns round. Why does the earth turn round? We can emulate this and, like the child, not be satisfied with first answers. Why is this interface better? Because it is consistent. Why does being consistent make it better? Because ... you answer that one! Children also ask 'what if?' What if we were on Mars, would it be dark at night? What if the earth didn't turn round? Again we can ask similar questions. What if we used this for a different purpose? What if the user gets interrupted? Rather like exploring boundaries, it is not so much the answers that are important as the understanding we gain in the process. In particular, this form of thinking often helps in establishing causal and other relationships between core concepts.

Formal representations: Some theoretical understanding can be embodied in some form of formal or mathematical model as described in Chapters 4 and 5. For example, if we are looking at selection from menus, we may model this as a sequence of actions of the form (1) visually scan menu for right item, (2) select option with mouse, (3) wait for screen to refresh, (4) repeat for next menu level. Given this model, stage (1) will be linear in the number of menu items, stage (2) is a Fitts' Law task and (3) is measurable for a given system. So we can build a model of how long selection will take from a particular menu hierarchy, and hence give ourselves a way of comparing different choices. Even qualitative theories may benefit from a more structured representation. For example, rather than a precise set of equations we can follow a diagram such as Figure 9.2 to see that increasing the number of items on screen will increase the time taken to make a selection.

Recoding dialectic: It is often hard to verify qualitative theories, especially to know if they are complete – have you entirely missed some important issue? Even when theories are built inductively from large data corpora, it is hard to know whether you have imposed some blinkers or pre-existing ideas that meant you missed things out. Recoding dialectic is a way to help give yourself confidence in the completeness of a qualitative theory, and to help you fill in the gaps you discover. All you do is go back to the primary data, whatever it is, perhaps utterances in a transcript, or results of a literature review, and, for each item, describe it using the vocabulary of the theory. Imagine a user has said 'I hate this system because it keeps logging me out.' You might encode this as 'timing problem in authentication procedures'. Sometimes you find that you cannot describe the utterance using the vocabulary. This might be because the utterance is irrelevant, but if not it suggests a gap in the theory. If you are able to describe an item using the vocabulary, you then say to yourself, 'this just says . . . ' – and feel the tension the word 'just' gives you. Is that really all the statement says? If the description using the terms in the vocabulary feels inadequate, try to describe why it is inadequate and in that description you often find the seeds of new concepts or relationships that belong in the theory.

As noted, these techniques are not a guaranteed way of building theories, but they are heuristics that can help. Look also at papers and books that describe new theories, or theoretical concepts; often these are presented as a *fait accompli*, but sometimes they also describe the process by which the insight was found.

9.3.3 Theory and the particular

We discussed earlier the paradigm shift in HCI in the later part of the 1980s with a move from more mechanistic models of human cognition to more situated and contextual models. For many this has led to a distrust in generalities and theoretical descriptions – each situation is different and special; any form of generalisation will miss important details.

Certain forms of ethnography (in particular the ethnomethodological school (Heritage, 1984), which has been so influential in HCI) can be particularly antagonistic to theory, largely in reaction to the perception that social science theories are often foisted onto the real world rather than expressing it. However, this stance is perhaps a little disingenuous, as there are clear theoretical stances underlying ethnomethodologically informed ethnography, in particular the focus on social accountability. In addition, the rich accounts and vignettes, while expressing particulars, are clearly also chosen to highlight behaviours and issues that one expects to see repeated elsewhere (generalisation through analogy).

Three strengths of ethnographic approaches are:

- **They start with real data:** While no human observation is without preconception, the aim is to be as open as possible to what is observed.

- **Limited generalisation:** While ethnographers bring with them past experience of similar contexts and situations, they expect any similarities to be limited and partial.
- **Reflexive practice:** Good ethnographers are aware that they do bring preconceptions and that they do influence the situation and so explicitly take this into account in their analysis.

Whilst eschewing theoretical approaches entirely seems an unproductive overreaction to its dangers, certainly these strengths are ones that are worth bearing in mind in more theoretical approaches. In particular, it is easy to forget the limited nature of more formalised theories.

One technique from the social sciences that is gaining support in HCI is grounded theory (Glaser and Strauss, 1967). Like ethnographic techniques it is focused on taking a very open approach to raw observation and experience, but uses this in order to construct theoretical descriptions from the particulars of the observations. See Chapter 7 for a lot more about this method in HCI. Its techniques are very much those of abstraction and organising described in the last section. In its purest form, it starts using open coding of the raw data: writing whatever terms make sense to describe each utterance or data item. These terms are then gathered, sorted, organised into taxonomies and relationships until a more abstracted theoretical account is created. While the standard methods for this do not include a specific validation step, recoding dialectic is directly applicable.

As well as building more general theories from observations, you may simply need sufficient theoretical understanding for the problem at hand – a *situated theory*. This is not an attempt to build a new theoretical framework that will generalise to different situations, but instead a building of theory (usually from existing pieces) that is just for what you are doing now. It may then turn out that this theoretical account generalises, but that is not its primary purpose.

Some while ago I was talking with a cleaner in our office block and we were discussing the problem of the paper getting unravelled in the toilet roll holders. The holder contains two toilet rolls, one above the other, so that as the paper is pulled from the lower roll, the upper one turns with it. We realised that a toilet roll unrolls if turned in one direction, and is held tight if turned in the other. If the toilet rolls are inserted in the same direction then the upper one will unroll with the lower one and get clogged up with loose paper; however, if they are in opposite directions then the upper one will be held tight as the lower one is pulled out. We had created a situated theory of toilet roll unravelling. In fact the theory was not ungeneralisable and the cleaner drew an analogy with the nuts on bicycle wheels, which are designed to tighten rather than loosen as the wheel turns, but this generalisation was not essential to solve the problem at hand.

Perhaps the hardest aspect of performing theoretical analysis is to hold *both* the abstract and the particular in mind at once. It is easier to either look only at the particular, or only at the abstract, but the greatest gains are usually from keeping both in mind. Even in school geometry you always draw a diagram – a particular example – and this helps you to think about the abstract proof.

9.4   Applying the method

Much of this discussion has been quite abstract, but now we will look at a few examples of how theory can be applied in the practice of research and design. We will look at three different kinds of application:

- Applying theory to the design of a new product
- Applying theory to understand design methods
- Applying theoretical thinking during analysis in order to develop new theories

These do not cover all the possible ways in which theory is used, but will give some indication of how theory can be used in practice.

9.4.1 Applying theory to design

From 1998–2000 I was involved in a dot-com company, aQtive, and our main product was an 'intelligent' internet desktop agent called onCue. The underlying software architecture was heavily influenced by status–event analysis, which we will discuss later in this section. However, for now we will focus on the user interface itself.

onCue usually sat as a small toolbar on the side of the screen, and whenever the user copied any text to the clipboard, onCue examined the text and then changed the toolbar to reflect the contents. If the text was a postcode, onCue might suggest an online mapping service; if it was a table of numbers, onCue might suggest adding them up or making a graph.

Of course the intelligent recognition algorithms behind onCue were not perfect, and we knew there was a history of failures in intelligent interfaces. In trying to make sense of how to design onCue we created a situated theory. In broad terms we realised that the important thing was to define the interaction around onCue so that when the recognition was wrong (which inevitably it would sometimes be), the interface would not be annoying. This we later formulated into the three rules of appropriate intelligence (Dix *et al.*, 2000), the generalisation of our situated theory, listed below. The first two are what you normally expect of an intelligent system, and look good in demos, but it is the last that makes a system work in practice.

1 Be right as often as possible
2 Do something useful when you are right
3 When things go wrong, don't mess up the user

As well as being 'intelligent', onCue was also proactive, and might make suggestions even when the user did not want them, so rule (3) was especially important. We needed to design onCue to be always readily available, but not to interrupt or distract the user – no bouncing Clippy from Microsoft Office.

First we made it non-modal (already a user-interface theoretic term) and small enough that it could be 'always on top', but not in the way; the user could choose to shrink it to a single small icon. When the user cut or copied to the clipboard, the contents of the onCue toolbar changed. Even though onCue was not modal, still there was the possibility of visual distraction. However, we knew that the fovea is very narrow and so the toolbar at the edge of the screen would be in peripheral vision. We also knew that in peripheral vision rods predominate and these are most sensitive to rapid movement and change. So instead of simply switching the icons in the onCue toolbar as the clipboard changed we slowly faded out the old icons and then faded in the new ones over a period of about one second. While this was fast enough for there to be no real delay for the user, it was slow enough that it did not register as a change in peripheral vision and so was not distracting.

Note how we made use of theoretical understanding of the human visual system as well as the situated theory of appropriate intelligence in order to make an effective design.

9.4.2 Applying theory to method

Personae and scenarios are heavily used in HCI practice. However, these vary substantially in detail. Some people create personae that are not very different from a user profile, 'Mary is a 30-year-old office worker with two children and a dog', while others create rich descriptions like a character in a novel. Similarly, scenarios vary from a bare list to something more like a short story. What is the right level? Is there any value to the irrelevant details that litter the richer descriptions?

Although the details are debated, it is generally accepted that in addition to logical/rational thinking, we also have different kinds of specialised knowledge at work, so-called 'multiple intelligences' (Gardner, 1983). For example, for interpersonal relations, we recognise the social intelligence that enables us to know what to do, or related emotional intelligence that gives us insights into what others feel; in contrast, when doing more physical things, we have an understanding of our own bodies and also of natural objects. These 'intelligences' work together in day-to-day life and in particular may allow us to make intuitive or subconscious judgements as well as engage in more explicit reasoning.

When we deal with very sparse propositional descriptions of the world, only the explicit encodings of these specialised forms of knowledge are available: 'person meets friend implies person smiles'. Yet we respond in real life more naturally and immediately than this. However, if we create a rich imaginary picture of a scene – imagine yourself meeting a long-lost friend – then these intelligences naturally swing into action. When you read a novel you may think 'Daniel wouldn't say that'; you 'know' the character and so know what he is or is not likely to do. If a person is acting 'out of character' in a novel, either (like real life) something is wrong with the person, or the author is not very good.

It is precisely the irrelevant details in a rich persona that allow us to 'get to know' the person and therefore be able to respond to the character in a scenario and say 'Mary would press that button now' or 'Mary wouldn't understand that.' Similarly the images elicited by a rich scenario allow your physical and spatial intelligence to kick in: 'he couldn't do that; it is too far across the room'.

See how theories of multiple intelligence allow us to understand *why* rich personae and scenarios work, and thus why it is important to retain 'irrelevant' details. Furthermore, because of this understanding we can consider other ways of recruiting a designer's multiple intelligences; for example, I suggest that students physically act out scenarios.

9.4.3 Applying theory during analysis (making theory)

Some years ago I was involved in formal modelling of user interfaces. Models of keystrokes, like KLM-GOMS described in Chapter 4, worked quite well: each key caused a change of state of the system and a resulting change in the display. However, things were not so good when it came to the mouse. Although you could model the mouse, a series of tiny movements each making a small change to the mouse pointer on screen, it did not 'feel' right; when you move a mouse it does not feel like a lot of tiny movements, but one continuous gesture.

This insight led to status–event analysis, the recognition that some phenomena, such as the screen contents and the mouse position, always have a 'value' – they are status, whereas others, like the key-presses, or beeps from the computer, happen at a particular moment – they are events. This is actually very obvious, and yet different from the event-dominated descriptions that are common across computing. This insight was first used in the formal modelling of mouse-based systems and later became a generic way of looking at a wide variety of phenomena.

One of the powerful things about status–event analysis is that it applies at many levels, from the internal electronics of the keyboard to social interactions. Actually, you should be cautious when you hear a claim like this; theories of everything usually turn out to be theories of nothing. However, this time it really did work (honest!). Using status–event analysis, not only can one examine phenomena at these very different levels, but often one can see similar behaviours at the different levels and with both electronic and human actors. For example, imagine you have to catch a train. You keep an eye on the time so that you leave on time, but you do not continuously look at the clock, every so often you look to see if it is the critical time. This is a polling behaviour, and the same technique is used in network applications to look for changes in remote databases, and by a keyboard controller when it looks to see if one of the keys is pressed.

Notice how a formal modelling of the interface led to a situated theory to deal with a particular problem. The problem came to light because the more abstract formal representation was considered alongside the 'gut' reaction to the real situation. When the disparity was noted it did not lead to an abandonment of the formal theory, but instead to an attempt to understand the nature of the discrepancy (boundaries and edges). This in turn led to both an improved formal model and also the formulation of a general qualitative theoretical position.

9.5   Critique

9.5.1 Focus or blinkers

We have already discussed one of the main criticisms of theoretical approaches, raised particularly by the ethnographers: by abstracting, theoretical views act as blinkers, meaning we only see the things that fit the theories and miss the rich details of each particular situation.

To some extent the examples in the last section show that it is possible to hold on to both the particular and the abstract and gain insight by doing so. Nonetheless, thinking only of the abstract and not the particular is a real danger. Many people do tend to separate the two. Academic disciplines in general and computing in particular tend to suggest that more abstracted thinking is good thinking. Of course this is true academically, as we need to abstract in order to generalise, but in addition we need to keep those abstractions continuously grounded.

If you do not naturally keep both in mind at once then you need to explicitly alternate between the two, sometimes reflecting on particulars and attempting to see the more abstract picture, and sometimes looking from your abstractions and seeking concrete examples (although this can be hard, see Dix (2007)). In particular, you need to be constantly on guard against trying to fit the world to your preconceptions, and instead actively look for discrepancies, not as 'faults' in your theories, but as opportunities to learn more.

9.5.2 Is it practical?

Theoretical is often seen as the opposite of practical. Again, the examples in the previous section show that this need not be the case. There is the old saying that 'those who can do, and those who can't teach'. Most academics, being teachers, would want to disagree with this, and in fact the knowledge required to teach something is often not the same as the knowledge or skills needed to do it. If we take a similar view of professionals and academics we could say:

professionals – do things
academics   – know about doing things

The theoretical reflection embodied in academic practice can be an ivory tower discussion, but can also lead back into practice. Consider an Olympic runner and her trainer. The trainer may not be able to run himself, but he understands nutrition and muscle groups, and has spent hours watching slow-motion footage of the runner. The trainer's theoretical knowledge *about* running helps the runner to run. Of course if the runner tried to think like a trainer while she was running she would probably fall over, but as part of reflective practice (how did that run go?) and when things go wrong (why did I hit that first hurdle?) more theoretical thinking comes into its own.

The onCue example shows this well. It is not necessary to think about the details of visual perception every time you choose an icon, but to solve a particular, difficult problem it can be very powerful to go back to basics. For more common decisions simple experience, standards or guidelines can help, but it is when you hit the unusual or apparently intractable that you need heavier intellectual armoury.

In HCI the most common development paradigm is an iterative cycle of prototyping and evaluation. However, iteration runs the danger of getting stuck in 'local minima' designs, which cannot be improved through small changes, and yet are not the best. This is particularly problematic when there are several facets that interact – for example, in onCue the slow change only works in combination with the positioning in peripheral vision and non-modal character. Theoretical understanding allows the designer to move from the 'ant steps' of iterative design to 'flea hops' – radically changing the design based on deep understanding of what doesn't work and why (and therefore how to change it) and what does work and why (and therefore what should be retained).

9.5.3 Validating theory

Because theories are very abstract they can be difficult to validate. And if you don't know whether a theory is right, how can you trust it?

Whilst it is possible to validate theories, it is first worth noting that theories are rarely completely 'true'; they are views of the world and may be more or less complete, accurate and faithful and then only to some facet of some portion of reality. Nonetheless, they are useful. When you fly a plane the engineers will have used the theory of Newtonian dynamics that was proved 'wrong' at the beginning of the twentieth century, and yet, despite being known to be 'wrong' for 100 years, it is still useful, because it is *right enough* for the speeds and sizes of normal life. So when we apply theories, whether in research or practice, we always need to be aware not only of their fallibility and limitations, but also of their value.

We have already seen one theory validation technique, recoding dialectic. This was especially focused on the completeness of qualitative descriptions. When looking at a theory we can ask about:

> **Correctness** – does it accurately represent what it purports to?
> **Completeness** – does it cover all the relevant phenomena and issues?

It is typically the second that is hardest, since it is difficult to know what you don't know – as Rumsfeld put it, the 'unknown unknowns'.[2] This can be addressed both from the particular and from the abstract.

From the particular, one can test the theory against as many specific situations and examples as possible, looking for adequacy of explanation. It is best if these examples are generated from external sources, as of course you tend to think of those that are already covered by your own theories. For example, some years ago I was looking at the coping strategies people use when communicating over channels with delays that are badly matched to the nature of their collaboration. I outlined a number of strategies and then looked through the literature at snippets of computer-mediated communication reported by other authors. In each case I found examples of the coping strategies I had outlined, and did not find examples of other kinds of behaviour. This therefore increased my confidence in the completeness/coverage of the strategies.

Recoding dialectic, as discussed earlier, is a more systematic approach to checking the completeness of a theory against a known corpus. If, as is the case with grounded theory, the corpus is the source for the theoretical constructs, then this is more of an internal check and should be supplemented by new cases. One technique used in quantitative methods (machine learning and statistical) is to deliberately hold back a portion of the data. You then analyse the rest to create a mathematical model, and test the effectiveness of the model on the 'unseen' cases. This can be applied equally well to experimental results, or even qualitative methods of analysis.

We'll turn now to correctness, which is perhaps easier than completeness, but nonetheless problematic.

In HCI it has almost become a joke that you cannot submit a paper without an 'evaluation' and that as long as referees can tick their mental 'evaluation' box the actual effectiveness of the evaluation is irrelevant. Now there is some truth in this as well as it being a caricature, and of course good referees look at papers on their own merits, not through preconceived templates. However, the truth behind the myth will continue unless as a discipline we understand what constitutes effective evaluation and, more importantly, validation of results.

The trouble is that many of the things we produce in HCI, including theories, are *generative artefacts*: things that are used (by people) to create other things. Theories are used to explain, to analyse, to design, to generate models, principles and even new theories. The success (truth, value, adequacy) of the theory is

---

[2] Donald Rumsfeld was awarded the Plain English Campaign's 'Foot in Mouth' award (Plain English Campaign, 2003) for his remark '...know, there are known knowns; there are things we know we know. We also know there are known unknowns; that is to say we know there are some things we do not know. But there are also unknown unknowns – the ones we don't know we don't know.' Although when spoken out loud it did sound rather enigmatic, and I do hate to defend Rumsfeld, I have never understood the hoo-hah about this. It is an important point and as clearly stated as I can imagine without far more words.

largely based on the effectiveness of the things it produces. Do the explanations it yields make sense? Do the things designed using it work? This is true of other things in HCI: guidelines, design principles, patterns, toolkits, algorithms and architectures. Even a particular system is generative in that the real thing of importance is the particular instance of its use.

For user interfaces, we get round this effectively by sampling: user testing with sufficient users, ideally (although actually rarely) over sufficient tasks, in sufficiently varied situations. Unless you test every user, doing every task, in every specific situation (occurrences which by definition are unique) you cannot prove that the interface is effective, but with sufficient users you can make reasonable conclusions (and of course to know what constitutes 'reasonable' you take recourse to implicit or explicit theories!).

Where the artefacts that we are evaluating are further abstracted (e.g. theories, guidelines, toolkits), life becomes far harder. They are used by particular designers or interface engineers in particular circumstances to produce specific user interfaces. We can test the interfaces produced, but how can we know whether it is the theory (design principle, architecture, etc.) that was the cause, or whether it was the skill (or otherwise) of the designer? We would need to experiment with many designers being given many briefs (since briefs may be biased to particular techniques). The closest you see is when a class of students are used as surrogate designers and asked to use multiple techniques, although they are usually given a single brief and often know that one of the techniques is the 'pet' one of the experimenter.

In a recent paper about evaluation in visualisation research (Ellis and Dix, 2006), we characterised this problem as: 'the evaluation of generative artefacts is methodologically unsound'. It is not just hard, but impossible and arguably *wrong*, as without great care in expressing your results such evaluations run the risk of appearing to produce general results that are in fact particular to the design situation tested. Happily all is not lost; while it is unsound to believe you can empirically evaluate generative artefacts, you can validate them and empirical evaluation can play a part in it!

Disciplines differ in the ways in which they validate their results; some focus on empirical testing, but not all – catch pure mathematicians doing statistics on a theorem – no, they *prove* them. You know the theorem is true, not because you try it out on lots of examples, but because the steps of the proof that led to it are its justification.

Because it is hard to validate generative artefacts, the justification becomes more important – why you thought the theory was a good idea in the first place. In mathematics the steps of the proof from axiom to theorem are indefeasible; if the proof is correct each step is entirely justified from its precursors. In most areas, and in particular HCI, this is not the case: our justification is sometimes from shaky premises (do we really believe the results of that experiment five years ago, which is poorly described?), or involves questionable deductions (can we really generalise from desktop use to mobile phones?).

While our justification will not have the decisive nature of a mathematical proof, we can make explicit and record the audit trail: the track of the argument from the assumptions we have worked on to the theory we have derived. The base points of this argument may be of many different kinds: previously published work by others, accepted practice, our own empirical data, or plain common sense (sadly undervalued!); and the 'reasoning' steps may range from formal deductions to a more vague feeling that something applies.

By knowing the strengths of different parts of the justification argument, we can know which aspects of our theoretical framework are strongly justified and which more problematic. Then empirical evaluation can be tuned towards the less well-established aspects. In fact it is common to see the opposite, empirical work tuned towards the most established parts of a theory (or other generative artefact). This is perhaps good for writing papers (as we can formulate very strong hypotheses that are likely to be upheld), but it teaches us little (because the outcome is nearly certain). When empirical evaluation addresses the weak points of the justification, then the two work together to build our confidence.

9.6   Related studies

Because HCI touches so many disciplines, there are many different theories that have been applied to it, from mathematical theories such as game theory or graph theory to social theories such as Actor-Network Theory or Structuration Theory. A good place to start is Carroll's *HCI Models, Theories, and Frameworks: Toward a Multidisciplinary Science* (Carroll, 2003). This edited volume includes formal techniques, activity theory, information foraging theory and much more. Like the present book, each chapter has a uniform structure, providing the scientific underpinnings of each theory or model, a detailed description of the theory, and one or more case studies. The case studies are particularly useful as they show how a wide range of different kinds of theory can be applied in practice.

In the early part of this chapter, we looked at some of the broad philosophical discussions about the nature of science in the works of Popper and Kuhn. Within HCI there has been considerable debate about the nature of the discipline, most notably whether it should be regarded as science, craft or engineering (Long and Dowell, 1989). Unlike traditional science disciplines where research and practice are distinct, in HCI the two intermingle. In particular, this leads to theoretical discussions of HCI methodology (see Chapter 8) and design practice, such as the task-artefact cycle (Carroll and Rosson, 1992).

Several of the terms used in this chapter are ones that I have coined at different times to describe concepts or techniques that may be widely practised, but did not have a name. These include synthetic theory in Section 9.2.4, critical transitions and recoding dialectic in Section 9.3.2 and generative artefacts in Section 9.5.3. More detail on these and other aspects of research methods in HCI can be found on my Research and Innovation Techniques web pages (Dix, 1996–2007).

10 Write now!

HAROLD THIMBLEBY

> *It is a delicious thing, to write, whether well or badly – to no longer be yourself.*
>
> Gustave Flaubert

10.1 Introduction

Writing is hard, and it is easy to postpone doing it. There seem to be many natural reasons to postpone writing, like you don't know what to write yet so you can't start. Our natural inclinations, however, are counter-productive. This chapter provides many reasons to start writing now. Writing now will improve your self-esteem, it will help you write better and it will help you do the work you are writing about – there are many other benefits this chapter covers. In short, writing is formative; it is the most important activity of your project, and is integral to it, not just a description of what you did. This chapter does not tell you everything you need to know about writing, but it tells you the most important secret: write now.

The advice in this chapter is written concretely as if for helping people write project reports (undergraduate, Masters or PhD theses). But the arguments apply equally to writing research proposals, job applications, novels or research papers.

10.2 Writing (noun) and writing (verb)

Writing (noun) was invented around six thousand years ago by the Sumerians. Today, we take writing for granted, yet in truth writing has a magic effect on us. Little marks, on a screen, on paper, on a road sign, anywhere, convey information – thoughts and emotions – from the writer to the readers. If you read a novel, your mind enters another world. Socrates is reputed to have said that writing would destroy memory. Yet we only know this because his student Plato wrote it down for us to read today. Without writing we would have forgotten.

All of us do a lot more reading than writing, and most writing we see just 'sits there', written by somebody else. It looks like passive stuff that just is. Thus, what you are reading right now is not going to change; it has no life of its own, it seems. You can skip to the end of this chapter, to see how I finish, and then you can come back. This sentence will still be here, unaffected by events around it.

Most writing (verb) we've done in our lives we did because we had to do it. Your teachers told you to write essays, and you did. Your teachers told you to fill in a lab book, and you did. You wrote; you got marks. If you weren't asked to write something, you didn't. Soon, you only wrote because you had to – and you only wrote just in time for the hand-in deadline. In short, you've been well trained by a lifetime of experience to write only for marks, and only to write when asked to. If you've come out well in this training process, now you only write when you have to, to get some marks or to pass a course.

Ironically, then, a lifetime of education behind you has become a recipe for passivity, and for missing some important things about writing.

A good piece of advice about writing is to read. If you read good books and good papers, especially ones you enjoy (even fiction), you will learn – if you reflect on it – a lot about how to write well, how to engage your reader. Why is this book gripping? How has the author structured it? What do you want to do that this author talks about, but this author puts you to sleep over? These are good questions, but unfortunately they can be misleading: the more we read, the more we come to see written text as just 'being there' as if by magic. Written text is static; it just 'is' – and it is a short step to believing that the author 'just wrote it'.

Almost certainly, anything good you read was written through a long process of writing, revising, and redoing everything. Probably as the author planned and wrote their story, they changed their story. Their writing changed what they were thinking, and their changed thinking resulted in a different, better, story. That final story is what you are reading, but all the work that led to the final result is hidden. Because we can't see that prewriting and rewriting work, it makes it seem even harder to write well, because we don't know how to begin to get that quality or quantity of writing done in our own work.

10.3 Writing a project into existence

Writing can bring benefits that, because you may already have bad writing habits, you are probably unaware of. These benefits include understanding your work better, understanding the tools you'll use to write and also the general benefit that comes simply from practice and having the time to practise.

To be concrete, let's say you are doing a project that must be written up and handed in to be marked in June. Today, let's suppose, it is February. You have four months to go. Obviously you are going to do your project then you will write it up. But your current rate of writing is zero pages per day. The word 'project' might mean anything from a small piece of coursework to a major grant proposal, or even a lifetime's work – your magnum opus you hope to get published as a book.

If we take the June deadline seriously, a simple calculation, based on the evidence to date (that is, you are writing zero pages per day), shows you should have started to write already, else you cannot possibly finish in time! Maybe you will ask for an extension when you get to June?

Of course, that's a joke, you are going to spend February, March and April working, then May writing up. What happens, then, if in May you find yourself writing something like: 'The experiments done on hot days got different results. There were ?? sunny days over the course of the experiments, thus accounting for the unexpected result.' Well, now we are in May, it's too late to find out what ?? is supposed to be. You could probably get away with ignoring the number altogether, basically by rewriting the sentence to conceal your ignorance. But that's only an option if you are lucky. Indeed, it isn't likely that your experiment will be clouded over by not knowing how sunny it is. The point is that you don't know what you want to say until you try saying it. Which means that you don't know how to run your experiment until you write it up. If you had tried writing that sentence before you did your experiments, you'd have anticipated that counting sunny days might be useful. Then, in June, you could put in the right number for ??. Now the best you can do is look up the weather reports and make a guess.

This is a trivial illustration but it has a general lesson: start writing your project now even before you've done the work. Then you'll know what to find out so you can write it up.

Many people will be working on their project, planning to write it up in time for June. People normally want to finish their lab work before writing up. They might well do work or experiments that don't need writing up. What happens when you are writing up and you find all the results from March are a mess? You aren't going to mention them in the write up. So why did you waste all of March doing that work? Looking at it the other way around: if you'd written your report first, it wouldn't have mentioned your wasted work from March, and you would have known you needn't do it. You could have done something else. Or you could have finished your project a month early. Or you could have done a better project.

So, start writing your project now even before you've done the work. Then you'll know what not to do so you needn't waste time on things you'll never write up.

If your project revolves around programming or software development, there is a very important synergy you can exploit. You can start writing now imaginatively, imagining how your software should be when it is finished. You can then change your program to make what you wrote become true. If you are doing an ordinary project, like collecting some data about rats, you are unlikely to be able to get the rats to change their behaviour to suit your imagination. But programming is more fun than experimenting with rats (in my opinion), because by programming you can create the stories you want to tell. That is deeply satisfying, when it works, and for it to work you only need to know what stories you want to tell! In fact, writing about programs (especially user manuals) often gives you strong clues on what to improve in your programming to make it better. If you find yourself writing a manual entry for your program that warns, 'You can't enter more than 100 characters' or similar (perhaps not so blatant!), surely this is a good clue that you could modify your program so the warning was not necessary? In this case, why have a limit at all? Again, that's a simple illustration, supporting an important rule: write now, maybe just sketches of your final work, so that you can see where to direct your work.

Most projects are quite big, and are probably amongst the longest documents you've ever written. Did you know that your word processor (probably) has an outliner, which will help you write a long document more easily? And if it doesn't have an outliner, why not use one that does? Did you know that there are tools to help organise bibliographies, and that you'll need them if you have more than a few references? Or you can generate tables of contents, indexes, cross-references, tables of figures, and many other things automatically – and hence easily get them right? If you are lucky, you will discover all this when you are writing up in May.

If you start your write-up now, you could find out whether you can print it. It sounds obvious, but guess what will happen if you write your project up during May, and you get round to printing it for the first time on 31 May. You will find your printer doesn't work, has run out of ink, or you need a password for it. If you start writing now, you can test out every part of doing your project well before you need to rely on every part working. When you really need to rely on a computer, the only thing you can rely on is that you can't rely on it.

Why not start writing up now, so that you learn how to use the writing tools you've got? Why not discover now, while you have months to go, how you are going to have to struggle with the tools? You might find that you want to include some nice pictures in your project. Are they in the right format? How do you keep captions and figures together? If the project involves a computer, you should be able to generate stuff, and as much as you want. Every picture, figure or table you generate from your program is another half page or more you don't need to write; it'll be well worth finding out how to do it reliably. In particular, if you develop a system (or find one that exists already) for generating and including pictures, you will be able to improve your project and then automatically get improved pictures (or tables or what have you) in the write-up.

You may even discover things about your writing tools you didn't even know were there to discover. You'll have time to learn these things but won't be under pressure and hence make mistakes.

If you were a musician preparing for a performance in June, you'd start practising, so that you got better and better. You'd practise even if there was nobody to listen to you. You'd practise because you want to get better, and because (as you start to get better) you actually enjoy playing. The same goes for writing. Write even if nobody else is going to read it; don't write only when you have to – that's a recipe to not enjoy your writing. If you don't enjoy writing, you won't write so well, and you enjoy it even less. The one way out of this vicious circle is to start writing as if you could enjoy it.

Why not start writing now, so you get better and better with practice? Each time you sit down with your writing you don't just add a bit, you can read it and improve it. If you read something a month after you wrote it, you'll have forgotten what you meant but you can see clearly what you said, and it's probably not half as clear as you thought it was when you wrote it last month! Now's a good time to clarify what you said. If you are going to write well, it means you need time to read it next month. If you read it next month, you have got to finish it a month earlier.

So, start writing your project now even before you've done the work. Then you'll have plenty of time to read what you've written. You'll be reading it more like all its other readers when you can't remember what you were thinking originally. So you'll have lots of ideas to improve your writing.

All of these arguments show that writing is alive. It's dynamic. It changes what you do. Put formally, writing is formative.

10.4   Talking to yourself

When you are writing you are not just communicating things you have done, to other people. You can communicate to yourself. You can tell yourself ideas, and you can think through those ideas yourself, just as you can think through my ideas when you read my writing. Do you agree with me? Do you agree with yourself? You usually agree with yourself – actually, you usually agree with yourself because you never thought of having an argument with yourself. Like Socrates feared, you've forgotten what you were thinking, so you think what you were thinking was just fine. But if you've made a mistake or been sloppy, hopefully you won't agree with yourself. You'll want to change what you said. In fact, you will only know how to improve your thinking if you write it down. Thinking that needs improving is often not clear to start with, and it's very hard to know your thinking is not clear if you're just thinking. If you're just thinking, your thoughts are wrapped up in themselves, and it is almost impossible to spot errors and weaknesses, because the thoughts themselves are erroneous and weak. You need to step out of yourself – write your thoughts down, and read them critically later.

So, again, start writing your project now even before you've done the work. You'll improve your thinking. If you start writing now, well before you've started 'real' work, you'll improve your planning too. Even today, you can write down your project title, your name, the beginnings of a table of contents and a few chapter headings. Introduction. Literature review. Conclusions. Future Work. References. Maybe an abstract? Acknowledgements? Pictures, certainly.

If my project has a literature review in it, maybe I should go and find some literature to review? If my project has pictures, maybe I should go and find a camera? Already, you can see how starting to write starts to define what is worth doing. Conversely, there are some things you are doing that you are never going to write about, so why are you wasting time doing them if nobody will ever know?

10.5   Nibbling

If you start this sketchy write-up now, you will have a framework you can extend any day you feel like it. You can nibble.

Nibbling is the way to get any big job done. If it's a huge job, this is inevitable; you'll need meals and sleep between nibbles! If it is an average sort of project write-up, nibbling has the advantage you can nibble when you feel like it. When you are energetic and efficient. When you are a good writer. You can even write when you are mediocre; you can write when you force yourself! If they don't nibble, many people put off writing until they think they can write perfectly, which of course they never can. Instead, nibble, and once you've started it will be easier to improve it than if you never start.

If you leave writing up till June, you will have to write, whether you like it or not. Mostly, it will be a chore if you have to do it, particularly if you have to do it under pressure of a deadline. You won't be able to party; you'll have to write.

Instead, you could have started now and nibbled when you felt like it. Partied when you felt like it. You would have enjoyed writing what you wrote, because you chose to write it when you felt like writing. You were nibbling, and you were happy because nibbling started soon enough is a fine way to write anything, however big. A happy writer writes happy things. It sounds obvious, but if you write boring dull stuff that you have to write, who ever reads it is going to find it, well, boring dull stuff too. You will get more marks for writing something your examiners enjoy reading. It's better than that, because if you enjoy writing it, you'll enjoy putting more time into it, and you will write it even better.

Nibbling is an attitude (if you believe in it) that will help you if you have 'writer's block' or low self-esteem about your writing. Today there is something you can write in your project. For example, your project will need an Acknowledgements section. Why not write a thank you to the friends who have helped you? Writing this small section, making a small contribution to your thesis, may be so different from writing the rest of it that it is enjoyable. Or at least you can see you will have got it completely written in the next half hour. You've done something useful. You've made progress. And the rest of the writing work you have to do is being nibbled away at.

10.6   Writing techniques

Word processors, and outliners, bring a great freedom that writers could never achieve before they were invented. You can write in any order. You can rearrange your writing any time you like. Outliners let you get an overview, and edit the overview without getting distracted by detail. Often, it is easier to write in an order that suits how you think; clearly, you cannot write down ideas until they occur to you! Once written, though, you are free to reorder your writing to suit the arguments and narrative you now see you are constructing, and that's most easily done in an outliner. Words differently arranged have a different meaning, as Blaise Pascal commented, and meanings differently arranged have a different effect. With an outliner, you can explore different effects, and find effects you wouldn't have found without the flexibility.

Another advantage of writing as soon as possible is that you will gradually learn how to use tools like the outliner when, in many ways, mistakes won't matter. You can experiment, and even have accidents. You will learn a lot about your editing tools, and as you get further into your project you will begin to use them more professionally to improve the quality of your writing. In the final stages of writing, you do not want any writing tools to be hindrances; you want to know these complex and powerful tools very well. And that means practice.

A useful thing to do with an outliner, especially if you are co-authoring your writing, is to have a section called Junk, where you move writing you don't yet have the heart to delete. I find a Junk section useful for my pedantry. Thus, my original opening of this chapter stated that Sumerian writing is not the oldest writing as everybody assumes, but merely the oldest we know about. Hardly a point that would improve the impact of the first few sentences. While I felt obliged to write it at the time, in the name of integrity, the point is so distracting from what I really wanted to say, I first moved it to Junk (that's easy), then once I had seen that it wasn't helping the story, I deleted it. Emotionally, it's far easier this way. Just deleting outright something that you think is cute is very hard to do. It took you effort to write the text the first time, and you will be proud of it! It will take less will power to move it to Junk than to delete it.

If you are co-authoring with somebody else, this is another good reason to move text to Junk, because it will upset them less than deleting it. Furthermore, their text that wasn't strong enough to keep (and therefore should have been deleted) might have been the beginnings of a good idea, which your co-author hasn't expressed very well as yet. If you delete it now, your co-author might forget all about the idea. If you move it to Junk, you are telling your co-author: 'this might be worth keeping if you rewrite it, but I don't like it as it currently is. Please, either delete it, or make it stronger.'

Instead of a section called Junk, I often find that using footnotes and appendices is easier. Some word processors have a 'track changes' feature. On the whole, I think these only work at the very last stages of writing: they do not cope very well with rewriting paragraphs. In LaTeX you can define macros to hide stuff into, or put as margin paragraphs or footnotes, as you and your co-authors prefer.

If you do start using footnotes and appendices seriously as a technique to help write better, remember to review whether you still want these footnotes in the final document. Generally, a document with lots of footnotes and appendices is probably trying to say 'delete some of this stuff that isn't of prime importance!'. If it isn't worth saying directly in the final document, why leave it in?

Some material becomes 'junk' because you change your mind about what your project is doing. Now, instead of deleting the junk text, you could consider moving it to your section Future Work. In the Future Work section of your project, you write about what you didn't do, but what you think is still worth doing in principle. So the text you wrote ages ago about what you thought you were going to do in the project can be moved into text about what somebody else could do, to carry on from where your project leaves off.

If you think this chapter is long, thank me for the text and ideas I have already deleted! A very good piece of advice (I don't know who said it) is that if you have any doubt at all in your own mind whether a bit of text, whether a chapter, paragraph or phrase, should be deleted, you should delete it. Your readers will be harsher critics than you. What you notice as redeemable thoughts, to them is certain rubbish. Delete!

Getting feedback is crucial to good writing – effectively it is user-testing your work. It can be very quick and easy to get feedback from your friends, your colleagues and your supervisor. Use them. There are five basic rules, worth keeping in mind about getting feedback:

1 Feedback is very useful, most especially when you don't like it.
2 You won't get feedback without doing some work; for example, you need to give people printouts of your chapters.
3 Just because some people don't give you feedback, don't give up – especially when your supervisor doesn't give you feedback.
4 Different people have different styles of giving feedback; find out what they are, and exploit them. For example, some supervisors want to read your complete project to see it as a whole; others would rather have a chapter at a time.
5 Tell the people who you've asked for feedback what sort of feedback you want. Do you want help with spellign? Do you want some high-level feedback, like encouragement? Do you want to know some short-cuts to finishing as quickly as possible, or do you want to make your project the best possible write-up ever?

If you are doing a big project, like a PhD or writing a book, a big project that takes a good few years to do, you have more time to write. The biggest danger of a big writing project is that it seems to make no difference whether you start writing today or tomorrow. There's so much time! So it seems you may as well start tomorrow or next week. That can't be true for ever, since sometime you will have to start writing something. There is a more insidious problem: if you put off writing today, even for the best of reasons, you are starting to train yourself not to write. The bigger the project, the easier it is to delay, and the longer you delay writing the more certainly you will have trained yourself into a habit of not writing. The only way out is to start writing today, to force yourself to overcome the temptation that you could procrastinate with little damage.

The second biggest danger of a big project is that there are more opportunities for it to go wrong. Working over a longer time, your computer is more likely to crash – and take with it more work than it would have done otherwise! Make sure you backup regularly, for instance onto a CD or something else that isn't going to get messed up, and occasionally check that you can read your backup. There's nothing worse than discovering your last backup itself is corrupted and useless, just when you need it most!

10.7   Killing two birds with one stone

With a big project, if you start writing now, some of your draft writing might be easy to turn into papers that you can publish. You can write a paper for a conference or journal. You may well find writing a paper for a conference helps in many ways: you get excited about the achievement and buzz of publishing; you can get that buzz writing something short; and when you hand in your thesis or project report you will be able to say somewhere prominent 'Chapter 4 was published at such-and-such conference' (so the examiners had better give lots of marks if it was good enough for that conference!).

Naturally, writing a paper for a conference will in itself define some of the work you need to do to support the writing for the paper – it's just a mini-project, and all the rules apply. It's exciting writing for conferences. Some people like the deadlines; it gets them writing. Some people like the buzz of the conference and being there. If you get a paper published, not only have you got a bit of writing that can go in your project, you've also got a piece of important evidence: your work is worth publishing. You'll get more marks, and be far more likely to pass the final exam.

One benefit is that writing a paper will give you more practice writing. It will help clarify your research ideas. It will help express them concisely, without all the history and confusion of your big project report. A paper has to be brief and to the point. Being brief makes it easier: there's less to do. Being to the point means you need to work out what your point is.

When you send off a paper to a conference or journal, it will get refereed. Your referees will give you lots of good feedback. Sometimes, though, your paper will be rejected and you think your referees were idiots! They missed the point! Three points: (1) your referees are representatives of your readers, so if they missed the point, maybe anybody else would have done – it's your responsibility to write more clearly. (2) you learn, you send off another version to another conference. It's not the end of the world! (3) unlike your friends and supervisor giving you feedback, the referees may not feel obliged to be nice to you, which can make their criticism a more honest reaction. This may also make it harder to bear but if you can bear it, you could get more insight out of it. Moreover, if the feedback is good, you can feel confident that the referee really did think it was good – they have no reason to be 'just saying that'.

Another benefit of writing a paper is that you could co-author it. Most likely, your project or thesis has to be written entirely by yourself, which is boring. But co-authoring means two or more people can get together and hammer out ideas and have even more fun, and write something that is even more polished. When you are bored writing, get your co-author to nibble, and vice versa. Only make sure you don't both nibble at the same time (unless you are in the same room or using a decent multi-authoring tool)!

10.8   Self-esteem

Your main enemy to writing may well be self-esteem.

Writing is very personal, and expressing yourself raises all sorts of anxieties. Is what I am writing going to be good enough? Might I be ridiculed for saying that?

Because low self-esteem makes it harder to start writing, you will find yourself putting off writing. When the deadline really looms over you and you know you must start writing, you've now probably given yourself an impossible task. You delayed because you lacked self-confidence, and now you haven't a chance of writing well because there is too much to do and not enough time. If you end up with a piece of bad writing, your already low self-esteem will seem confirmed. Your self-esteem will plummet. It's a terrible vicious cycle.

Realising that low self-esteem feeds on itself may be some help to you; other helps are to draw other people into your writing, to get encouragement from them. In fact, if you start writing early and simply, you can show people drafts before you get anxious – and with the nice excuse that any weaknesses in your writing can be laid at the door of starting early, you followed my advice even, and obviously you don't yet know what you are writing about! It's all Thimbleby's fault! Your self-esteem will recover if you blame me rather than yourself.

You may be worried what other people (particularly your supervisor) will think of your writing. The obvious thing to do is to work harder, polish what you are writing and to try hard to make it perfect. This obvious response couldn't be more wrong. The more you try to polish your work, the harder it will be to show it to anyone. They might criticise what you thought was perfect. If they want you to make major revisions, you'll be devastated. Instead, write a little, show it to your supervisors or friends and ask for feedback and help. If you give it to them knowing it isn't finished, you'll be happier with any feedback; and they will be able to give you more useful feedback, too.

Other people can be bad for your self-esteem and motivation. Ironically, the people you see most of are (with rare exceptions) not actually writing when you see them, so you will tend to believe that they achieve whatever success they have by putting little effort into their writing. It does not help to compare what you see them doing with what you know you try to do. In particular, if you work in a laboratory with other students, say PhD students who started ages ago and seem mature, the students you see most of and who seem the most experienced are ironically the ones who haven't finished writing their thesis! The longer a student takes, the more you will see of them. Efficient students, on the other hand, who get on and write their thesis efficiently, finish on time, and disappear. The students who are around, then, are mostly the ones who are writing slowly, if at all. Statistically, familiar people are not examples to follow nor to set your personal standards by.

Inevitably, a consequence of writing and writing by nibbling is that some of your writing will be 'wasted'. You might write something today that next week you'll want to delete. You mustn't take deleting stuff personally. Deleting writing is no different from a musician practising a piece and nobody else hearing it. The unheard sound of music is lost; the deleted writing is lost. But both the musician and you got better for the practising.

10.9 Scaffolding

Since writing material that later needs deleting is part of the process of good writing, it's useful to give it a name, not least so you can feel positive about deleting stuff you put so much effort into! Writing that helps you write, but which is not needed in the final document I call *scaffolding*. You can't erect a decent building without putting a lot of care into scaffolding, but you take it all away before you hand over the building to its users. So, review your writing and look for scaffolding: stuff you needed to write at the time, but is it helping your readers? And then delete it, or squirrel it away in another file for another document. Pascal once apologised, 'This letter is very long only because I didn't have the leisure to make it shorter.' Even for him, then, good writing meant putting scaffolding up, because you need to say things and get them off your chest, then deleting and editing them, because you want to communicate.[1]

Often, I find, what I want to say first is not what I really want to say, but until I've started writing and got some ideas off my chest and out of the way, the key new thoughts won't surface. And, it's good to write down familiar things, it gets your writing up to speed, speeding up with the easy bits – like the project outline – and then being on the ball when the harder work starts.

---

[1] Actually, Pascal's Letter XVI of his Provincial Letters, where he makes this point, is rhetorical, so here he is saying something contrived in order to make the lengthy fictitious letter sound more plausible. In 1660 Louis XIV ordered Provincial Letters banned and burned: the letters were not just irritating, but were so well written they attracted too much attention for the king's liking.

The popular film *The League of Extraordinary Gentlemen* is typical of making a virtue of the necessity of deleting scaffolding material: the DVD box boasts that you can watch 12 deleted scenes!

Should this footnote be deleted? Doesn't the detail distract from my arguments?

10.10 The best is the enemy of the good

Though nibbling is a good way of starting, it can become a problem in the long run: how do you know when to stop? Nibbling makes it seem you can always add a bit more (in fact, that's the point of nibbling as a writing strategy).

Ironically, following my advice to write has got you into a lifetime's habit of writing, but it may have also developed in you a habit of writing far too long, and not letting go. You have got yourself into the habit of continually improving what you write, and improvements are always possible. While it's true you can always improve, it's worth remembering that at some stage your readers are not going to notice when you make what you think is an 'improvement'. At some stage, after lots of work on your writing, your writing will be good enough, and spending more time on it will merely delay its completion.

The pithy way of putting this is Voltaire's comment: 'the best is the enemy of the good' – which means that trying to write perfectly, you may never write well. If you are always improving, you will never finish. Too many people want to have the perfect idea before they write it up. They think, rightly, that writing will make the idea better. It's a short step from this to wanting your writing to be perfect before you show it to anyone else, or hand it in, or hand it over to a publisher, or send it off to a conference or journal. The longer you perfect your writing, the more pride you will have, and the harder it will be to get it finished or to get really helpful comments from friends or colleagues.

(I thought about deleting the next paragraph, but by leaving it in, you can see a paragraph I wrote that ought to have been deleted. Fortunately, you can't see the many other paragraphs I really deleted!)

~~It's far better to give somebody a draft and ask for their comments now. Both you and they know a draft needs improving, so you'll get useful feedback. Give them a highly polished piece of writing (if you ever finish!) and they won't know how to avoid upsetting you, and you won't know how to deal with even the slightest criticism. In short, take breaks in your writing and let somebody read it as soon as possible.~~

10.11 Other advice on writing

A great deal has been written about writing. A lot of it is very sensible advice, particularly about reading and learning from material you admire. (Do you know what writing you admire? Why do you admire it?) You can read a lot from different genres, too. A good novel envelops you in another world, and is hard to put down. How does the author achieve that? Wouldn't it be nice to write project reports that examiners found so gripping?

Almost all of this very sensible advice is about the facts and knowledge you need to write well. Some advice you can get, however, is mad: like, if you want to write clearly, you should know what you want to say. No! Rather, you should work out what your readers would like to hear. You can work out what your readers want by being a reader yourself: work it out through writing, and deleting some of what you thought you wanted to say. In particular, if your readers are people who are going to mark your writing, what do they want to hear? How can you play the game to get more marks? Have you read all the instructions? Do you know the criteria you will be marked against?

Unfortunately, to write in a way that your readers regard highly, or mark highly, is also a slippery route to moral stagnation. The most popular newspapers are probably the least useful in improving the world, precisely because they write what their readers want to hear. However, if you don't write well, and your readers don't like reading your writing style, you will never change the world. You must know what your readers want and like, just as you should know what you want and like, but you do not need to pander to any of it.

10.12 Writing style

When you write you have to choose how to express yourself, and how to communicate to your readers. These goals are often in conflict; for example, you may feel like screaming at a wrong-doer, but the legal expressions of a lawyer may be more effective – though it all depends! That's an extreme example, but it makes the point. Indeed, it takes a very long time to learn to write effectively as a lawyer.

Typically in writing you have a particular audience, who have expectations. If you are writing a project, there may be advice provided on writing style; if so, you should know it, and follow it. It may be important that your references follow APA (American Psychology Association) style, or Harvard, or Chicago. Here, it is easy to get more marks by merely knowing the rules. Similarly, when submitting a paper to a conference, you want 'more marks'; irritating referees on your bad style will be counter-productive.

Editing references to follow a style is a relatively light task, and you can do it and double-check your references at the same time. Or you could use a tool like Bibtex, and leave the style of references up to a program. However, changing the style of your whole project can be very tedious. It's best to think about style early on, and it may be worth trying a few styles out consciously to see how effective they are for you.

One of the most common problems is the voice of the writing. Do you use the first person in the active mood, 'I wrote the program'? Do you use the third person in passive, 'The program was written'? How do you refer to other people, such as experimental subjects and users? 'The user pressed a button, and then they pressed another . . .'? You can certainly avoid choosing between he/she/they by circumlocution, but your writing can become more tedious to read.

Some people think you can be more objective, more scientific, if you write impersonally – which means third person passive. They think it is subjective to write in the first person. My view is that it depends, though too many people insist without thinking that you have to write science in the passive. In fact (in my opinion), to admit that you did things is scientifically more honest than to pretend things just happened, which is what the passive literally implies. If 'a test tube was heated' did you do this, did a technician, did an electric heater, or what?

You should take responsibility. On the other hand, if you are writing formal material (such as law, maths or philosophy) the argument in the writing should stand on its own feet, and the passive is then more appropriate. An argument is no stronger or weaker simply because *you* made it. But an experiment might get a certain result (or ignore a certain outcome) because *you* did it.

You will notice that throughout this chapter, I have referred to the writer as you. Obviously, if you are reading this, you want to write. Other authors (that is, people other than me) might have written 'one' (as in, 'When one writes references, the required style should be used'). Some writers like to be completely impersonal, as in 'The references should be written in APA style.'

Personally, I prefer my style; if I had used the words 'author' or 'writer' too often, you would have got confused. Are you the author or am I? Actually, we both are. For a chapter about writing, then, it would take a pedantic style to make clear who's who, except by using the first person (me) and second person (you).

As the goal of this chapter is to encourage you and make you enthusiastic about writing, I have not adopted a 'scientific' tone. This chapter has a voice and a tone suitable to the goals of the chapter. Likewise you must find the right voice and tone to communicate the goals of whatever you write.

In short, there is no agreement on how to write well. My advice therefore has five levels:

1 If there are any writing rules provided, follow them. If there are no explicit rules, read examples of what has been successful in the past, and follow their style.
2 Read Strunk and White (2000) *The Elements of Style*, a pleasantly short book, on writing style, and follow their advice.
3 Read David Crystal's *The English Language* (2000), and enjoy learning about the history and varieties of English writing, and then make your stylistic choices in an informed way that you can justify.
4 In some documents, such as thesis projects and books, which have the space, it may be worthwhile taking a paragraph or two to explain your choice of style. You may wish to refer to Crystal (2000).
5 If you get really serious, read an established publisher's style guide, such as the *Chicago Manual of Style*. (Make sure you get the latest edition, not a dusty old one from a library.) Also, if you get really serious, buy a smaller dictionary – if, as a writer, you find yourself turning to a big dictionary (or the web!) to

look up a word to use, your readers won't know what it means either; so get a smaller dictionary.

You will write best if you enjoy what you are writing about. People marking or reading what you write will prefer writing that is enjoyable. Put the other way around: when you choose a project, choose one you will enjoy writing about. When you find that time is running short, and you cannot write about everything you'd like to, choose to write first about what you enjoy most.

10.13 Write now

Very few people say the best way to get good at something is not just to understand but to *do* it too. It's not enough to know how to write; it's not enough to do your project and wait until you know what to write; it's not enough to write as an afterthought. Hindsight in writing comes too late to help. Real writing is transforming; real writing is forethought.

When you get right into writing you are using writing to transform and polish your own thinking – as it were, leaving just the shine of the polish for other readers, not all the work you did to get there.

Now you've got to the end of your writing, it's time to go back to the beginning. Your readers will start with your title and abstract. Now you know what you've written, it's time to review and probably rewrite the title and abstract – that is, assuming you wrote them some time ago, when *the writing* was driving the project!

10.13.1 Key points

Start writing now, even before you've done the work.

1 Start to write straight away. Get into a habit of nibbling.
2 Your initial writing will make clear the holes in your argument, plan or program.
3 Address the holes:
   (a) Plan your work to fill in those holes in your writing.
   (b) If you are programming, modify your program to help remove the holes, warnings, verbiage and hedges from your writing.
   (c) Or move 'holes' to your Further Work section if you are not going to fill them in yourself.
4 Find out what writing tools, outliners, Computer Supported Co-operative Work (CSCW) or version control, etc., will help your writing requirements best.
5 Refine and revise your writing as the holes get filled in.
6 Remove scaffolding.
7 Find out how to use people, like your supervisor, to get the feedback you need.

Whereas: if you write at the end, once you've done the work, you will discover the holes too late to do anything about them. And, very likely, you will have spent time doing work that does not need to be written up – and therefore was wasted effort.

10.14 Acknowledgements

This chapter was much improved with help from my colleagues, family, students and friends: Tim Bell, Paul Cairns, Graeme Harper, Tony Hoare, Prue Thimbleby, Sam Thimbleby, Will Thimbleby, Ian Witten.

Earlier versions were sent to these and others, who very kindly made all sorts of constructive comments. They probably found it easier to comment on drafts: my drafts were shorter, less polished (so my colleagues could find things they could help me with easily) and I wasn't too precious about my draft ideas. I'd love to hear your comments, too.

This chapter was written with support from a Royal Society-Wolfson Research Merit Award.

11 Applying old research methods to new problems

PAUL CAIRNS AND ANNA L. COX

> *The History of every major Galactic Civilization tends to pass through three distinct and recognizable phases, those of Survival, Inquiry and Sophistication, otherwise known as the How, Why and Where phases. For instance, the first phase is characterized by the question 'How can we eat?' the second by the question 'Why do we eat?' and the third by the question 'Where shall we have lunch?'*

> Douglas Adams

11.1 Overview

Given the complex and dynamic nature of HCI, it could be argued that the methods described here, whilst successful so far, may not be sufficient to address the challenges of HCI research in future. The purpose of this chapter is to show that even in the new area of user experience, these methods are still able to structure investigations and so provide insights and knowledge that we hope will be valuable to other researchers. Of course, this new area also shows up some of the limitations of the existing methods and this leads us to discuss the relationship between HCI as it might be in future and the research methods it has and may come to need.

Before describing our research into user experience, it is worth discussing the move in HCI towards user experience and why it seems a natural trajectory for HCI to take.

11.2 From usability to user experience

Traditional usability, as embodied in standards such as ISO 9241, have focused on users being able to interact with a system in a given context in a way which is effective, efficient and satisfying. These three features are still widely represented in usability research and practice (Hornbaek and Law, 2007), possibly because they can be measured quantitatively: effectiveness is tasks completed, efficiency is time to complete and satisfaction can be measured with a variety of bespoke or general questionnaires such as SUS or QUIS. However, what has also emerged is that these measures do not seem to provide insight into how interfaces work and whilst a design may be effective, efficient and satisfying, it can somehow still not be a good user interface.

There have therefore been many attempts to provide a theoretical basis for usability and hence to predict in advance whether a system is usable. The design of an interface is built to meet some particular criteria set out by the theory, such as task action mappings (Young, 1983), or performance criteria specified using GOMS (see Chapter 4). By satisfying the criteria, the system is expected to be more usable. However, often these systems are no more usable than other designs. This is not so surprising in hindsight – a theory is all very well but, in general, theories of interaction never seem to go far enough to cover all the things that need to be sorted for a design to be usable. In this sense, usability is something of a contingent state – something is usable until a usability problem is found. Some theories help avoid particular types of usability problem. Some heuristics help avoid others. But avoiding one set of problems does not mean that there are no other usability problems that are important to address in the design.

To better understand this, it is worth going back to the work of Aristotle (Aristotle and Ackrill, 1975). He identified that within the physical world there were concepts that were defined not through the presence of some object or attribute but through its absence. Thus, death is the absence of life, cold is the absence of heat and light is the absence of dark. These concepts that are based on the absence (or privation) of another concept are accordingly called privatives.

The problem with privatives is that linguistically they can be treated the same as positive concepts. Thus, it is perfectly reasonable to make comments like 'Close the curtains to keep the cold out' when in fact curtains are closed in order to provide an insulating layer to keep the heat in. Whilst such statements do not generally cause confusion, it is not a hard stretch to make statements that are clearly absurd. So if dark is a positive concept, the American comedian Steve Wright asks, 'What is the speed of dark?' and this is elaborated by writer Terry Pratchett who observes that the speed of dark must be faster than the speed of light because whenever light gets somewhere, all the dark has gone away.

Some confusions with privatives are not so easily noticed. It is perfectly reasonable to treat cold as the positive concept and heat as the privative of cold in many circumstances, such as cooling things down and keeping the cold out. Problems come when you try to do things like focus cold. Heat can be focused, like light, with a lens as any child with a magnifying glass can tell you. Cold cannot. This is because heat can radiate from an object but cold, being the absence of heat cannot radiate.

Thus, whilst we might talk about usability as a positive concept, 'This system is more usable than the old system', actually it seems in the traditional sense of usability it makes more sense to consider usability as a privative. A system declared usable is usable because no usability problems have been found. Or put another way, the positive concept is a usability problem. These are generally easy to identify, name and even measure. However, it is very difficult to fully qualify all of the usability problems that must be absent to make the system usable. Indeed, it may be that a system becomes unusable in the face of a new type of user not considered in the development of the system, say one who is elderly or one who is partially sighted, or because of a new context of use. Thus, the statement 'This system is usable' is always a contingent statement waiting on someone to come along and find a problem in using it.

Designing for usability is therefore difficult. It is much more straightforward to design out unusability, that is features that will cause usability problems, but it is not clear how to design so that there are no usability problems at all. From this privative perspective, HCI is therefore mostly about trying to find out all the problems in advance. This has given HCI something of negative role and HCI researchers behave like critics. They are very able to point out the problems with a system as they have spent a long time thinking about all the different types of problems. Unfortunately, they are not able to make suggestions that guarantee no further problems. In fact, it could be argued that any design is potentially flawed since any design features are potentially unusable given the wrong people or the wrong context.

Norman has railed against this negative role for HCI and so was motivated to look at how HCI could stop moaning about unusable systems, as Norman himself did in *The Design of Everyday Things* (1998) and start promoting a positive usability (Norman, 2004). In this positive usability, the role of the usability engineer is to suggest design features that would promote a positive experience and thus help people to overcome minor usability problems on a tide of good feeling. Norman's work is an important work in this move within HCI, but also typical of a growing tide of usability researchers and practitioners trying to understand HCI as developing a user experience rather than just avoiding problems (Garrett, 2002; Veen, 2001; Saffer, 2006).

The consideration of positive usability has coincided with a move of technology away from work-oriented, desktop computing to handheld, mobile and ubiquitous systems. People are using enormous amounts of computing power to play music whilst sitting on the bus or to goof around with a mobile phone camera with their friends. Thus, the need to study these contexts and goals has also driven HCI to consider a more general understanding of usability that is not about being effective, efficient and satisfying but to having fulfilling experiences that are fun (Blythe *et al.*, 2003) and pleasurable (Jordan, 2002). Perhaps the ultimate end point for this is to no longer consider technology as something with which many can achieve a task, but something that provides an experience unique to the individual (McCarthy and Wright, 2006).

Obviously experiences can be both negative and positive. But experiences, unlike traditional usability, do not seem to make sense as privatives. An experience is an accumulation of something, such as happiness, intrigue, tension, fear or frustration, and none of these things would make sense as privatives. For instance, happiness is not the absence of sadness. The absence of sadness might be a sense of calmness or unity, but happiness is something more, a provoking sensation in itself. Happiness is something in its own right that is not suited to being described as the absence of something else. As an aside, note that a system that provokes fear and tension could also be an excellent system in the right context: just think of a really good Hitchcock film like *The Birds* or *Rear Window*.

Understanding these experiences and understanding them in relation to computers and interactive systems could be a very positive way forward for HCI. It may be that people will still have some problems with interactive systems, or to paraphrase Abraham Lincoln, you can make some of the features usable all of the time and all of the features usable some of the time, but you cannot make all of the features usable all of the time. However, what HCI may be able to do is to predict the general experience that people could have when interacting with a system. Moreover, such predictions could also suggest design elements that would enhance the intended experience.

HCI, then, could be going through the phases of Galactic Civilization described by Douglas Adams in the opening quote to this chapter. Initially, it was difficult to get computers to do anything and this was the survival phase in which computer science began. However, as more powerful computers were built, it became clear that just because a system could do something, it did not mean that its users could get it to do that something. Thus, HCI developed as inquiry into why computers were difficult to use. Now, however, it seems there are an awful lot of successful systems out there and HCI's role is no longer to understand why computers are difficult to use but to add the sophistication to systems of providing the different experiences that different users seek.

11.3   Researching user experience

Whilst it may seem reasonable, then, to use HCI knowledge to promote user experiences, what would be the goals of HCI research to do this? It is very hard to make a definitive statement on what the goal of any research should be. In some ways, the need to satisfy the inquisitive drive that seems to dominate human nature is the goal of any form of research, be it understanding how the Universe came into being or how earthworms function. But as an ideal for HCI research into user experience, it would be thrilling to start from wanting to provide users with a particular experience with a system, regardless of the goal of the system, and to be able to design the system that guarantees the experience. This is the ultimate synthetic theory for HCI (see Chapter 9).

Thus, user experience research is no different from any other sort of research: to be able to predict the outcome of actions. Only in this case, the outcome is some vaguely defined thing called user experience and the actions are to design a system. To do this, HCI needs theories on user experience and interactive systems that can be used to make predictions on the consequences of particular interactive designs. Of course, this is an ideal and HCI is currently a very long way from achieving this.

We feel that a good place to start is to understand more fully exactly what is meant by a user experience. Only when we know what a user experience is, do we feel we would be able to take steps to providing users with that experience. To this end we have looked at various sorts of user experience but we discuss here only two: the experience of playing computer games and the experience of using information visualisations.

Computer games or videogames provide an excellent domain in which to study user experience because the only purpose of games (usually) is simply to provide the user with an experience. When players play a game they do not expect to achieve anything except in terms of rules and progression within the game. And even then, the players may be perfectly happy with the experience even if they did not measurably achieve anything inside or outside the game except to pass some time.

Of course, computer games are rich and varied. The games themselves vary enormously from racing games, puzzles and sports to massively multiplayer fantasy games and simulations of everything from ordinary life to world domination. The outcomes of games are also enormously varied and may be as trivial as distracting someone during their teabreak (Bibby, 2007) or as important as providing an experience that will influence the player's politics and actions (Gee, 2004). The focus we have taken is on something that we believe to be an essential part of any gaming experience, namely that of becoming immersed in the game. Indeed, we would hold that immersion in games is just a particular facet of the ability to become immersed in other activities such as reading or watching films.

This still does not tell us what the experience of immersion is. Whilst a lot of game players are able to say that they become immersed, there are questions like: What do they mean by immersion? Do they all mean the same thing? To address this, the starting point for work in this area was to conduct a grounded theory interview study (see Chapter 7) to investigate what immersion in games meant to gamers (Brown and Cairns, 2004). It turned out that whilst gamers were not precise about what immersion was, there were clear barriers to immersion such as poor controls on the game, or not enough content in the game. This suggested that overcoming these barriers led to increasing immersion. Gamers also were very clear that full immersion in a game, periods when the experience of the gamer was solely contained within the game, did occur with some games but even then it was only fleeting. Interestingly, the theory saturated with only seven gamers which suggested that immersion was a generally agreed upon concept.

This led us to formulate a theory that immersion was not a single thing but a scale of experience where people could become more or less immersed depending on the game and circumstances of playing. To this end, we developed an immersion questionnaire (see Chapter 2) to probe for people's experience of immersion. We then devised a simple experiment with two conditions to manipulate immersion (see Chapter 1). In one condition, participants played a game, Half Life 2, and in the other they 'played' a simple task of clicking on squares as they appeared on the screen. Immersion was measured after ten minutes using the questionnaire. The scores on the questionnaire were found to be significantly different between the two conditions, as predicted (see Chapter 6). This suggests that the questionnaire was working. However, as with all questionnaires, we could not be sure that we were measuring immersion, but only something to do with measuring the experience of games. We tested for this with a simple question at the end of the experiment which simply asked people to rate their degree of immersion on a scale of 1 to 10. As hoped, this rating of immersion correlated well with the scores of the questionnaire which gave us confidence that we were actually measuring immersion (Jennett *et al.*, in press).

Our work building on immersion has continued by considering the relationship between immersion and a player's personality and also between immersion and other aspects of psychology such as attention. However, to return to Brown and Cairns' original study, the notion of barriers to immersion and engagement was key and one of the first such barriers was the controls of the game.

We therefore turned to considering how the controls of the game affect the experience of playing the game. Obviously immersion is affected but what else is affected? Once again, it is not clear what constitutes the gaming experience in this broader sense. So again a qualitative study was used to develop a rich description of the gaming experience offered by a game. That is, how does a game produce a gaming experience for the gamer? Rather than interview gamers, it was decided to use game reviews as the source material for a grounded theory. This way the theory would focus on the experiences intended by the games rather than those the gamers actually had. From this, a theory was developed describing how the controls of a game allowed the player to become present in a game like a puppeteer controlling a puppet. From the puppetry within the gameplay presented by the game, the players would have an experience that they could then relate to others in the form of a narrative. This notion of experience resulting in narratives agreed with the work of McCarthy and Wright (2006).

As before, we intended to use this theory to develop an approach to manipulating and measuring the gaming experience. The obvious measure seemed to be through the narratives that players produced. However, despite three different experimental approaches to eliciting narratives from players using different controls, it was difficult to ascertain which narratives indicated a good experience and which a poor one. Narratives were too deeply embedded in the previous experiences and personalities of the players to be abstracted in some general, comparable way. What is the way forward here? If we decide narratives are not a good probe for user experience, we could replace narratives with some other concept that is easier to measure, but the theory suggests that this would not have the same connection to user experience as narratives. The solution is not at all clear. Hence, this work is still in progress and is the primary research focus of PhD student, Eduardo Calvillo Gámez.

Information visualisation systems offer a very different domain in which to understand user experience. These systems are intended to help a user understand large and complex sets of data by representing multiple facets of the data in some visual form (Spence, 2001). Whilst it is well understood that a good visual presentation of data can be highly illuminating (Tufte, 1992), it is hard to qualify further what it is that makes a visualisation work. A phrase commonly used is that information visualisations 'amplify cognition'. This clearly puts the effects of visualisations in the domain of thoughts and ideas, but does not say which bits of cognition, or even less what it means for cognition can be amplified!

Information visualisations make a good domain in which to study user experience because they are more goal oriented. People use visualisations in order to understand data better. What motivates them is generally external to the visualisation itself thus making information visualisations more like a traditional task-oriented system. However, unlike task-oriented systems, the visualisation may be used with very different objectives. In the area of literature knowledge domain, visualisations present a representation of the academic literature in a particular field of study. These visualisations could have a multitude of purposes from allowing the viewer to identify influential figures in the field, to helping a researcher new to the domain understand the broad areas of study (Faisal, Cairns and Craft, 2005) and thence to pursue a specific line of inquiry. Also, the end point of an exploration is ill defined. It may in principle be never ending as new literature is added and a field grows or it may be limited by time pressures to complete a paper or it may just be a brief, one-off activity to see if there is anything of relevance a researcher should know about.

This combination of the visualisation allowing users to perform tasks but those tasks being unspecified and possibly even being unspecifiable makes information visualisations possibly more about the experience a user has rather than about performing a task in a measurable effective, efficient and satisfying way. What sets information visualisation systems apart from static presentations of data is that they are interactive. Thus, through the user performing actions, the visualisation is adapted and so enables the user to gain different views and ultimately different insights into the data. It seems, then, that interaction is key to the user experience of information visualisations. It is the way in which users engage with a system in order to 'amplify cognition'. Arguably, given the acknowledged importance of doing something for learning that something, it is possibly the interaction, the ability to do something, that makes visualisations so useful.

How then are we to understand the user experience of an information visualisation? Like many systems, we can evaluate the usability – the ability of the user to perform tasks – but the usability of a visualisation is like evaluating the quality of grammar of piece of text. It is good for text to have good grammar but it does not tell you about the value of what is written. We need in some way to evaluate the semantics of the interaction rather than the syntax. To investigate this domain, PhD student Sarah Faisal has produced a literature knowledge domain visualisation. It is intended to meet the needs of users as identified in an earlier grounded theory study with users of literature, that is, researchers. She will then try to understand how users interact with this visualisation, not to evaluate the interface but to understand the sorts of experiences they have and hence to bring some structure to our understanding of user experience in this domain.

In this work, a system itself is being used as a research tool. This is common within HCI research but it is not clear exactly what the contribution of such research is and how it can be assessed. Zimmerman, Forlizzi and Evenson (2007) are beginning to formulate how designing can be used as a research methodology within HCI, but as Chapter 8 discusses, any methodology development is necessarily a long process and the current thinking in this area is far from mature.

Both of these strands of our work show that the methods described in this book can lead to a deeper understanding of a new and difficult idea like user experience. As illustrated though, there are limitations. Narratives seem to be emerging as something crucial to understanding user experience, but how can these be analysed or even deconstructed to form a base of knowledge from which to generalise across systems and domains? Systems can be used to probe for user experience, but to what extent do the systems themselves guide and structure the user experience? If we cannot account for this, then user experience understood via systems will always be particular to the systems used. New methods are clearly needed to keep pushing back the boundaries of our knowledge of this domain. What is clear though is that the new methods should not be seen as replacing existing methods but should complement them, taking up the research effort when the existing ones reach their limits.

11.4   Our hopes for the future of HCI

We hope that this book will be more than just a textbook that students find useful when conducting their research projects. We hope that it may be a resource that all researchers in the HCI community might find useful both for when they would like to check to see whether or not they are applying methods correctly, and when they wish to broaden their understanding of methods from other disciplines that contribute to HCI.

Researchers of HCI come from a variety of backgrounds and bring with them a selection of skills from their discipline. Once they have begun their careers, researchers often become aware of other methods which appear to be useful for their research, but they perhaps underestimate the amount of diligence required to apply a method with which they are not familiar. Some of our recent work (Cairns, 2007) has shown just how often research methods are misapplied. A survey of two BCS HCI conferences (2005 and 2006) and one year (2006) of two leading HCI journals showed that 50 per cent of the papers covered included some form of inferential statistics. Yet only one of these papers had conducted the appropriate analysis and reported the results correctly. In that paper we suggest that some 'HCI specific education could be of some benefit' to researchers trying to get to grips with methods, so perhaps this book can serve that purpose.

Thimbleby's paper (2004a) raises a problem being faced by the HCI community regarding the difficulties that are experienced in obtaining funding for HCI research and getting papers accepted for publication. In theory, with research councils such as the EPSRC having themes such as People and Interactivity, one might imagine that HCI would be top of the list of areas to receive funding. In practice however it does not seem as though it is straightforward to obtain funding for HCI. One of the reasons for this may be the very multidisciplinary nature of HCI. As a community we are often proud of the fact that we can draw on different disciplines when tackling challenging problems in our research, but when it comes to evaluating the research of others we are not always so supportive. Reviewers of papers and grant proposals tend to see someone else's research from their own disciplinary perspective and therefore see an alternative way of tackling a particular problem. So rather than congratulating the author of the paper or proposal on their well thought out research, they instead suggest the approach that they themselves would have taken and argue that that would have been better. This appears to be a criticism of the work (and is sometimes meant to be exactly that) and therefore fewer HCI papers are published and grant proposals funded. Although we have aimed this book at those at the beginnings of their research careers, we hope that it may be of interest to those further on in their careers who might be interested to know a little more about methods used in HCI that they are not particularly familiar with. If we embrace the multidisciplinary nature of HCI by trying to learn more about the methods that others in the community use, and why they find them useful when trying to answer particular problems, we may as a community be encouraged to be more supportive of each other. Therefore, rather than not valuing, say, qualitative research, researchers might develop a more mature attitude and appreciate that all methods are valuable when applied appropriately. If we are unable to change the attitudes of existing researchers, then perhaps this book might educate the new researchers in our field about the value of alternative methods so that in a few years time we might see the tide turning.

References

Abelson, R. P. 1995. *Statistics as Principled Argument*. Mahwah, NJ: Lawrence Erlbaum Associates.

Adams, A., Blandford, A. and Lunt, P. 2005. 'Social empowerment and exclusion: a case study on digital libraries.' *ACM Trans. on Computer–Human Interaction* 12(2):174–200.

Adams, A. and Sasse, M. A. 1999. 'The user is not the enemy.' *Comm. of ACM* 42(12):40–6.

2001. 'Privacy in multimedia communications: Protecting users, not just data.' In Blandford, A., Vanderdonckt, J. and Gray, P. (eds.) *People and Computers XV: Interaction without Frontiers* (Joint Proc. of HCI 2001 and ICM 2001, Lille, Sept. 2001). London: Springer, pp. 49–64.

Adams, A., Sasse, M. A. and Lunt, P. 1997. 'Making passwords secure and usable.' In Thimbleby, H., O'Conaill, B. and Thomas, P. (eds.) *People and Computers XII – Proc. of HCI 1997,* Berlin: Springer, pp. 1–19.

Aiken, L. R. 1996. *Rating Scales and Checklists*. New York: Wiley.

Aldridge, A. and Levine, K. 2001. *Surveying the Social World: Principles and Practice in Survey Research*. Maidenhead, UK: Open University Press.

Allendoerfer, K., Aluker, S., Panjwani, G., Proctor, J., Sturtz, D., Vukovic, M. and Chen, C. 2005. 'Adapting the cognitive walkthrough method to assess the usability of a knowledge domain visualization.' In *INFOVIS 2005: IEEE Symposium on Information Visualization*, London: IEEE, pp. 195–202.

Anderson, J. R. and Lebiere, C. 1998. *The Atomic Components of Thought*. Mahwah, NJ: Lawrence Erlbaum Associates.

Apro, B. and Hammond, G. 2005. *Hackers: The Hunt for Australia's Most Infamous Computer Cracker.* Rowville, Australia: Five Mile Press.

Aristotle and Ackrill, J. L. 1975. *Categories*. Oxford: Clarendon Press.

Aula, A., Majaranta, P. and Rih, K. J. 2005. 'Eyetracking reveals the personal styles for search result evaluation.' In Constabile, M.F. and Paternò, F. (eds.) *Proc. of INTERACT 2005*, Lecture Notes in Computer Science, Berlin: Springer, 3585:1058–61.

Barnard, P. J. and May, J. 1999. 'Representing cognitive activity in complex tasks.' *Human–Computer Interaction* 14(1–2):93–158.

Baumeister, L. K., John, B. E. and Byrne, M. D. 2000. 'A comparison of tools for building GOMS models.' In *Proc. of CHI 2000*, New York: ACM Press, pp. 502–9.

Behrmann, G., David, A. and Larsen, K. G. 2004. 'A tutorial on Uppaal.' In Bernardo, M. and Corradini, F. (eds.) *Formal Methods for the Design of Real-time*

Systems, Springer Lecture Notes in Computer Science, Berlin: Springer, 3185: 200–36.

Bérard, M., Bidoit, M., Finkel, A., Laroussinie, F., Petit, A., Petrucci, L. and Schnoebelen, P. 2001. *Systems and Software Verification: Model-Checking Techniques and Tools*. Berlin: Springer.

Beyer, H. and Holtzblatt, K. 1998. *Contextual Design*. San Francisco: Morgan Kaufmann.

Bibby, J. 2007. *Jay Is Games (Casual Gameplay)*, jayisgames.com.

Blackmon, M. H., Kitajima, M. and Polson, P. G. 2003. 'Repairing usability problems identified by the cognitive walkthrough for the web.' In *Proc. of CHI 2003*, New York: ACM Press, pp. 497–504.

Blackmon, M. H., Polson, P. G., Kitajima, M. and Lewis, C. 2002. 'Cognitive walkthrough for the web.' In *Proc. of CHI 2002*, New York: ACM Press, pp. 463–70.

Blandford, A., Adams, A., Attfield, S., Buchanan, G., Gow, J., Makri, S., Rimmer, J. and Warwick, C. (2008). 'PRET A Reporter: evaluating digital libraries alone and in context.' *Information Processing and Management*.

Blandford, A. E., Buckingham Shum, S. and Young, R. M. 1998. 'Training software engineers in a novel usability evaluation technique.' *Int. J. of Human–Computer Studies* 45(3):245–79.

Blandford, A., Green, T. and Connell, I. 2005. 'Formalising an understanding of user-system misfits.' In Bastide, R., Palanque, P. and Roth, J. (eds.) *Proc. of EHCI-DSVIS 2004*, Lecture Notes in Computer Science, Berlin: Springer, 3452:253–70.

Blandford, A. E., Harrison, M. D. and Barnard, P. J. 1995. 'Using Interaction Framework to guide the design of interactive systems.' *Int. J. of Human–Computer Studies* 43:101–30.

Blandford, A. E., Hyde, J. K., Green, T. R. G. and Connell, I. (in press) 'Scoping usability evaluation methods: A case study.' *Human–Computer Interaction*.

Blandford, A., Keith, S., Connell, I. and Edwards, H. 2004. 'Analytical usability evaluation for digital libraries: A case study.' In *Proc. of ACM/IEEE Joint Conference on Digital Libraries*. New York: ACM Press, pp. 27–36.

Blandford, A., Keith, S. and Fields, B. 2006. 'Claims analysis 'in the wild': A case study on digital library development.' *Int. J. of Human–Computer Interaction* 21(2):197–218.

Blandford, A. E. and Young, R. M. 1996. 'Specifying user knowledge for the design of interactive systems.' *Software Engineering* 11(6):323–33.

Blythe, M. A., Overbeeke, K., Monk, A. and Wright, P. C. (eds.) 2003. *Funology*. Dordrecht: Kluwer Academic Publishers.

Boden, M. A. 1988. *Computer Models of Mind*. Cambridge: Cambridge University Press.

Bojko, A. 2005. 'Eyetracking in user experience testing: How to make the most of it.' In *Proc. of the UPA 2005*, Bloomingdale, IL: Usability Professionals' Association.

  2006. 'Using eyetracking to compare web page designs: A case study.' *J. of Usability Studies* 3(1):112–20.

Bowers, J., Pycock, J. and O'Brien, J. 1996. 'Talk and embodiment in collaborative virtual environments.' In *Proc. of CHI 1996*, New York: ACM Press, pp. 58–65.

Brewster, S., McGookin, D. and Miller, C. 2006. 'Olfoto: Designing a smell-based interaction.' In *Proc. of CHI 2006*, New York: ACM Press, pp. 653–62.

British Psychological Society 2006. *Code of Ethics and Conduct*. Available from www.bps.org.uk/ (viewed 7 November 2006).

Brown, E. and Cairns, P. 2004. 'A grounded investigation of immersion in games.' In *Proc. of CHI 2004*, New York: ACM Press, pp. 1297–300.

Brumby, D. P., Cutrell, E. and Sarin, R. 2006. 'Eyetracking in practice: The path to evaluating a new interface for personal desktop search.' In Webb, N. and Renshaw, J. A. (eds.) *Getting a Measure of Satisfaction of Eyetracking in Practice*, CHI 2006 workshop, Broomfield, USA, www.amber-light.co.uk/CHI2006/CHI2006ETWkshop.htm

Bruseberg, A. and McDonagh-Philp, D. 2002. 'Focus groups to support the industrial/product designer: A review based on current literature and designers' feedback.' *Applied Ergonomics: Human Factors in Technology and Society* 33(1):27–38.

Bryman, A. 1988. *Quantity and Quality in Social Research.* London: Unwin Hyman.

Burke, M., Hornhof A., Nilsen E. and Gorman N. 2005. 'High-cost banner blindness: Ads increase perceived workload, hinder visual search and are forgotten.' *ACM Trans. on Computer–Human Interaction* 12(4):423–45.

Butts, L. and Cockburn, A. 2001. 'An evaluation of mobile phone text input methods.' *Proc. of AUIC 2002*, New York: ACM Press, pp. 55–9.

Cairns, P. (2007) 'HCI . . . but not as it should be: Inferential statistics in HCI.' In *Proc. of BCS HCI*, vol. 1, pp. 195–201.

Campos, J. C. 1999. 'Automated Deduction and Usability Reasoning.' PhD thesis, Department of Computer Science, University of York, UK.

Campos, J. C. and Harrison, M. D. 1998. 'The role of verification in interactive systems design.' In Markopoulos, P. and Johnson, P. (eds.) *Proc. Eurographics Workshop on Design Specification and Verification of Interactive Systems, 1998*, Berlin: Springer, pp. 155–70.

    2001. 'Model checking interactor specifications.' *Automated Software Engineering* 8:275–310.

Carbon C., Hutzler F. and Minge, M. 2006. 'Innovativeness in design investigated by eye movements and pupillometry.' *Psychology Science* 48(2):173–86.

Card, S., Moran, T. and Newell, A. 1983. *The Psychology of Human–Computer Interaction.* Hillsdale, NJ: Lawrence Erlbaum Associates.

Carroll, J. M. (ed.) 2003. *HCI Models, Theories, and Frameworks: Toward a Multidisciplinary Science.* San Francisco: Morgan Kaufmann.

Carroll, J. M. and Rosson, M. B. 1992. 'Getting around the task-artifact cycle: How to make claims and design by scenario.' *ACM Trans. on Information Systems* 10(2):181–212.

The Chicago Manual of Style (15th edn). Chicago: University of Chicago Press.

Cimatti, A., Clarke, E., Giunchiglia, E., Giunchiglia, F., Pistore, M., Roveri, M., Sebastiani, R. and Tacchella, A. 2002. 'NuSMV 2: An open source tool for symbolic model checking.' In Larsen, K. G. and Brinksma, E. (eds.) *Computer-Aided Verification (CAV 2002)*, Lecture Notes in Computer Science, Berlin: Springer, 2404: 241–68.

Clarke, E. M., Grumberg, O. and Peled, D. A. 1999. *Model Checking.* Cambridge, MA: MIT Press.

Clarke, S. 2005. 'Describing and measuring API usability with the cognitive dimensions.' In *Proc. Cognitive Dimensions of Notations 10th Anniversary Workshop.* www.cl.cam.ac.uk/afb21/CognitiveDimensions/workshop2005/Clarke_position_paper.pdf

Cochran, W. G. and Cox, G. M. 1992. *Experimental Designs*. New York: Wiley Classics Library.

Cockburn, A., Gutwin, C. and Alexander, J. 2006. 'Faster document navigation with space-filling thumbnails.' In *Proc. of CHI 2006*, New York: ACM Press, pp. 1–10.

Cohen, P. R. 1992. 'The role of natural language in a multimodal interface.' In *Proc. of UIST 1992*, New York: ACM Press, pp. 143–9.

Connell, I., Blandford, A. and Green, T. 2004. 'CASSM and cognitive walkthrough: Usability issues with ticket vending machines.' *Behaviour and Information Technology* 23(5):307–20.

Cooper, R. P. 2002. *Modelling High-Level Cognitive Processes*. Mahwah, NJ: Lawrence Erlbaum Associates.

Cowen, L., Ball, L. J. and Delin, J. 2002. 'An eye movement analysis of web page usability.' In Faulkner, X., Finlay, J. and Detienee, F. (eds.) *People and Computers XVI: Memorable Yet Invisible*, Berlin: Springer, pp. 317–35.

Cox, A. L., Cairns, P., Walton, A. and Lee, S. (in press) 'Tlk or txt? Using voice input for SMS composition.' *Personal and Ubiquitous Computing*.

Creswell, J. W. 2003. *Research Design: Qualitative, Quantitative, and Mixed Methods Approaches*. London: Sage Publications.

Cross, N. 2004. 'Expertise in design: An overview.' *Design Studies* 25:427–41.

Crystal, D. 2000. *The English Language: A Guided Tour of the Language*. London: Penguin Books.

Cuomo, D. L. and Bowen, C. D. 1994. 'Understanding usability issues addressed by three user-system interface evaluation techniques.' *Interacting with Computers* 6(1):86–108.

Czaja, R. and Blair, J. 1996. *Designing Surveys*. Thousand Oaks, CA: Pine Forge Press.

Dearden, A. and Finlay, J. 2006. 'Pattern languages in HCI: A critical review.' *Human–Computer Interaction* 21:5–47.

Degani, A. 1996. 'Modeling Human–Machine Systems: On Modes, Error, and Patterns of Interaction.' PhD thesis, Georgia Institute of Technology, USA.

DeGraef, P., Christiaens, D. and d'Ydewalle, G. 1990. 'Perceptual effects of scene context on object recognition.' *Psychological Research* 52:317–29.

Desurvire, H. W., Kondziela, J. M. and Atwood, M. E. 1992. 'What is gained and lost when using evaluation methods other than empirical testing.' In Monk, A., Diaper, D. and Harrison, M. D. (eds.) *People and Computers VII – Proc. of HCI 1992*, Cambridge: Cambridge University Press, pp. 89–102.

Dix, A. 1996–2007. *Research and Innovation Techniques*. www.hiraeth.com/alan/topics/res-tech

   2002. Teaching Innovation Keynote at Excellence in Education and Training Convention, Singapore Polytechnic, May.

   2007. 'Why examples are hard, and what to do about it.' *Interfaces* 72:16–18.

Dix, A., Beale, R. and Wood, A. 2000. 'Architectures to make Simple Visualisations using Simple Systems.' In *Proc. of Advanced Visual Interfaces – AVI 2000*, New York: ACM Press, pp. 51–60.

Dix, A., Finlay, J., Abowd, G. and Beale, R. 1998. *Human–Computer Interaction* (2nd edn). London: Prentice-Hall Europe.

Doherty, G. J., Campos, J. C. and Harrison, M. D. 2000. 'Representational reasoning and verification.' *Formal Aspects of Computing* 12(4):260–77.

Drury, C. G. and Clement, M. R. 1978. 'The effect of area, density, and number of background characters on visual search.' *Hum. Factors* 20:597–602.

Duchowski, A. 2006. 'High level eye movement metrics in the usability context.' In Webb, N. and Renshaw, J. A. (eds.) *Adding Value with Eyetracking*, UPA workshop, Montreal, Canada, www.amber-light.co.uk/UPA2006/UPA2006ETWkshop.htm

2007. *Eye Tracking Methodology Theory and Practice* (2nd edn). London: Springer-Verlag.

Duncker, E. 2002. 'Cross-cultural usability of the library metaphor.' In *Proc. of JCDL 2002*, New York: ACM Press, pp. 223–30.

Dwyer, M. B., Avrunin, G. S. and Corbett, J. C. 1999. 'Patterns in property specifications for finite-state verification.' In *21st International Conference on Software Engineering 1999*, Los Angeles, California.

Eger, N., Ball, L. J., Stevens R. and Dodd, J. 2007. 'Cueing retrospective verbal reports through eye movement replay.' In Ball, L. J., Sasse, M. A., Sas, C., Ormerod, T. C., Dix, A., Bagnall, P. and McEwan, T. (eds.) *People and Computers XXI – HCI . . . but not as we know it*. Swindon: The British Computer Society, pp. 129–38.

Ehmke, C. and Wilson, S. 2007. 'Identifying web usability problems from eyetracking data. In Ball, L. J., Sasse, M. A., Sas, C., Ormerod, T. C., Dix, A., Bagnall, P. and McEwan, T. (eds.) *People and Computers XXI – HCI . . . but not as we know it*. Swindon: The British Computer Society, pp. 119–28.

Ellis, G. and Dix, A. 2006. 'An explorative analysis of user evaluation studies in information visualisation.' In *Proc. of the 2006 Conference on Beyond Time and Errors: Novel Evaluation Methods for Information Visualization, BELIV 2006*, New York: ACM Press, pp. 1–7.

Fafchamps, D. 1991. 'Ethnographic workflow analysis: Specifications for design.' In Bullinger, H. J. (ed.) *Human Aspects in Computing: Design and Use of Interactive Systems and Work with Terminals*. Amsterdam: Elsevier, pp. 709–15.

Faisal, S., Cairns, P. and Craft, B. 2005. 'InfoVis experience enhancement through mediated interaction.' *ICMI 2005 Workshop on Multimodal Interaction for the Visualization and Exploration of Scientific Data*, Lake Como, Italy.

Fawcett, J. and Downs, F. 1986. *The Relationship of Theory and Research*. Norwalk, CT: Appleton Century Crofts.

Feynman, R. P. 1992. *Surely You're Joking, Mr. Feynman!* London: Vintage.

Field, A. and Hole, G. J. 2002. *How to Design and Report Experiments*. London: Sage Publications.

Fitts, P. M. 1954. 'The information capacity of the human motor system in controlling the amplitude of movement.' *Journal of Experimental Psychology* 47(6):381–91. (Reprinted 1992, *Journal of Experimental Psychology: General* 121(3): 262–9.)

Folstad, A., Bark, I. and Gulliksen, J. 2006. 'How HCI practitioners want to evaluate their own practice.' In *Proc. of the 4th Nordic Conference on Human–Computer Interaction, NordiCHI 2006*, New York: ACM Press, pp. 417–20.

Foster, J. J., Barkus, E. and Yavorsky, C. 2005. *Understanding and Using Advanced Statistics*. London: Sage Publications.

Franconeri, S. L. and Simons, D. J. 2003. 'Moving and looming stimuli capture attention.' *Perception and Psychophysics* 65(7):999–1010.

Friedman, A. 1979. 'Framing pictures: The role of knowledge in automatized encoding and memory for gist.' *Journal of Experimental Psychology. General* 108(3):316–55.

Furniss, D. 2004. 'Codifying Distributed Cognition: A Case Study of Emergency Medical Dispatch.' MSc thesis, UCLIC (UCL Interaction Centre).

Furniss, D. and Blandford, A. 2006. 'Understanding emergency medical dispatch in terms of distributed cognition: A case study.' *Ergonomics Journal* 49(12/13):1174–203.

Gallivan, M. 2000. 'Examining workgroup influence on technology usage: A community of practice perspective.' In *Proc. of SIGCPR 2000*, New York: ACM Press, pp. 54–66.

Gardner, H. 1983. *Frames of Mind: The Theory of Multiple Intelligences*. New York: Basic Books.

Garret, J. J. 2002. *The Elements of User Experience*. Indianapolis: New Riders.

Gee, J. P. 2004. *What Videogames Have to Teach Us about Learning and Literacy*. New York: Palgrave Macmillan.

Gilroy, S. W., Olivier, P. L., Cao, H., Jackson, G. D., Kray, C. and Lin, D. 2006. 'CROSS-BOARD: Crossmodal access of dense public displays.' Paper presented at the International Workshop on Multimodal and Pervasive Services (MAPS06), Lyon, France.

Glaser, B. G. 1978. *Theoretical Sensitivity*. Mill Valley: Sociology Press.

Glaser, B. G. and Strauss, A. 1967. *The Discovery of Grounded Theory*. New York: Aldine De Gruyter.

Gluck, K. A. and Pew, R. W. (eds.) 2005. *Modeling Human Behavior with Integrated Cognitive Architectures*. Mahwah, NJ: Lawrence Erlbaum Associates.

Goldberg, J. H. and Kotval, X. P. 1999. 'Eye movement based evaluation of the computer interface: Its psychological foundation and relevance to display design.' *Int. J. of Industrial Ergonomics* (24)6:631–45.

Goldberg, J. H., Stimson, M. J., Lewenstein, M., Scott, N. and Wichansky, A. M. 2002. 'Eyetracking in web search tasks: Design implications.' In *Proc. of Eye Tracking Research and Applications 2002*, New York: ACM Press, pp. 51–8.

Goldberg, J. H. and Wichansky, A. M. 2003. 'Eyetracking in usability evaluation: A practitioner's guide.' In Hyönä, J., Radach, R. and Deubel, H. (eds.) *The Mind's Eye: Cognitive and Applied Aspects of Eye Movement Research*, Oxford: Elsevier Science, pp. 493–516.

Gong, R. and Kieras, D. 1994. 'A validation of the GOMS model methodology in the development of a specialized, commercial software application.' In *Proc. of CHI 1994*, New York: ACM Press, pp. 351–7.

Gow, J., Thimbleby, H. and Cairns, P. 2006. 'Automatic critiques of interface modes.' In Gilroy, S. and Harrison, M.D. (eds.) *Proc. 12th International Workshop on the Design, Specification and Verification of Interactive Systems*, Springer Lecture Notes in Computer Science, Berlin: Springer, 3941:201–12.

Graf, P. and Mandler, G. 1984. 'Activation makes words more accessible, but not necessarily more retrievable.' *Journal of Verbal Learning and Verbal Behavior* 23:553–68.

Graf, P. and Schacter, D. 1985. 'Implicit and explicit memory for new associations in normal and amnesic subjects.' *Journal of Experimental Psychology: Learning, Memory, and Cognition* 11:501–18.

Granka, L., Joachims, T. and Gay, G. 2004. 'Eyetracking analysis of user behaviour in WWW search.' *Proc. of SIGIR 2004*, New York: ACM Press, pp. 478–9.

Gray, W. D. and Boehm-Davis, D. A. 2000. 'Milliseconds matter: An introduction to microstrategies and to their use in describing and predicting interactive behavior.' *Journal of Experimental Psychology: Applied* 6:322–35.

Gray, W. D., John, B. E. and Atwood, M. E. 1993. 'Project Ernestine: Validating a GOMS analysis for predicting and explaining real-world performance.' *Human–Computer Interaction* 8:237–309.

Gray, W. D. and Salzman, M. C. 1998. 'Damaged merchandise? A review of experiments that compare usability evaluation methods.' *Human–Computer Interaction* 13(3):203–61.

Gray, W. D., Young, R. M. and Kirschenbaum, S. S. 1997. Introduction to Special Issue on Cognitive Architectures and Human–Computer Interaction. *Human–Computer Interaction* 12(4):301–9.

Green, T. R. G. 1989. 'Cognitive dimensions of notations.' In Sutcliffe, A. and Macaulay, L. (eds.) *People and Computers V.* Cambridge: Cambridge University Press, pp. 443–60.

1994. 'The cognitive dimensions of information structures.' *Technical Communication* 41(3):544–8.

Green, T. R. G. and Benyon, D. 1996. 'The skull beneath the skin: Entity-relationship models of information artefacts.' *Int. J. of Human–Computer Studies* 44(6):801–28.

Green, T. R. G., Blandford, A. E., Church, L., Roast, C. R. and Clarke, S. 2006. 'Cognitive dimensions: Achievements, new directions, and open questions.' *J. of Visual Languages and Computing* 17(4):328–65.

Green, T. R. G. and Petre, M. 1996. 'Usability analysis of visual programming environments: A cognitive dimensions framework.' *J. of Visual Languages and Visual Computing* 7:131–74.

Greene, J. and D'Oliveira, M. 2006. *Learning to Use Statistical Tests in Psychology.* Maidenhead, UK: Open University Press.

Gregory, R. L. 1998. *Eye and Brain: The Psychology of Seeing.* Oxford: Oxford University Press.

Guan, Y. H. 2006. 'Eye movement analysis in multimedia based learning scenarios.' In Webb and Renshaw, 2006b.

Harel, D. 1987. 'Statecharts: A visual formalism for complex systems.' *Science of Computer Programming* 8:231–74.

Harris, P. 2002. *Designing and Reporting Experiments in Psychology.* Maidenhead, UK: Open University Press.

Hawes, L. 1975. *Pragmatics of Analoguing: Theory and Model Construction in Communication.* Reading, MA: Addison-Wesley Publishing Company.

Henderson, J. M. and Ferreira, F. (eds.) 2004. *The Interface of Language, Vision and Action: Eye Movements and the Visual World.* London: Psychology Press.

Henwood, K. L. and Pidgeon, N. F. 1992. 'Qualitative research and psychological theorising.' *British J. of Psychology* 83(1):97–111.

Heritage, J. 1984. *Garfinkle and Ethnomethodology.* Cambridge: Polity Press.

Hertzum, M. and Jacobsen, N. E. 2001. 'The evaluator effect: A chilling fact about usability evaluation methods.' *Int. J. of Human–Computer Interaction* 13(4):421–43.

Hindus, D., Ackerman, M., Mainwaring, S. and Star, B. 1996. 'Thunderwire: A field study of an audio-only media space.' In *Proc. of ACM CSCW 1996*, New York: ACM Press, pp. 238–47.

Hirotaka, N. 2003. 'Reassessing current cell phone designs: Using thumb input effectively.' In *Proc. of CHI 2003*. New York: ACM Press, pp. 938–9.

Hitchings, J. 1995. 'Deficiencies of the traditional approach to information security and the requirements for a new methodology.' *Computers and Security* 14:377–83.

Hollan, J. D., Hutchins, E. L. and Kirsh, D. 2000. 'Distributed cognition: Toward a new foundation for human–computer interaction research.' *ACM Trans. on Computer–Human Interaction* 7(2):174–96.

Hollnagel, E. 1993. *Human Reliability Analysis: Context and Control*. London: Academic Press.

Holmqvist, K., Holsanova, J., Barthelson, M. and Lundqvist, D. 2003. 'Reading or scanning? A study of newspaper and net paper reading.' In Hyönä, J., Radach, R. and Deubel, H. (eds.) *The Mind's Eye: Cognitive and Applied Aspects of Eye Movement Research*, Oxford: Elsevier Science, pp. 657–70.

Holzmann, G. J. 2003. *The SPIN Model Checker, Primer and Reference Manual*. Harlow, UK: Addison Wesley.

Hornbaek, K. and Law, E. L. C. 2007. 'Meta-analysis of correlations among usability measures.' *Proc. of CHI 2007*, New York: ACM Press, pp. 617–26.

Horrocks, I. 1999. *Constructing the User Interfaces with StateCharts*. Harlow, UK: Addison Wesley.

Hutchins, E. 1995. *Cognition in the Wild*. Cambridge, MA: MIT Press.

Huth, M. R. A. and Ryan, M. D. 2000. *Modelling and Reasoning about Systems*. Cambridge: Cambridge University Press.

Hyde, J. K. 2002. 'Multi-Modal Usability Evaluation.' PhD thesis, Middlesex University, London, UK.

ICCM 2006. iccm2006.units.it/index.html

ICCM 2007. sitemaker.umich.edu/iccm2007.org/home

Iqbal, S., Adamcyzk, P. D., Zheng, X. S. and Bailey, B. P. 2005. 'Towards an index of opportunity: Understanding changes in mental workload during task execution.' In *Proc. of CHI 2005*, New York: ACM Press, pp. 311–20.

Iqbal, S. T., Zheng, X. S. and Bailey, B. P. 2004. 'Task evoked pupillary response to mental workload in human–computer interaction.' In *Proc. of CHI 2004*, New York: ACM Press, pp. 1477–80.

Jackson, D. 2006. *Software Abstractions: Logic, Language and Analysis*. Cambridge, MA: MIT Press.

Jacob, R. J. K. 1991. 'The use of eye movements in human–computer interaction techniques: What you look at is what you get.' *ACM Trans. on Information Systems* 9(3):152–69.

Jacob, R. J. K. and Karn, S. K. 2003. 'Eyetracking in human–computer interaction and usability research: Ready to deliver the promises.' In Hyönä, J., Radach, R. and Deubel, H. (eds.) *The Mind's Eye: Cognitive and Applied Aspects of Eye Movement Research*, Oxford: Elsevier Science, pp. 573–606.

Jeffries, R., Miller, J. R., Wharton, C. and Uyeda, K. M. 1991. 'User interface evaluation in the real world: A comparison of four techniques.' In *Proc. of CHI 1991*, New York: ACM Press, pp. 119–24.

Jennett, C., Cox, A., Cairns, P., Dhoparee, S., Epps, A., Tijs, T. and Walton, A. (in press) 'Measuring and defining the experience of immersion in games.' *Int. J. of Human–Computer Studies*.

John, B. E. 1988. 'Contributions to Engineering Models of Human–Computer Interaction' (volumes I and II). Phd Thesis, Carnegie Mellon University, USA.

1996. 'TYPIST: A theory of performance in skilled typing.' *Human–Computer Interaction* 11(4):321–55.

John, B. E. and Kieras, D. E. 1996a. 'The GOMS family of user interface analysis techniques: Comparison and contrast.' *ACM Transactions on Computer–Human Interaction* 3(4):320–51.

1996b. 'Using GOMS for user interface design and evaluation: Which technique?' *ACM Transactions on Computer–Human Interaction* 3(4):287–319.

John, B. E. and Packer, H. 1995. 'Learning and using the cognitive walkthrough method: A case study approach.' In *Proc. of CHI 1995*, New York: ACM Press, pp. 429–36.

John, B. E., Vera, A., Matessa, M., Freed, M. and Remington, R. 2002. 'Automating CPM-GOMS.' In *Proc. of CHI 2002*, New York: ACM Press, pp. 147–54.

Johnson P. 1992. *Human–Computer Interaction: Psychology, Task Analysis and Software Engineering*. London: McGraw-Hill.

Jordan, P. 2002. *Designing Pleasurable Products*. London: Taylor and Francis.

Josephson, S. and Holmes, M. E. 2002. 'Visual attention to repeated Internet images: Testing the scanpath theory on the World Wide Web.' In *Proc. of Eye Tracking Research and Applications 2002*, New York: ACM Press, pp. 43–9.

Just, M. A. and Carpenter, P. A. 1976. 'Eye fixations and cognitive processes.' *Cognitive Psychology* 8:441–80.

Karat, C. M., Campbell, R. and Fiegle, T. 1992. 'Comparison of empirical testing and walkthrough methods in user interface evaluation.' In *Proc. of CHI 1992*, New York: ACM Press, pp. 397–404.

Karn, K. S. 2000. ' "Saccade pickers" vs. "Fixation pickers": The effect of eyetracking instrumentation on research.' In *Proc. of Eye Tracking Research and Applications*, New York: ACM Press, pp. 87–8.

Kasarskis, P., Stehwien, J., Hickox, J., Aretz, A. and Wickens, C. 2001. 'Comparison of expert and novice scan behaviours during VFR Flight.' In *Proc. of 11th Int. Symp. on Aviation Psychology*, Columbus, OH: The Ohio State University.

Keele. S. 1968. 'Movement control in skilled motor performance.' *Psychological Bulletin* 70:387–402.

Kieras, D. E. 1994. 'A Guide to GOMS Task Analysis.' Unpublished manuscript, University of Michigan.

1997. 'A guide to GOMS model usability evaluation using NGOMSL.' In Helander, M., Landauer, T. and Prabhu, P. (eds.) *Handbook of Human–Computer Interaction* (2nd edn), Amsterdam: North Holland, pp. 733–66.

2001. 'Using the Keystroke-level Model to Estimate Execution Times.' Unpublished manuscript, University of Michigan.

Kline, P. 1993. *An Easy Guide to Factor Analysis*. London: Routledge.

Kray, C., Kortuem, G. and Krüger, A. 2005. 'Adaptive navigation support with public displays.' In St. Amant, R., Riedl, J. and Jameson, A. (eds.) *Proc. of IUI 2005*, New York: ACM Press, pp. 326–8.

Kuhn, T. 1962/1970. *The Structure of Scientific Revolutions*. Chicago: University of Chicago Press. (1962, 1st edn; 1970, 2nd edn, with postscript.)

Latour, B. 1987. *Science in Action*. Milton Keynes, UK: Open University Press.

Lave, J. and Wenger, E. 1991. *Situated Learning: Legitimate Peripheral Participation*. Cambridge: Cambridge University Press.

Lewis, C. H., Poison, P. G., Wharton, C. and Rieman, J. 1990. 'Testing a walkthrough methodology for theory-based design of walk-up-and-use interfaces.' In *Proc. of CHI 1990*, New York: ACM Press, pp. 235–41.

Li, S. Y. W., Cox, A. L., Blandford, A., Cairns, P. and Abeles, A. 2006. 'Further investigations into post-completion error: The effects of interruption position and duration.' In *Proc. of the 28th Annual Meeting of the Cognitive Science Society*, Vancouver, BC, Canada.

Loer, K. 2003. 'Model-based Automated Analysis for Dependable Interactive Systems.' PhD thesis, Department of Computer Science, University of York, UK.

Loer, K. and Harrison, M. D. 2005. 'Analysing user confusion in context aware mobile applications.' In Constabile, M. F. and Paternò, F. (eds.) *Proc. of INTERACT 2005*, Springer Lecture Notes in Computer Science, Berlin: Springer, 3585: 184–97.

   2006. 'An integrated framework for the analysis of dependable interactive systems (ifadis): Its tool support and evaluation.' *Automated Software Engineering* 13(4):469–96.

Lohse, G. L. 1993. 'A cognitive model for understanding graphical perception.' *Human–Computer Interaction* 8:353–88.

Long, J. and Dowell, J. 1989. 'Conceptions of the discipline of HCI: Craft, applied science, and engineering.' In Sutcliffe, A. and Macaulay, L. (eds.) *People and Computers V – Proc. of HCI 1989*, Cambridge: Cambridge University Press, pp. 9–32.

Lunt, P. and Livingstone, S. 1996. 'Rethinking the focus group in media and communications research.' *J. of Communications* 46(2):79–98.

MacKenzie, D. 1994. 'Computer-related accidental death: An empirical exploration.' *Science and Public Policy*, 21(4):233–48.

MacKenzie, S. I., Kober, H., Smith, D., Jones, T. and Skepner, E. 2001. 'Letter wise: Prefix-based disambiguation for mobile text input.' In *Proc. of CHI 2001*, New York: ACM Press, pp. 111–20.

Marshall, S. P. 2002. 'The Index of Cognitive Activity: Measuring cognitive workload.' In *Proc. of IEEE 7th Human Factors Meeting*, London: IEEE, 7-5-7-9.

Matessa, M. 2004. 'An ACT-R framework for interleaving templates of human behavior.' In *Proc. of the 26th Annual Conference of the Cognitive Science Society*, Mahwah, NJ: Lawrence Erlbaum Associates.

May, J., Barnard, P. and Blandford, A. 1993. 'Using structural descriptions of interfaces to automate the modelling of user cognition.' *User Modelling and User-Adapted Interaction* 3(1):27–64.

McCann, T. and Clark, E. 2003. 'Grounded theory in nursing research: Pt 1.' *Nurse Researcher* 11(2):7–18.

McCarthy, J., Sasse, M. A. and Riegelsberger, J. (2003). 'Could I have the menu please? An eyetracking study of design conventions.' In O'Neill, E., Palanque, P. and Johnson, P. (eds.) *People and Computers XVII: Designing for Society*, Berlin: Springer Verlag, pp. 401–14.

McCarthy, J. and Wright, P. C. 2006. *Technology as Experience*. Cambridge, MA: MIT Press.

McGuffin, M. and Balakrishnan, R. 2005. 'Fitts' law and expanding targets: Experimental studies and designs for user interfaces.' *ACM Trans. on Computer–Human Interaction* 12(4):388–422.

McMillan, K. L. 1993. *Symbolic Model Checking*. Dordrecht: Kluwer.

Meyer, D., Abrams, R., Kornblum, S., Wright, C. and Smith, J. 1988. 'Optimality in human motor performance: Ideal control of rapid aimed movements.' *Psychological Review* 95:340–70.

Milekic, S. 2003. *The More You Look the More You Get: Intention based Interface Using Gaze-Tracking*. www.archimuse.com/mw2003/papers/milekic.html

Minsky, M. 1965. 'Matter, mind and models.' In *Proc. Int. Federation of Information Processing Congress 1965*, vol. 1, pp. 45–9. web.media.mit.edu/minsky/papers/ MatterMindModels.html

Morgan, M. 1996. 'Qualitative research: A package deal?' *The Psychologist: Bulletin of the British Psychological Society* January:31–2.

Moyle, M. and Cockburn, A. 2005. 'A flick in the right direction: A case study of gestural input.' *Behaviour and Information Technology* 24(4):275–88.

Newell, A. 1990. *Unified Theories of Cognition*. Cambridge, MA: Harvard University Press.

Nielsen, J. 1992. 'Finding usability problems through heuristic evaluation.' In *Proc. of CHI 1992*, New York: ACM Press, pp. 249–56.

    1994a. 'Heuristic evaluation.' In Nielsen, J. and Mack, R. (eds.) *Usability Inspection Methods*, New York: John Wiley, pp. 25–62.

    1994b. 'Estimating the number of subjects needed for a thinking aloud test.' *Int. J. of Human–Computer Studies* 41(3):385–97.

    1995. 'Technology transfer of heuristic evaluation and usability inspection.' Keynote paper presented at *Interact 1995*. Available from www.useit.com/papers/ heuristic/learning_inspection.html

Nielsen, J. and Landauer, T. K. 1993. 'A mathematical model of the finding of usability problems.' In *Proc. of CHI 1993*, New York: ACM Press, pp. 206–13.

Nielsen, J. and Molich, R. 1990. 'Heuristic evaluation of user interfaces.' In *Proc. of CHI 1990*, New York: ACM Press, pp. 249–56.

Nightingale, D. and Cromby, J. (eds.) 1999. *Social Constructivist Psychology*. Maidenhead, UK: Open University Press.

Nilsson, J., Sokoler, T., Binder, T. and Wetcke, N. 2000. 'Beyond the control room: Mobile devices for spatially distributed interaction on industrial process plants.' In Thomas, P. and Gellersen, H. W. (eds.) *Handheld and Ubiquitous Computing, HUC 2000*, Springer Lecture Notes in Computer Science, Berlin: Springer, 1927: 30–45.

Nipkow, T., Paulson, L. C. and Wenzel, M. 2002. *Isabelle/HOL: A Proof Assistant for Higher-Order Logic*. Springer Lecture Notes in Computer Science, Berlin: Springer, 2283.

Nodine C. F., Kundel, H. L., Lauver, S. C. and Toto, L. G. 1996. 'Nature of expertise in searching mammograms for breast masses.' *Academic Radiology* 3:1000–1006.

Norman, D. 1998. *The Design of Everyday Things*. Cambridge, MA: MIT Press.

    2004. *Emotional Design*. New York: Basic Books.

OED 1973. 'Theory (definition).' In Little, W., Fowler, H., Coulson, J., Onions, C. and Friedrichsen, G. (eds.) *The Shorter Oxford English Dictionary on Historical Principles* (3rd edn, vol. II), Oxford: Clarendon Press, p. 2281.

Owre, S., Rushby, J. and Shankar, N. 1992. 'PVS: A prototype verification system.' In Kapur, D. (ed.) *11th International Conference on Automated Deduction (CADE 92)*, Lecture Notes in Artificial Intelligence, Berlin: Springer, 607:748–52.

Pace, S. 2004. 'A grounded theory of the flow experiences of web users.' *Int. J. of Human–Computer Studies* 60:327–63.

Pagano, R. 2006. *Understanding Statistics for the Behavioral Sciences* (6th edn). London: Wadsworth.

Pahl, G. and Beitz, W. 1984. *Engineering Design*. London: The Design Council.

Palmer, S. E. 2002. *Vision Science: Photons to Phenomenology*. Cambridge, MA: MIT Press.

Partala, T., Jokiniemi, M. and Surakka, V. 2000. 'Pupillary responses to emotionally provocative stimuli.' In *Proc. of Eye Tracking Research and Applications 2000*, New York: ACM Press, pp. 123–9.

Payne, S. J., Duggan, G. B. and Neth, H. (in press). 'Discretionary task interleaving: Heuristics for time allocation in cognitive foraging.' *Journal of Experimental Psychology: General*.

Payne, S. J. and Green, T. R. G. 1986. 'Task-Action Grammars: The model of the mental representation of task languages.' *Human–Computer Interaction* 2:93–133.

Peebles, D. and Cheng, P. C.-H. 2001. 'Extending task analytic models of graph-based reasoning: A cognitive model of problem solving with Cartesian graphs in ACT-R/PM.' In *Proceedings of the 4th International Conference on Cognitive Modeling*, Mahwah, NJ: Lawrence Erlbaum Associates.

  2002. 'Extending task analytic models of graph-based reasoning: A cognitive model of problem solving with Cartesian graphs in ACT-R/PM.' *Cognitive Systems Research* 3:77–86.

  2003. 'Modeling the effect of task and graphical representation on response latency in a graph reading task.' *Human Factors* 45:28–46.

Peebles, D., Cheng, P. C.-H. and Shadbolt, N. R. 1999. 'Multiple processes in graph-based reasoning.' In *Proceedings of the 21st Annual Conference of the Cognitive Science Society*, Mahwah, NJ: Lawrence Erlbaum Associates.

Plain English Campaign 2003. *Foot in Mouth Award 2003*. www.plainenglish.co.uk/footinmouth.htm#2003

Polk, T. and Seifert, C. 2002. *Cognitive Modeling*. Cambridge, MA: MIT Press.

Pomerantz, J. 1986. 'Visual perception: An overview.' In Schwab, E. and Nusbaum, H. (eds.) *Pattern Recognition by Humans and Machines*, vol. II, London: Academic Press, pp. 1–30.

Poole, A. and Ball, L. J. 2005. 'Eyetracking in human–computer interaction and usability research: Current status and future prospects.' In Ghaoui, C. (ed.) *Encyclopedia of Human Computer Interaction*, Hersley, USA: Idea Group, pp. 211–19.

Popper, K. 1959. *The Logic of Scientific Discovery*. New York: Basic Books.

Radach, R., Lemmer, S., Vorstius, C., Heller, D. and Radach, K. 2003. 'Eye movements in the processing of print advertisements.' In Hyönä, J., Radach, R. and Deubel, H. *The Mind's Eye: Cognitive and Applied Aspects of Eye Movement Research*, Oxford: Elsevier Science, pp. 609–32.

Rayner, K. 1998. 'Eye movements in reading and information processing: 20 years of research.' *Psychological Bulletin* 124(3):372–422.

Razavim, M. N. and Iverson, L. 2006. 'A grounded theory of information sharing behavior in a personal learning space.' In *Proc. of CSCW 2006*, New York: ACM Press, pp. 459–68.

Read, J., MacFarlane, S. and Casey, C. 2002. 'Endurability, engagement and expectations: Measuring children's fun.' In Bekker, M. M., Markopoulos, P. and Kersten-Tsikalkina, M. (eds.) *Interaction Design and Children: Proceedings of the International Workshop*, Eindhoven: Shaker Publishing.

Renshaw, J. A., Stevens, R. C. and Finlay, J. E. 2006. *Eyetracking for Dynamic Scenes: Enhancing the Study of Game Playing Behaviour.* Innovation North: Research in Progress Workshop. Leeds Metropolitan University. www.leedsmet.ac.uk/inn/rip2006.htm

Renshaw, J. A., Finlay, J. E., Tyfa, D. and Ward, R. D. 2003. 'Designing for visual influence: An eyetracking study of the usability of graphical management information.' In Rauterberg, G.W.M., Menozzi, M. and Wesson, J. (eds.) *Human Computer Interaction, INTERACT 2003*, Amsterdam: IOS Press, pp. 144–51.

2004a. 'Regressions re-visited: A new definition for the visual display paradigm.' In *Proc. of CHI 2004*, New York: ACM Press, pp. 1437–40.

Renshaw, J. A., Finlay, J. E., Ward, R. D. and Tyfa, D. 2004b. 'Understanding visual influence in graph design through temporal and spatial eye movement characteristics.' *Interacting with Computers* 16:557–78.

Renshaw, J. A., Finlay, J. E., Tyfa, D. and Ward, R. D. 2005. 'A Back track to satisfaction.' In *Proc. of British Human Computer Interaction 2005,* vol. II, Swindon: British Computer Society, pp. 73–6.

Ritter, F. E. 2004. 'Choosing and getting started with a cognitive architecture to test and use human–machine interfaces.' *MMI-Interaktiv-Journal* 7:17–37.

Roast, C. R., Khazaei, B. and Siddiqi, J. 2000. 'Formal comparison of program modification.' In *IEEE Symposium on Visual Languages 2000*, London: IEEE Computer Society, pp. 165–71.

Rowntree, D. 2000. *Statistics without Tears.* London: Penguin Books.

Sadasivan, S., Greenstein, J. S., Gramopadhye, A. K. and Duchowski, A. T. 2005. 'Use of eye movements as feedforward training for a synthetic aircraft inspection task.' In *Proc. of CHI 2004*, New York: ACM Press, pp. 141–9.

Saffer, D. 2006. *Designing for Interaction: Creating Smart Applications and Clever Devices.* Indianapolis: New Riders.

Salvucci, D. D. 2001. 'Predicting the effects of in-car interface use on driver performance: An integrated model approach.' *Int. J. of Human–Computer Studies* 55:85–107.

Salvucci, D. D. and Goldberg, J. 2000. 'Identifying fixations and saccades in eyetracking protocols.' In *Proc. of Eye Tracking Research and Applications 2000*, New York: ACM Press, pp. 71–8.

Salvucci, D. D. and Lee, F. J. 2003. 'Simple cognitive modeling in a complex cognitive architecture.' In *Proc. of CHI 2003*, New York: ACM Press, pp. 265–72.

Santella, A. and DeCarlo, D. 2004. 'Robust clustering of eye movement recordings for quantification of visual interest.' In *Proc. of Eye Tracking Research and Applications 2004*, New York: ACM Press, pp. 27–34.

Savage, J. and Cockburn, A. 2005. 'Comparing automatic and manual zooming methods for acquiring off-screen targets.' In McEwan, T., Gulliksen, J. and Benyon, D. (eds.) *People and Computers XIX: the Bigger Picture – Proc. of HCI 2005*, Berlin: Springer, pp. 439–54.

Schiele, F. and Green, T. R. G. 1990. 'Formalisms in HCI: The case of Task-Action Grammar.' In Harrison, M. and Thimbleby, H. (eds.) *Formal Methods in Human–Computer Interaction*. Cambridge: Cambridge University Press, pp. 9–62.

Schmidt, A. 2000. 'Implicit human computer interaction through context.' *Personal and Ubiquitous Technologies* 4(2):191–9.

Sears, A. 1997. 'Heuristic walkthroughs: Finding the problems without the noise.' *Int. J. of Human–Computer Interaction* 9(3):213–34.

Sennersten, C., Alfredson, J., Castor, M., Hedström, J., Lindahl, B., Lindley, C. and Svensson, E. 2007. 'Verification of an experimental platform integrating a Tobii eyetracking system with the HiFi game engine.' In *Proc. of The Scandinavian Workshop on Applied Eye Tracking*, Lund University, Sweden. www2.foi.se/rapp/foir2227.pdf

Sharp, H., Robinson, H., Segal, J. and Furniss, D. 2006. 'The role of story cards and the wall in XP teams: A distributed cognition perspective.' In *Proc. of Agile 2006*, London: IEEE Computer Society, pp. 65–75.

Sherrard, C. 1997. 'Qualitative research: Never mind the bath water, keep hold of the baby.' *The Psychologist: Bulletin of the British Psychological Society* April: 161–2.

Sibert, L. E. and Jacob, R. J. K. 2000. 'Evaluation of eye gaze interaction.' In *Proc. of CHI 2000*, New York: ACM Press, pp. 281–8.

Silfverberg, M., MacKenzie, I. S. and Korhonen, P. 2000. 'Predicting text entry speed on mobile phones.' In *Proc. of CHI 2000*, New York: ACM Press, pp. 9–16.

Silva, M. and Cox, A. L. 2006. 'Can parafoveal processing explain skipping behaviour in interactive menu search?' *J. of Vision* 6(6):524.

Spence, R. 2001. *Information Visualization*. New York: ACM Press.

Spencer, R. 2000. 'The streamlined cognitive walkthrough method: Working around social constraints encountered in a software development company.' In *Proc. of CHI 2000*, New York: ACM Press, pp. 353–9.

Star, S. L. and Griesemer, J. R. 1989. 'Institutional ecology, "translations" and boundary objects: Amateurs and professionals in Berkeley's museum of vertebrate zoology, 1907–1930.' *Social Studies of Science* 19(3):389–420.

Stevenson, C. and Cooper, N. 1997. 'Qualitative and quantitative research.' *The Psychologist: Bulletin of the British Psychological Society* April:159–60.

Strauss, A., Bucher, R., Ehrich, D., Schatsman, L. and Sabshin, M. 1964. *Psychiatric Ideologies and Institutions*. Chicago: Free Press.

Strauss, A. and Corbin, J. 1990. *Basics of Qualitative Research: Grounded Theory Procedures and Techniques*. London: Sage Publications.

1998. *Basics of Qualitative Research: Techniques and Procedures for Developing Grounded Theory*. Thousand Oaks, CA: Sage Publications.

Strunk, W. and White, E. B. 2000. *The Elements of Style* (4th edn). Needham Heights, MA: Allyn and Bacon.

Suchman, L. 1987. *Plans and Situated Actions*. Cambridge: Cambridge University Press.

Thimbleby, H. 2004a. 'Supporting diverse HCI research.' In Dearden, A. and Watts, L. (eds.) *Proc. of BCS HCI Conference*, vol. II, Bristol: Research Press International, pp. 125–8.

2004b. 'User interface design with matrix algebra.' *ACM Transactions on Computer–Human Interaction* 11(2):181–236.

Tobii User Manual (2006) Tobii Eye Tracker. Clearview Analysis Software. Tobii Technology AB. www.tobii.se/linkpage.asp?sid=826

Tufte, E. R. 1992. *The Visual Display of Quantitative Information*. Cheshire, CT: Graphics Press.

Underwood, J. 2005. 'Novice and expert performance with a dynamic control task: Scanpaths during a computer game.' In Underwood, G. (ed.) *Cognitive Processes in Eye Guidance*, Oxford: Oxford University Press, pp. 303–24.

Uppaal 4.0.6 (2007). www.uppaal.com/

Veen, J. 2001. *The Art and Science of Web Design*. Indianapolis: New Riders.

Vera, A., John, B., Remington, R., Matessa, M. and Freed, M. (2005) 'Automating human-performance modeling at the millisecond level.' *Human–Computer Interaction* 20(3):225–65.

Ware, C. 2003. 'Design as applied perception.' In Carroll, J. M. (ed.) *HCI Models, Theories and Frameworks: Toward a Multidisciplinary Science*, San Francisco: Morgan Kaufmann, pp. 11–26.

Webb, N. and Renshaw, J. A. 2006a. *Adding Value with Eyetracking*. UPA 2006 Workshop, Montreal, Canada. www.amber-light.co.uk/UPA2006/UPA2006ETWkshop.htm

2006b. *Getting a Measure of Satisfaction of Eyetracking in Practice*. CHI 2006 Workshop Broomfield, USA. www.amber-light.co.uk/CHI2006/CHI2006ETWkshop.htm

West, J. M., Haake, A. R., Rozanski, E. P. and Karn, K. S. 2006. 'eyePatterns: Software for identifying patterns and similarities across fixation sequences.' In *Proc. of Eye Tracking Research and Applications 2006*, New York: ACM Press, pp. 149–54.

Wharton, C., Rieman, J., Lewis, C. and Polson, P. 1994. 'The cognitive walkthrough method: A practitioner's guide.' In Nielsen, J. and Mack, R. (eds.) *Usability Inspection Methods*. New York: John Wiley, pp. 105–40.

Wickens, C. D. 1992. *Engineering, Psychology and Human Performance* (2nd edn). New York: Harper Collins.

Willig, C. 2001. *Introducing Qualitative Research in Psychology: Adventures in Theory and Method*. Buckingham, UK: Open University Press.

Winograd, T. and Flores, F. 1985. *Understanding Computers and Cognition*. Greenwich, CT: Ablex Publishing Corp.

Wixon, D. 2003. 'Evaluating usability methods: Why the current literature fails the practitioner.' *Interactions* 10(4):28–34.

Woolrych, A. and Cockton, G. 2000. 'Assessing heuristic evaluation: Mind the quality, not just percentages.' In Turner, S. and Turner, P. (eds.) *Proc. of HCI 2000*, vol. II, London: British Computer Society, pp. 35–6.

2001. 'Why and when five test users aren't enough.' In *Proc. of IHM-HCI*, vol. II, Berlin: Springer, pp. 105–8.

Yamamoto, S. and Kuto, Y. 1992. 'A method of evaluating VDT screen layout by eye movement analysis.' *Ergonomics* 35:591–606.

Yang, G. Z., Gillies, D. and Hansell, D. 2004. 'ViTAL: Visual Tracking for Active Learning. A general framework for knowledge gathering in Diagnostic Decision Support System for Medical Imaging.' wwwhomes.doc.ic.ac.uk/gzy/vital/

Yarbus, A. L. 1967. *Eye Movements and Vision.* New York: Plenum Press.

Yoon, D. and Narayanan, N. H. 2004. 'Mental imagery in problem solving: An eyetracking study.' In *Proc. of Eye Tracking Research and Applications 2004*, New York: ACM Press, pp. 77–84.

Young, R. M. 1983. 'Surrogates and mappings: Two kinds of conceptual models for interactive devices.' In Gentner, D. and Stevens, A. L. (eds.) *Mental Models*, Mahwah, NJ: Lawrence Erlbaum, pp. 35–52.

Young, R. M., Green, T. R. G. and Simon, T. 1989. 'Programmable user models for predictive evaluation of interface designs.' In *Proc. of CHI 1989*, Reading, MA: Addison-Wesley, pp. 15–19.

Zimmerman, J., Forlizzi, J. and Evenson, S. 2007. 'Research through design as a method for interaction design research in HCI.' In *Proc. of CHI 2007*, New York: ACM Press, pp. 493–502.

Index

Lightning Source UK Ltd.
Milton Keynes UK
UKOW07f0458280417

300098UK00004B/109/P

9 780521 690317